DATA PROCESSING CONCEPTS

DATA PROCESSING CONCEPTS

DOUGLAS A. COLBERT

U.S. Army Data Command

Formerly of
Tacoma Technical Institute

McGraw-Hill Book Company

New York   St. Louis   San Francisco
London   Toronto   Sydney

DATA PROCESSING CONCEPTS

Library of Congress Catalog Card Number: 68–13625

11667

1 2 3 4 5 6 7 8 9 10 (HDBP) 7 4 3 2 1 0 6 9 8

Preface

In recent years the use of automatic data processing equipment has been extended into almost every area of business, government, and science. As a result, the need for people who are experienced and knowledgeable in this challenging field is continuing to multiply at an ever-increasing rate. Therefore, the purpose of this book is to reach beginners who must study about or work with data processing. The text and illustrations offer the most extensive coverage available in an introductory volume on computers, their supporting equipment, and their uses. Emphasis has been placed on making this an easy-to-understand textbook, progressing from the simple to the complex. It is written in a logical sequence, as the machines and related subjects should be learned. To be a ready reference, it covers the machines separately by chapters. However, all chapters are related and must be considered as a unit to understand data processing as an integrated concept.

This book has been designed to provide the serious student an opportunity to develop a concept of data processing. However, the concept is more than a generalization, as is revealed by a brief glance through the table of contents. The material is discussed in depth, but is presented in a most elementary manner, since the student is assumed to have little or no knowledge of data processing. For this reason the text is suitable for study both in the classroom and by oneself. The opportunity is available to gain a background in general wiring methods and computer programming, as well as to become acquainted with data processing terminology. Various applications and related subjects are used as vehicles to demonstrate the use and purpose of the machines.

The student studying data processing as a career can gain an understanding during the early stage of his schooling that will enhance his learning as he studies each machine in depth. College and high school students considering other occupations can learn how data processing may affect their careers. Within the data processing installation, semiskilled machine operators and programmers can increase their knowledge of the field. A background in the major areas of data processing—electrical punched-card systems, electronic computer systems, programming, and systems development—combined with sound and effective work habits, permits working with a minimum of supervision. This in turn leads to greater opportunities for advancement.

Those not working directly in or with data processing are influenced by it strongly. A basic knowledge is necessary in order to handle the source documents and mechanized reports prepared by the data processing department—nerve center of the company's operation. For the business manager, this book provides orientation leading to a better understanding of data processing in his business. For the office worker and others who must deal with data processing technicians and their outlandish dialect, this book bridges the communications gap. Thus an appreciation is developed for the management and operation tools made available by mechanization.

The student is exposed to two generations of machines. The first, a set of machines called a punched-card system, is covered in Chaps. 3 to 11. This system often comprises the entire data processing operation of an organization. The second generation, called a computer system, is normally found in larger companies and is covered in Chaps. 12 to 19. Although the former can function as a data processing unit for a small or beginning operation, the latter is generally an expansion of the punched-card machines. As a general rule, we can say that mechanization begins with installation of a punched-card system. The expansion of mechanized areas or growth of business eventually necessitates the speed of a computer system and justifies its cost. Although some companies do convert directly from a manual system to a computer system, at least some punched-card machines are needed for support.

The machines selected for study, such as IBM 1400 series computers, are popular models used in business, rather than the hypothetical equipment that is frequently taught. They were selected for their instructional adaptability and because their characteristics are found not only in IBM equipment, but also in machines of other manufacturers. The student progresses to the point where he can actually wire control panels and write programs for these machines. As a result, the student is prepared to encounter similar machines in the business world, and he can easily transfer principles he has learned to different models if necessary.

Since two types of processing systems are covered, this book can be used as a study guide or reference for either. However, it is strongly recommended that the student study the chapters in the order presented. After completing each chapter, evaluate your understanding of the machine and its use by solving the problems and answering the review questions. Most of the problems are intended to create understanding; if you fail to solve them or to answer the questions, restudy the chapter. You can expect to return to the chapter in search of answers for a majority of the questions and problems. Only when you understand each machine, before proceeding to the next, will its use and rightful place in the data processing installation be clear.

The student is reminded that even the experienced data processing technician's wired or stored program seldom works the first time. When it fails, the technician returns to the drawing board for analysis and further study of the problem and technical manuals. His determination to succeed in the presence of failure is the mark of a dedicated data processor. Do not be discouraged if you cannot immediately understand or remember terms and technical information. Concentrate on learning where to find them in the book and how to apply them.

This book is the outgrowth of a data processing course developed for adult education and taught by the author in the public school system of the state of Washington. Although there are numerous worthwhile data processing books written for the intermediate-level student, I was unsuccessful in my search for a suitable textbook for an introductory course in all phases of data processing. As the demand increased, I continued teaching the course for three years in Washington and another year in Okinawa. I revised and improved the course outline to satisfy the requirements of the class, which included not only students but employees attending at their companies' request. Thus, *Data Processing Concepts* was conceived and written for students studying data processing as a career and for those who are already working with data processing.

I wish to extend my great appreciation to International Business Machines Corporation. Without their permission for the use of IBM technical references and cooperation in reviewing certain problems, this book in its present form would not have been possible. As a result of working with IBM representatives and equipment for several years, it is only natural that my background, and thus this book, is IBM-oriented. It is impossible for me to extend in words enough credit.

Competent typing and proofreading are often forgotten and never are given enough recognition. I am deeply indebted to Mrs. Bette D. Thornton for correcting my grammatical errors and typing a very suitable manuscript from a very unsuitable draft. The "honor" of reading, reading, and more proofreading went to my wife, Ann, whom I expressly thank. Their effort and assistance have proved immeasurable. To both of these assistants I extend a sincere acknowledgment. Lastly, I would like to thank my colleague William E. Simon for his review and helpful comments on some of the material.

DOUGLAS A. COLBERT

Contents

Printing
Selection
Wiring the Counters
Programming
Control Panel Diagram Summary

Introduction to Flowcharting
Systems Flowchart
Program Flowchart
Developing a Flowchart

Concepts of an Electronic Data Processing System
Need for Computers
History of Computers
Beginning of Electronic Data Processing
Classification of Computers
Conversion to EDP

Decimal Numbering System
Binary Numbering System
Octal Numbering System
Binary Coded Decimal
Binary Arithmetic
Octal Arithmetic
Binary-Coded Decimal Arithmetic

Functional Units of a Computer System
Processing of Data
Movement of Data
Magnetic Core Storage
Buffer Storage
Magnetic Disk Storage
Magnetic Tape Storage
Other Storage Devices

Communicating with the Computer
IBM 1401 Electronic Data Processing System

DATA PROCESSING CONCEPTS

1
Evolution to data processing

Data processing, as recognized and applied in this modern age, has evolved in recent years. Man has made more technological advances since the beginning of World War II than in all previous years combined. This has resulted in an industrial revolution, creating an expanded need for mechanization.

HISTORY OF DATA PROCESSING

The need to count has been recorded throughout history. The decimal system gives a clue that man's fingers were the first counting device.

The earliest man-made counting device was invented in China around 5000 B.C. It was called the *abacus* (Fig. 1-1), and counting was accomplished with beads on strings of wire. The Chinese abacus migrated to Japan in a slightly different version. The Egyptians also had their version of the abacus, which used pebbles for counting in the sand. The Romans, as well, used a similar abacus counting board with marbles.

Of particular importance, this remarkably efficient calculator is widely used in the Orient today. Another widely used manual calculator is the *slide rule,* invented around 1632 by the English mathematician William Oughtred. Both are still used today, even in modern data processing offices.

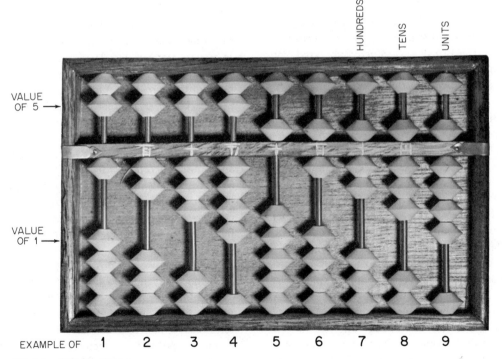

Fig. 1-1 Chinese abacus.

The next milestone preceding the advent of modern data processing machines was the first known mechanical computer. Around 1642, in Rouen, France, Blaise Pascal invented a gear-driven machine to count long columns of figures. His machine, the size of a shoe box, was used in his father's tax office.

In 1801, in Lyons, France, Joseph Marie Jacquard invented the first successful machine to operate from *punched cards*. His machine was capable of weaving decorative, elegant designs into cloth according to instructions given by the punched cards. Fear of automation caused a mob to burn the loom and beat Jacquard. Fortunately, this act gained the attention of Napoleon. The emperor's interest in the loom caused Jacquard to build other looms, and thousands were placed in French textile plants. His loom gained worldwide attention, and a monument was erected for him in 1840 on the spot where the first loom was burned.

In 1812 Charles Babbage, an English mathematician at Cambridge University, conceived the idea of a calculator he called the *difference machine*. In 1913, its basic principles were employed in Burroughs accounting machines. Due to the worldwide publicity and success of France's loom, the British government supported Babbage through grants. He finished and demonstrated his machine in 1822.

Around 1830, Babbage turned his attention to a more complicated *analytical engine* based on the punched-card pattern. This switch alarmed the government and resulted in withdrawal of its support, dooming the project. Without giving up hope, Babbage continued with drawings of his machine to store numbers, calculate them, and restore them for later use. His versatile computer would follow instructions automatically, when fed a predetermined sequence of cards. But the inventor never had a chance to construct his engine. He spent 20 years blueprinting his plans and spending most of his personal fortune. After hundreds of engineering drawings, his analytical engine, if developed, would have operated similarly to present-day electronic computers with stored programs and punched-card input-output.

In 1939, Howard Aiken, a mathematics professor at Harvard University, began work on the first large-scale computer. The machine, called the *Automatic Sequence Controlled Calculator,* or *Mark I,* was completed in 1944. He was well along with his work when he read that Babbage had been there over 100 years before with the analytical engine.

So only today's techniques are new, the concept having been known for more than a century. Pascal, Jacquard, and Babbage merely had the misfortune of being born too early.

DEVELOPMENT AS RELATED TO NEED

The development of data processing machines has been slow, not because of lack of knowledge, but lack of need for them due to the agricultural economy of the past.

At the turn of the twentieth century, 1 out of every 25 wage earners worked in an office. By 1940, the ratio was up to 1 in 10. The ratio increased to 1 in every 8 during the 1950s and will continue to climb unless challenged. If this rate of growth continued until the turn of the century, there would not be enough people in the labor force to process clerical work. Data processing machines have helped solve this problem. For instance, one IBM computer of the early 1950s is capable of equaling the work of 8500 people using desk calculators. More recent computers operate at hundreds of times the rate of this early one.

The Social Security system has been called the biggest accounting operation of all time. In 1936, the initial job required setting up accounts for 30 million people. A family of punched-card data processing machines, including the keypunch, sorter, collator, calculator, and tabulator, made the undertaking possible. Within a year the agency was using these machines to handle more than 1 million personal records a day. During the next 20 years the system added almost 100 million new accounts.

Scientific needs also became greater. In 1950, Los Alamos Atomic Energy Laboratory had a problem calling for 9 million mathematical operations. "Problem Hippo" was presented to the Selective Sequence Electronic Calculator, which contained 21,400 electrical relays and

12,500 vacuum tubes. The machine produced the answer in 150 hours; a mathematician would have taken 1500 years.

BEGINNING OF PUNCHED-CARD DATA PROCESSING

Mechanization was stimulated by the needs of the U.S. Census Bureau. The 1880 census was not completed until 1888. The statistics were compiled with large, handwritten cards and handled or sorted countless times for different reports. The growing population, relocation of the population, and increasing need for more statistics pushed the demand for mechanization. Since the population grew from 50 million to 62 million between 1880 and 1890, there was concern that the 1890 census would not be completed before the 1900 census. This delay would have prevented Congress from reallocating its seats as required by the Constitution.

Dr. Herman Hollerith, statistician for the Census Bureau, and his assistant, engineer James Powers, worked out a mechanical system using long strips of paper. This was changed to punched cards, which were counted by the *Hollerith tabulating machine*. The tabulator counted by rows of telescoping pins which dropped through the holes into mercury-filled cups, completing an electrical circuit which caused a pointer to move one position on a dial.

Hollerith left the Census Bureau before the 1890 census was completed to work on the first mechanized job: a mortality rate for the city of Baltimore. He established a tabulating service bureau and extended his method to railroad accounting. His bureau became the forerunner of the giant corporation, International Business Machines.

Powers followed through with the 1890 census, completing it in 2½ years using the Hollerith method. Powers left to form his own company, which became the forerunner of another giant corporation, Remington Rand.

In 1908, Powers patented his 20-column punching machine based on the simultaneous punching method which permitted correction of an error before punching. Also in 1908, Hollerith developed a machine to arrange

cards into a desired sequence. His vertical sorter operated at nearly 200 cards per minute. In 1911, he introduced the horizontal sorter which operated at the rate of 270 cards per minute.

Later developments in 1913 resulted in a *tabulator* to print numeric information as well as to accumulate totals. In 1928, a tabulator was developed to subtract, and recent tabulators have been made to multiply and divide. The IBM 400 series *accounting machines* were introduced in 1931, followed by the IBM 405 in 1934. The IBM 402 and 403 accounting machines were introduced in the late 1940s. A more versatile family of accounting machines was introduced later: the IBM 407, 408, and 409.

A *calculator* to multiply was developed in 1931. The IBM 603 calculator, capable of dividing, was introduced in 1946, followed by the IBM 602 calculator in 1947 and the more powerful IBM 604 calculator in 1948. Other 600 series calculators were developed, resulting finally in the transistorized IBM 609 calculator.

HISTORY OF DATA PROCESSING COMPANIES AND THEIR LEADERS

In 1911, Dr. Herman Hollerith's Tabulating Machine Company merged with the International Time Recording Company of New York and the Dayton Scale Company to form the Computing, Tabulating and Recording Company. In the same year, James Powers formed Powers Accounting Machine Company.

In 1914, Thomas J. Watson, Sr., sales manager of National Cash Register Company, became the president of the Computing, Tabulating and Recording Company. The company now had four basic business machines: the keypunch, the gangpunch, the sorter, and the tabulator. In 1924, the company adopted its present name—International Business Machines. IBM products are used in virtually every country, and the company has manufacturing plants in many countries.

Powers' company merged with several office-supply companies in 1927 to form the Remington Rand Corporation. Subsequently, Remington Rand merged with Sperry Gyroscope Company to form the present company,

Sperry Rand Corporation. Its computers are marketed under the trade name of Univac. For half a century, Sperry Rand was second to IBM. However, innovations occur rapidly, and several companies are offering progressive competition. Honeywell Corporation is now runner-up to IBM with other companies close behind. Nevertheless, IBM still controls three-fourths of the data processing market.

Electrical punched-card machines are manufactured primarily by International Business Machines and Univac Division of Sperry Rand Corporation. Electronic data processing systems or computers are manufactured by numerous companies. Some are IBM, Honeywell Corporation, Univac, Burroughs Corporation, National Cash Register Company, Philco Corporation, General Electric Company, and RCA Corporation. There are also numerous smaller companies that specialize in custom-made computers.

EFFECT OF AUTOMATION

This frequently abused word applies to the use of labor-saving devices. Many critics, without searching for the real reason, point an accusing finger at automation as the cause of unemployment. Yet many experts maintain that automation creates jobs.

Let us look first at some of the facts pertinent to employment. Elimination and creation of jobs is a by-product of our recent technological boom. In a single decade, 50 million manual jobs were destroyed. This was caused primarily by the upward movement of wages. During this same period, 60 million jobs were created. And most important, the number of new jobs is increasing faster than the number of people pursuing them, due mainly to the high number of unskilled among the jobless. Workers with higher education and skills are required for jobs created as a result of technological advancement. Yesterday's skill may be insufficient today; employees must prepare for the new jobs resulting from automation. This is corroborated by the fact that half of the labor force will be of a professional or technical level in the immediate

future. Workers who fail to prepare themselves will be victims of technological unemployment.

Those concerned about automation should welcome rather than fear it. Generally, automation does not reduce the number of jobs available. Instead, high-speed data processing machines make possible many job-producing activities that otherwise would probably not exist. An earlier fear of automation caused a mob to burn Jacquard's weaving loom, which was the first machine to operate by punched cards. Yet employment in the textile industry increased from 40,000 to 1.5 million workers during the century preceding 1860. During this same period, machines were built that were capable of producing as much as 300 could in former times.

A more recent example is the dial telephone system, which comprises the world's largest computer. If automatic switchboards were not available, all the single women in the country, it is estimated, would be required to handle the approximately 100 billion telephone calls Americans make each year. The result would not be employment for millions, but lack of communication. We just would not make the 100 billion calls each year. The service could not be sold on the scale it is today, and many of the men and women who now work for the telephone companies would be unemployed, victims of a lack of automation. What, then, is there to fear from automation? While the controversy over automation continues, the number of people in new jobs and employees holding second jobs continues to multiply.

NEED FOR DATA PROCESSING TODAY

Data processing came into being to meet an increasing need for information under increasingly complex conditions. High-speed machines were not essential until recently, because ours was an agricultural economy. But now more people are engaged in handling, processing, and distributing goods and services than are engaged in their production.

Data processing machines can assist in handling the paperwork for an ever-increasing volume of data. The processing of data usually requires performing repetitive operations with few variations on one document after another. Once the data have been correctly recorded, they can be sorted, calculated, listed, and filed mechanically.

Through elimination of clerical operations, accuracy is ensured. An average of 5 errors can generally be expected for every 100 manual calculations. Data processing machines are virtually 100 percent accurate. However, machines in general are no better than the data fed them or the people programming them—they process incorrect data just as fast as correct data. As safeguards, controls and editing functions are built into the processing instructions.

Economy can also be expected through mechanization. Management can gear production and supply to equal demand. Improved reporting and scheduling allow management to discover and correct potential problem areas. It is the companies that do not learn such economies that competition forces out of business.

Data processing can meet a company's needs, both financial and nonfinancial. It meets the financial needs by allowing the company to reduce costs through maintaining fewer clerical personnel, retaining less inventory, and overhead costs. Revenue can be increased as a result of more sales-handling capacity and better customer service. It meets the nonfinancial needs and helps achieve long-range goals by improving the company's competitive position, allowing for greater flexibility, and providing the potential for rapid expansion. Operating objectives can be reached by handling volumes that would be impossible manually.

FUTURE OF DATA PROCESSING

In the war years of the early 1940s, mechanization became more essential to the national effort as paperwork mounted in both industry and government. At a most critical time, jobs outnumbered the civilian labor force. Large business concerns contributed to the national effort by releasing hundreds of punched-card machines to the government. This was necessary for projects such as writing 8 million checks monthly, required by the dependency law passed by Congress in 1942. The United States government is now the second largest computer user, representing about 40 percent of the market. Business data processing is in first place with 45 percent of the market. The remaining 15 percent of the computer market is in the field of science and engineering.

The punched-card machines were not fast enough nor were they capable of solving the problems of engineering and scientific applications, so giant computers were built. One such giant, called Maniac for *Mathematical Analyzer Numerical Integrator and Computer,* was developed by the late John Von Neumann in the late 1940s. This machine has been given credit for making possible the development of the hydrogen bomb before the Soviet Union. The computer was developed at the Institute for Advanced Study, Princeton, New Jersey, and installed at Los Alamos, New Mexico.

This new generation of data processing machines went beyond bookkeeping and accounting. In 1952, a differential equation in aircraft wing design required 8 million calculations. The problem would have required seven years to complete manually using desk calculators. The IBM 701 computer solved the problem, and within the next few years other computers were operating 100 times faster.

Computers are being used to search equations to determine the best of many possible answers, such as the design of the 1955 Chevrolet engine. Computers can be used to determine the best itinerary for a salesman. In order to visit 15 cities, a salesman has a choice of 1.3 trillion different routes.

Other uses of computers are in reckoning probabilities to determine likelihood, such as oil in certain kinds of underground strata; simulation by reducing complicated processes to mathematical formulas and logical progressions, such as performance of an oil refinery in advance of its actual construction; computing time and space factors, such as daily routing of railway freight cars and centralization of airline reservations.

Most monetary transactions are settled by checks.

Many companies give the employee the option of having the payroll department send his check directly to the bank handling his account. The employee then does his purchasing by writing checks. This method can be carried one step further to be even more efficient for the company and for concerns servicing the employee.

A payroll chain reaction would occur where each employee's bank account would be credited by the employer for the amount earned and the company account would be debited by a like amount. Information relating to earnings, withholding tax, deductions, etc., would be entered into the company computer for processing and storage.

To make a purchase, the customer would identify himself to the store clerk by an identification card that would be automatically verified by a centralized computer. The punched holes or other means in the identification card would be transmitted to the centralized computer along with other information relating to the purchase. The clerk would key information into a store device similar to a cash register that would instruct the bank computer to decrease the customer's account by the amount of the purchase. Simultaneously, information on the sale would go to the store computer for processing sales, inventory, financial, and tax data. As with present-day checking accounts, the customer would be notified regularly by a statement of deposits and transactions. If the prophecy comes true that paper money and checks will become rarities, the savings will be passed on to the customer.

When computers were commercially offered in the early 1950s, the experts and computer inventors predicted that, because of their size and cost, only a few dozen would be manufactured for use by large corporations. However, this prediction fortunately was incorrect, and there are now more than 55,000 computers being used both in and outside the United States. There are even more punched-card data processing systems in use.

While the future of data processing cannot be predicted accurately, its growth can be envisioned by the fact that the data processing industry will employ 3 million people by 1970.

QUESTIONS

1. What is the major need for data processing machines?
2. Name the first machine to operate from punched cards.
3. Today's computers operate similarly to which historical invention?
4. What recurring event demanded the first need of data processing machines?
5. How may our monetary exchange of the future be affected by mechanization?
6. Does automation create unemployment? Explain.
7. What is the oldest man-made calculator?

2

Introduction to data processing

interpreters, collators, reproducers, calculators, and tabulators (synonymous with accounting machines). An *electronic data processing* (EDP) *system* (Fig. 2-2) is defined as a set of input and output devices connected to a central processor (which is the heart of the system) to perform as a unit. The EDP system (also referred to as a computer) is capable of performing a series of data processing functions without operator intervention, such as sorting, collating, calculating, and printing. Punched-card machines are electromechanical, as opposed to computers, which are entirely electronic.

As seen in the preceding chapter, data processing machines can save time and money when properly applied. In some cases they merely provide a means of accomplishing a job that would be unfeasible to do manually. As the machines accomplished these objectives, the public began forming misconceptions about data processing. This happened mainly as a result of erroneous articles in news media and over-glamorized television advertisements. However, most of the misconceived public statements were intended as factual and were reported otherwise because of a lack of knowledge.

MISCONCEPTIONS OF DATA PROCESSING

Due to abuse in definition, data processing means different things to different people. It has been referred to as automatic data processing, machine accounting, punched-card accounting machines, electronic data processing, electrical accounting machines, and tabulating machines. The machines themselves have been called "brains." With the exception of the latter, all are correct terms because a universal name has not been agreed upon. Until a universal name is adopted, data processing remains the most common term, but refers to the field as a whole.

Data processing is divided into two categories. A *punched-card data processing system* (Fig. 2-1) is defined as a set of conventional machines including sorters,

DEFINITION OF DATA PROCESSING

A characteristic of data processing is that once the data are recorded onto punched cards or magnetic tape, they may be used for many different purposes. They may be mechanically sorted, filed with other cards, tabulated, and listed, without further manual transcription or copying.

Data processing is the mass processing of data. It also provides the solution to highly complex problems. We shall be concerned with the definition that data processing is a group of people and machine units of the type described in the following chapters that are organized to process the data requirements of a company.

DATA PROCESSING FUNCTIONS

Preparing checks, writing invoices and statements, maintaining inventory, and record keeping of all types are just the beginning of an endless list of jobs performed by data processing machines. In carrying out these functions, the information must first be recorded or punched onto a card, which is the most common means of initial recording. The information is recorded in the form of punched holes. The holes in the card cause the machines to automatically perform operations such as reading, printing, comparing, classifying, adding, subtracting, multiplying, and dividing.

IBM 514 REPRODUCER

IBM 188 COLLATOR

IBM 84 SORTER

IBM 407 ACCOUNTING MACHINE

IBM 108 CARD-PROVING MACHINE

IBM 26 KEYPUNCH

IBM 557 INTERPRETER

IBM 609 CALCULATOR

Fig. 2-1 Typical punched-card data processing system. (IBM Corp.)

MACHINE FUNCTIONS

The basic functions performed by data processing machines can be broadly explained as follows. These definitions begin a new language called *data processing terminology.*

Card punching (Fig. 3-1) is the basic method of converting source data into punched cards. The operator reads a source document and presses the keys of the keyboard to punch the cards, much as a typist types a letter or form. The machine (Fig. 4-3) automatically feeds, positions, and ejects the card after manual punching. *Duplication* is the process of automatically punching repetitive information, such as the current date, onto all cards after the operator punches the common information onto only the first card.

Card verification is a means of checking the accuracy of the original keypunching. A second operator verifies the original punching by pressing the keys of a verifier while reading from the same source data. The machine, similar to the keypunch, compares the key pressed with the hole already punched in the card. A difference causes the machine to stop, indicating a discrepancy between the two operations.

Interpreting (Fig. 7-2) is the translating of punched holes into printed information on the card. Alphabetic or numeric information can be printed on any location of the card. Interpreting is advantageous when punched cards are used as documents on which additional information is written or marked, or whenever personnel unfamiliar with punched cards must handle them.

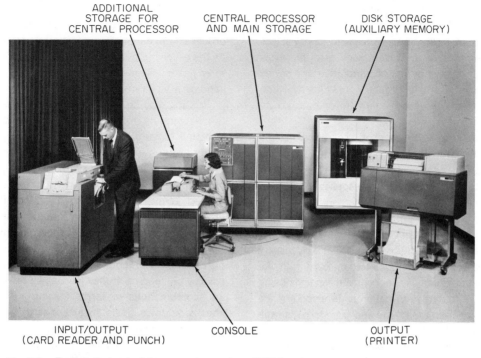

Fig. 2-2 Typical electronic data processing system. (IBM Corp.)

Sorting, or classifying, and selecting are accomplished on a sorter (Fig. 5-1). *Sorting* is the process of grouping cards in numeric or alphabetic sequence according to any classification punched in them. To arrange cards into social security number sequence, the cards are sorted on columns in the card containing social security number. *Selecting* is the function of pulling certain items, such as cards punched with specific numbers, from a mass of data.

Editing of the punched data to ensure a maximum of accuracy and compiling statistics from the cards are performed on a statistical machine (Fig. 6-1). Proving the punched data before producing the report substantially reduces error and correction time costs. This machine performs operations such as high-speed sorting, editing, sequence checking, adding, subtracting, obtaining different classes of totals, crossfooting, and balance checking.

Mechanized filing is performed on the collator (Fig. 8-1). *Merging* is the combining of two sets of punched cards into one set by a given sequence. This makes possible high-speed filing of new cards into an existing file of cards and eliminates human error. *Matching* is a checking function used to check the agreement between two sets of cards. Unmatched cards or groups of cards in either file may be selected from the files. This function is frequently performed with merging.

Reproducing, gangpunching, and mark-sensed punching are accomplished on a reproducer (Fig. 9-1). *Reproducing* is the function of copying information from one set of punched cards onto another set of cards. Information from the punched set of cards is compared with the newly punched cards and differences are automatically detected. *Mark-sensed punching* is the function of reading marks made on the card, such as hours worked, and translating these facts into punched-hole form. *Gangpunching* is the function of punching repetitive information, such as pay rates, onto groups of all the new cards.

Calculating is the computing and punching of the result onto the card. Any combination of addition, subtraction, multiplication, or division can be performed. Factors to be calculated may be read from each card, or series of cards, and developed by the accumulation of a series of calculations. For example, regular hours plus overtime hours equals computed total hours times hourly rate equals gross pay.

Summary punching is the function of creating a single card to replace a group of cards. It can be used to reduce card volume, thus reducing the number of cards to be processed by the machine. A payroll application, where an employee fills out a time card daily, can be summarized at the end of the pay period by summary punching one card for each employee with the tabulated hours punched. To carry balance figures forward, it is necessary only to include the previous total-to-date card with the current-transaction cards. While a current report is being run, new balance-to-date information is developed by the computer or accounting machine and transferred to the punch unit by cable.

In-line processing means posting transactions, as they occur, to all ledger accounts affected. For example, processing a customer order changes the inventory status of all items ordered and alters accounts receivable and sales records, too. All these accounts can be updated at one time to make them represent today's status, not last week's. This type of data processing requires a computer with high-capacity storage (Fig. 2-2), so that all types of accounts can be included. Data enter the system from punched cards, magnetic tape, or information previously stored on the magnetic disks.

Converting coded information (machine-language media) from one form to another allows flexibility and facilitates a wider range of operations. Punched cards may be converted to magnetic tape, which can be processed at faster speeds. Magnetic tape may also be converted to punched cards. Machine-to-machine communication is possible. This eliminates the time lag, such as in transmitting payroll checks from the central data processing preparation point to a distant location for payment. Two machines are necessary, one to read the data to be transmitted and the other to receive the data

at the receiving point. For example, data on punched cards or paper tape may be transmitted from one data processing installation to another via telegraph circuits. At the receiving point, the data will be converted to the form needed. Transmission of data may be compared to sending a telegram.

Printing may be accomplished in many variations on the accounting machine (Fig. 2-1) or by the printer attached to the computer (Fig. 2-2). *Detail printing* is the printing of information from each card as it passes through the machine. During this listing operation, computations may be made and many combinations of totals printed. *Group printing* is the function of summarizing groups of cards, printing the total, and listing the complete descriptive information to identify the totals.

Form control is the rapid, accurate positioning of reports and documents on which machine results are printed. A tape-controlled carriage feeds various sizes and combinations of forms (registers, reports, cards, checks, address labels, invoices) as the desired printing occurs at predetermined locations.

Report preparation is the end result of a series of processing steps. This function is to print numeric and alphabetic data from punched cards in a meaningful and desired format and to total data by proper classifications.

Data processing machines perform a variety of functions other than the major ones covered. You will see in the following chapters how to wire and program the machines to perform many functions.

QUESTIONS

1. Name five machine functions necessary in processing business data.
2. Define the term "data processing."
3. What is the most time-consuming machine function?
4. Form control is associated with which machine(s)?
5. What is the correct data processing term for printing on the card?

3
Data representation

In the last chapter we defined some of the functions performed by a data processing department. We also related some functions to the machines. In this chapter, we introduce a means of communicating with the machines in order to accomplish these functions. In the next chapter we begin the discussion of how the many machines of a data processing system work in unison to produce the desired processing.

CODE FORMS OF DATA PROCESSING

Symbols convey information, but the symbol itself is not the information. It merely represents the data or information. The characters $ and % are symbols and, when understood, convey the writer's meaning. The dollar sign, when used with numbers, tells us that the representation is of monetary value and not the number of occurrences of an event. The percent sign, likewise, indicates a fractional part and not money.

Presenting data to a data processing machine is similar in many ways to communicating with another person by letter. That is, the symbols, which are letters, numbers, and punctuation, are recorded on paper in a prescribed sequence and transported to another person who reads and interprets them.

Similarly, communication with a data processing machine requires that information be reduced to a set of symbols that can be read, interpreted, and acted upon by a certain machine. Some machines do not accept the same language as other machines, but there are data processing techniques and machines to convert the symbols to a compatible language. The important fact is that information can be represented by symbols, which become a language of communication between people and machines.

Information to be used as input to data processing machines may be in the form of punched cards (Fig. 3-1), magnetic tape (Fig. 15-12), paper tape, similar in image to magnetic tape, and forms of direct input described in the next chapter. Data are represented on the card by the presence or absence of small, rectangular holes in specific locations. In a similar manner, small, circular holes along a paper tape represent data. On magnetic tape, the symbols are small, magnetized areas, called *spots* or *bits,* arranged in specific patterns.

In the machines, data are stored by many electrical and electronic components: magnetic core, transistors, magnetic disks and drums, wheels, and relays. The storage and flow of data through these devices are represented as electronic signals. The presence or absence of these signals is the method of representing data. The representation and physical makeup are covered in detail in subsequent chapters.

SYMBOL REPRESENTATION

The ordinary decimal system has the digits 0 to 9, thus a base of 10. The nature of electronic machines makes it difficult to deal with a base-10 numbering system. Computers function in a *binary mode,* meaning that the computer components can indicate only two possible states or numbers. For example, a light switch operates in a binary mode; it is either off or on. Likewise, the vacuum tubes, transistors, or magnetic cores of a computer are off or on, thus representing data in a binary form.

Decimal numbers can be represented with a device of four *vacuum tubes* (Fig. 10-2), each assigned an arbitrary decimal value of 1, 2, 4, or 8. When a tube is on, it represents the decimal value associated with it. When a tube is off, the decimal value is ignored. The decimal numbers 0 to 9 can now be represented. For example, the

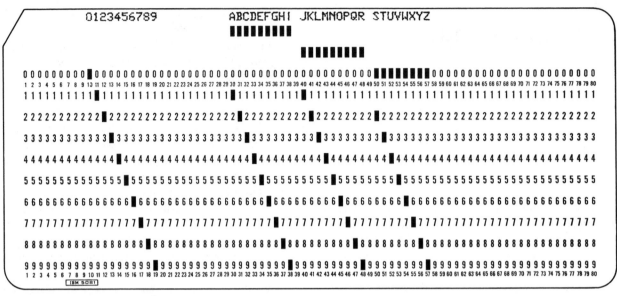

Fig. 3-1 Hollerith punched-card codes.

decimal value of 0 is represented by all lights off; the value of 6, by having the 2 and 4 tubes on; the value of 9, with the 1 and 8 tubes on; and so forth.

Because computers function in binary, a binary method of notation is used to illustrate these values. The two states of binary, on or off, are given a value of 1 to represent an on condition or a value of 0 to represent an off condition. Thus, the value of 6 in binary notation would be 0110, the value of 9 would be 1001, the value of zero would be 0000, and so on.

Data in punched-card machines are represented by various electromechanical devices. One such device is a *wheel,* much like the speedometer in an automobile. Two or more wheels placed next to each other may represent a counter. Each wheel has the digits 0 to 9. The wheel on the right stores the units position, the next wheel the tens position, and so on. In operation, all wheels are turned to 0. The addition of a 1 results in the units wheel being moved to the 1 position. Each wheel is internally connected to the wheel to its left. Therefore, each time a wheel turns beyond 9, the wheel to its left advances one position to record the carry.

Since our first chapters of study are on machines using punched cards as input, this chapter is devoted in detail to the punched card and the recording of data on it. More on internal representation will be covered as the need arises.

The most widely used method of recording data is the *Hollerith punched card.* Data are represented on the card in the form of punched holes. The horizontal face of the card is divided into rows, and each row is subdivided into columns. Each row is given a value of from 0 to 9, and a hole in any row represents the value associated with it. For example, a hole in the 9 row has the decimal value of 9.

Once the information is punched onto the card, it is a permanent record that may be repeatedly processed at machine speeds. Various reports may be prepared from the same cards, thus eliminating the need to recopy the information.

UNIT RECORD

The *unit record principle* is that all data concerning a single transaction are recorded in one punched card and the punched data remain the same for each use of the card.

The Hollerith card measures 7⅜ by 3¼ inches and is 0.007 inches in thickness. It is composed of 80 vertical columns, numbered from left to right. There are 12 vertical punching positions in each column, of which the punching positions for 0 to 9 are identified by printing on the card. The punching positions are designated from the top to the bottom of the card by 12, 11, 0, 1, 2, 3, 4, 5, 6, 7, 8, and 9. The top edge of the card is known as the *12 edge* and the bottom of the card is known as the *9 edge*. These designations are made because cards are fed through machines either 9-edge first or 12-edge first.

Each column of the card is designed to accommodate one of the digits 0 to 9, the letters A to Z, or certain special characters such as the dollar sign. We shall concern ourselves primarily with the numbers and letters, since special characters are generated inside the machines for the purpose of punctuation. *Numeric* information is recorded on the card by punching a single hole in a given column in the position that represents that digit. For example, employee number 25 punched in columns 1 and 2 would be recorded by a hole punched in the 2 position of column 1 and a hole punched in the 5 position of column 2.

Alphabetic information is represented by a combination of two punches, a numeric punch and a zone punch. The three *zone punches* are the 12 zone, associated with the letters A to I; the 11 zone, associated with the letters J to R; and the 0 zone, associated with the letters S to Z. The 0-zone position is the same as the numerical 0. It is not important to memorize the letters, but it is wise to remember the 12 and A, 11 and J, 0 and S relationship. That is, the A is 12 and 1, the B is 12 and 2; the J is 11 and 1, the K is 11 and 2; the S is 0 and 2, the T is 0 and 3, and so forth. If an unprinted column is punched with the 11 and 5, it is easy to count five letters from the J and interpret the representation as an N.

Some cards have a distinguishing color or have one of the corners cut. These features are provided as means of recognition to personnel handling the cards and have no meaning to the machine. For example, a corrected card in a file may be a different color in order to easily locate the card at a later time. When it is necessary for a machine to be able to distinguish between different types of cards, the distinguishing information must be punched in the card. This may be done in many ways. One of the most frequently used control punches is the 11-zone punch, which is usually referred to as an X punch. For instance, master address cards will contain an X punch (11 zone) in some column in order to separate them from current-purchase cards. The master cards may then be filed for use in the next billing period.

A predetermined number of columns set aside for specific information is known as a *field* (Fig. 3-2). We cannot punch characters in random columns and expect the machine to know where the needed information is punched. If we reserve columns 26 to 28 for employee number, then we can instruct the machine to process the employee number in the desired manner. If the field contains fewer digits than the number of columns in the field, the normal rule is to precede the number with zeros. For example, employee number 1 would be punched 001 in columns 26 to 28.

The design of fields on a card provides us with the first important control in data processing. Suppose that four columns of a card contain the punches 0591. Does this mean customer number 0591, a quantity of 591, $5.91, or something else? We have no way of knowing what the numbers mean without knowing what they are intended to mean. It is the responsibility of the person who is planning the operation to assign the desired meaning to these columns and to document it in the procedure. This provides the keypunch operator with instructions about how the fields should be punched. The documentation also provides instructions that tell the machine operator how to print the data on the card, which columns are to be sorted, and how to set up other card-handling steps so that the information in the card is handled in the intended way. The computer or accounting machine can be instructed so that the desired processing will be achieved, if the documentation is complete and accurate.

It is necessary to consider also how the data are organized in the card since the arrangement of the information has a most significant effect on how the proc-

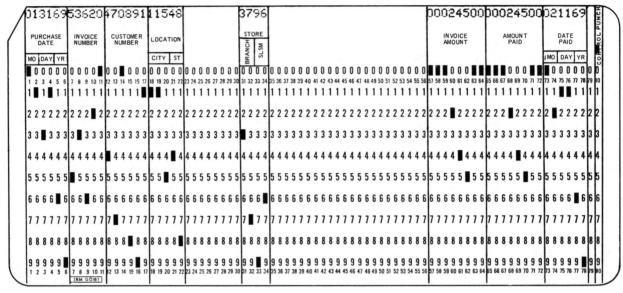

Fig. 3-2 Accounts receivable card fields.

essing is done. This brings us to one of the most fundamental concepts in data processing, that of a file.

A *file* is a collection of unit records containing information about a group of related accounts, people, inventory items, etc. There are two types of files. The *master file* contains semipermanent data that are used time after time in preparation of reports, checks, invoices, etc. In a payroll file, the master file includes a record for each employee containing such data as name, employee number, department, sex, social security number, withholding exemptions, and so forth. A *detail* or *transaction file,* on the other hand, contains data to be used in the current processing and then filed as history. The payroll transaction card representing time attendance records might include a minimum of information such as employee number, regular hours, and overtime hours. The card would be matched with the master card by employee number to obtain the pay rate necessary for computations, the authorized deductions, tax, and so forth.

CODING DATA

Coding is fundamental to all types of business systems for identifying data items. A *code* may be defined as a brief title, composed of either letters or numbers and used to identify an item of data and express its relationship to other items of the same or similar nature. For instance, employee number is used for identification purposes, is easier to control both manually and by machine than employee name, and eliminates erroneous processing resulting from duplicate or similar names. Ordering is simplified by ordering part number xyz instead of "bolt, stove type, stainless steel, ¼ inch diameter, 1 inch long."

One purpose in assigning codes to data is to enable presentation of the data in the most meaningful, orderly, and useful fashion. The ability to present related data in report form depends greatly upon the coding structure used. The complexity of the relationship between items governs the complexity in the coding structure.

The use of a coding structure usually permits faster machine processing in sorting, classifying, and filing because the machine acts upon the code number rather than the longer designation of the data. By coding, the number of card columns utilized is often reduced, thus reducing the amount of card punching. The user does not necessarily have to familiarize himself with the coding structure involved, since the data designation is usually reflected by both name or description and code number.

The simplest type of coding is the assignment of numbers in sequence to items on a list. Another type is the assignment of numbers in sequence to data in alphabetic order, such as a listing of names or firms. More sophisticated codes take into consideration family relationships of data, such as related items of hardware, screws, nails, and so forth. Some codes are constructed so that each segment of the code is descriptive of a specification of an object, such as bolt, steel, hexagonal head, 2 inch.

The next chapter concerns various means of recording data and tells how to operate the machine to punch data in the card.

QUESTIONS

1. Name the different means by which information may be used as input to data processing machines.
2. How does the machine distinguish between different types of cards? The operator?
3. Define a field punched in a card.
4. How are data represented in a computer? A punched-card machine?
5. How many punching positions are on a card?
6. What is the difference between a master file and a detail file?
7. What is the purpose of coding data?

4
Recording

Converting source documents into a language the machines will accept has long been recognized as the bottleneck of data processing. Although machines can process information at seemingly impossible speeds, most original input data have been recorded previously by manual means.

PROBLEMS IN PROCESSING SOURCE DATA

The solution would be to use source data in its original state, thus eliminating retranscription or coding to facilitate machine processing. However, the problems confronting engineers in developing machines to digest raw data are staggering. Some of the reasons are: different document sizes, handwritten data, numerous methods for recording data, and multiple or dissimilar transactions on a single document.

Some industries have solved the bottleneck with custom-built machines. In 1958, an estimated 10 billion checks circulated in the United States. Each check required handling six or more times. The rate had risen to 13 billion by 1961 and to over 18 billion in 1967. To cope with this uncontrollable mountain of paper, computer manufacturers, in cooperation with the American Banker's Association, developed *magnetic character sensing*. Specific information, such as the bank of origin, depositor's account number, and other essential data, is preprinted at the bottom of the check by magnetic recording. The amount of the check is recorded with magnetic ink when it is presented at the bank for payment.

Then the check can be processed as many times as necessary at mechanical speed, eliminating manual handling at banks and clearinghouses.

The advantages gained have been the limitation of keypunching and verifying, and the ability of both man and machine (Fig. 4-1) to directly read the recorded data. From an ultimate recording solution standpoint, disadvantages exist. Magnetic-character-sensing machines will read only certain kinds of type and will not read handwriting; production cost is high since each machine is custom-built for specific applications.

The oil industry has, perhaps, come closest to solving the input bottleneck. Some major oil companies issue their customers embossed plastic credit cards containing their account numbers. Briefly, the recording necessary to bill a customer occurs as follows. After filling the gas tank, the service station attendant inserts the customer's embossed plastic credit card and a billing form in a data recorder (Fig. 4-2). He moves variable keys to the numeric position corresponding to the gas purchase. When he actuates the impression lever, the customer's account number and the purchase amount are imprinted onto the hard copy of the billing form. The imprinted card is processed at the oil company's data processing center. Optical character recognition equipment scans the imprinted codes and punches the data onto the card. The card is processed by other machines, discussed later, to complete the billing operation. Again, the end results are elimination of manual punching and increased accuracy.

While progress is being made in the document-recording area, the keypunch (Fig. 4-3) is the machine most used for transcribing written data into punches in a card. Although it is not the intent of this chapter to teach card punching, the essentials should be known to anyone studying data processing.

KEYPUNCH FUNCTIONS

The card punch, also referred to as a keypunch, is similar to a typewriter. When a typist depresses a key on the typewriter, a character is printed on a piece of paper.

Fig. 4-1 Magnetic Character Reader. (IBM Corp.)

When a keypunch operator depresses a key, a hole or combination of holes representing a character is punched onto a card. The operator reads a source document and presses the keys on the keyboard to punch the data onto the card. Keypunch features allow feeding, card positioning, skipping, duplicating, printing, and ejecting the card automatically, thus increasing speed and punching efficiency.

Card punching is the operation of punching characters onto predetermined fields of the card according to information read from the source document. *Manual duplication* is the automatic punching of data from the preceding card onto the card presently being punched. Manual duplication occurs at 10 columns per second. *Automatic duplication* is the same as the previous function except that duplication occurs under the control of the program unit at twice the speed. Automatic skipping also occurs when directed by the program unit. Skipping proceeds at the rate of 80 columns per second, whereas normal skipping is 20 columns per second. Printing on

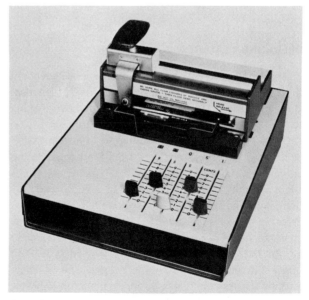

Fig. 4-2 Data Recorder Model 12-85. (Addressograph-Multigraph Corp.)

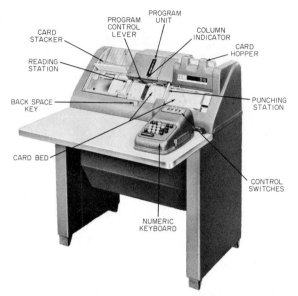

Fig. 4-3   IBM 24 Keypunch with numeric keyboard. (IBM Corp.)

grouped together similar to the way they are on an adding machine.

Now, assume that an error is made when we reach column 50. The card must be repunched, column 50 corrected, and punching resumed. We remove the card by depressing the *release* key (REL). This moves the card to the read bed. Since columns 1 to 49 are correct, we can take advantage of the manual duplication feature. Another card is fed into the punch bed and both cards are registered. Then, by depressing the *duplicate* key (DUP), an internal connection between the reading station and punching station is made. As long as the duplicate key is held down, each character from the erroneous card is relayed to the punching station and is punched onto the new card. Watching the column indicator, we continue duplication until column 50. The correct character is punched in column 50 and the remaining data to be punched continues. When a new card is fed in, the error card automatically moves to the card stacker and can be destroyed.

The *backspace* key, located below the read bed, is

the card occurs at the top, directly over the column being punched.

OPERATING FEATURES

The control keys on the alphanumeric keyboard (Fig. 4-4) are shaded and will be explained as needed. Our example of card punching is explained by referring to the keypunch (Fig. 4-3) and the keyboard chart.

Cards are placed in the card hopper, and depression of the *feed* key moves one card from the hopper to the punching station. Depression of the *register* key (REG) aligns column 1 under the punching station ready for punching. The keyboard is in lower shift; therefore, depressing any keys labeled A to Z punches an alphabetic character. To punch a numeric digit, depress the *numeric* key (NUM), which places the keys labeled 0 to 9 in upper shift, allowing the 10 numeric digits to be punched. Spacing occurs automatically, and the column indicator rotates one position to display column 2 as the next punching position. Note that the numeric keys are

Fig. 4-4   Combination alphabetic and numeric keyboard. (IBM Corp.)

used to backspace the card one column at a time. This is convenient when we skip a column that should be punched. A card jammed at either station can be manually removed by pressing the *pressure-roll release* lever located next to the column indicator.

PROGRAM CARD

A program card, which controls the program unit, is prepared for each different punching application. However, once punched, it can be used repeatedly. Its function is to allow repetitive operations to be accomplished automatically. The program unit controls automatic skipping over columns not to be punched, automatic duplicating of repetitive information, and shifting for punching numeric or alphabetic characters. Each of these operations is designated by a specific code punched in the programmed card. The program card is fastened around a program drum and inserted in the program unit. The punches in the program card are read by sensing mechanisms, called *star wheels*. The program drum revolves simultaneously with the movement of the cards under the reading and punching station. The program codes control the operations, column by column. Four of the twelve possible program codes are described below.

Field definition is controlled by a 12 punch in every column of the field, except the high-order position (left-hand column). The 12 punches cause a *skip* or *duplication* instruction to continue to the end of the field. The absence of a 12 punch in any column indicates the beginning of a field.

Automatic skipping is controlled by an 11 punch in the first column of the field to be skipped. A single-column field to be skipped is punched only with an 11.

Automatic duplication is controlled by the 0 punch and the rules are the same as for the 11 code.

Alphabetic shifting is controlled by punching a 1 in each column of a field containing predominantly alphabetic characters. When the keypunch is under the control of program unit, the keyboard is in numeric shift. Therefore, every column in the data card containing alphabetic information must be punched with a 1 in the corresponding column of the program card. If a field in the data card may be alphabetic or numeric, the field in the program card is programmed for the predominant pattern. During automatic duplication, 1s permit spacing over blank columns and prevent unwanted skipping that may result from 11 punches in the data card.

Three switches on the keyboard are used in conjunction with the program unit. The *print* switch is turned ON if printing on the card is desired. Its use is optional. The *automatic feed* switch must be ON to cause the card at the read station to register, the card in the punch bed waiting to be punched to register, and another card to be fed to the punch bed. Automatic feeding occurs when column 80 of the card passes the punching station. The *automatic skip* and *duplicate* switch is turned ON to activate the 11 and 0 program codes. The *program control* lever, located above the read bed, must be turned ON for program control. The program-sensing star wheels are lowered onto the program drum, and the codes punched in the program card control the automatic operations. An example of a program card used in preparing a master employee name and address file is shown in Fig. 4-5.

Numerous other time-saving devices are optional. Two of these devices are briefly described.

The *alternate-program feature* allows two program setups to be punched in a single program card. It is advantageous when two different source documents, such as purchase orders and purchase requests, are received intermingled. The two documents, when punched onto cards or unit records, can be separated by the sorter, covered in Chap. 5. Two other program codes are optional. One causes insignificant zeros in a field to print, for example, 000416. The other prevents certain fields from printing, although the *print* switch is ON.

The *decimal-tabulation feature* permits automatic punching of insignificant zeros in a field. This can be especially effective in large, variable money amount fields. To punch the amount 150 into an eight-position field would require five separate keypunch strokes for the insignificant zeros. The decimal-tabulation device causes the five zeros to be punched automatically with one stroke.

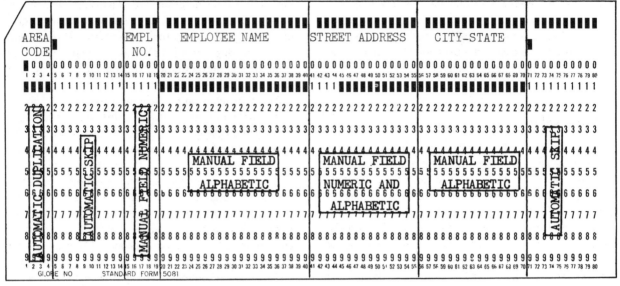

Fig. 4-5 Master employee name program card.

VERIFYING PUNCH CARDS

Accurately punched cards are essential to record keeping. Since mistakes may occur due to misinterpretation of handwritten characters or erroneous punching, cards are usually verified by a different operator immediately after they are punched.

The verifier is the same in appearance and operation as the keypunch. The significant difference is that sensing occurs, rather than punching. The operator depresses the keys corresponding to the data read from the source document. When a difference exists between the punch in the column and the key depressed, an *error* light turns on and the keyboard becomes inoperative. Provision is made for three trials in verification of a column in case the verifying operator depresses the incorrect key.

When a card is verified, a notch is cut in the right end of the card between the 0 and 1 punching rows. If a column is in error, a notch over the column containing an error is cut on the third attempt at verification.

ORDER WRITING AND BILLING

This section concerns the way keypunches may be used in handling order writing once the order is received by the seller and what means are taken to request reimbursement from the buyer.

Once an order is secured, the company's prime objective is to disburse to the buyer the commodities or services ordered in the fastest, most economical manner and be reimbursed accordingly. *Ordering* is the sequence of operations commencing with writing of the sales order and terminating with shipment of the goods.

There are numerous reasons for order writing. The source document, or customer order, originates with the vendor's salesmen or is received by mail. Customers occasionally order by phone. These orders are not going to follow any standard, resulting in poor legibility, confusion in nomenclature, and incomplete description. The advantages gained from rewriting the order are standard order forms, assured legibility, correct and complete description, and correct pricing and packing.

By-products available from order writing are acknowledgment to the customer that his orders have been received, a shipping and packing list, shipping labels showing the name and address of the customer, a bill of lading to authorize a shipping company to move the order, back-order control, notification to the customer, and order analysis. Order analysis gives management an up-to-date picture of how sales are moving and gives ample warning of demand so that production can be geared to handle the volume of orders. Order analysis can be combined with tabulations of shipments in order to report on efficiency in filling orders.

Billing refers to operations commencing with shipment of merchandise and terminating with forwarding of the completed invoice. Since over 90 percent of the information on the invoice appeared on the order, the original card punched for order writing, or a reproduced card, can be used for billing. The difference between the order and the invoice is item prices and their extensions, which must be calculated for the invoice. The total for the invoice is added by the accounting machine or as the invoice is prepared.

A typical invoice would include heading information such as customer name and address, ship-to address, and invoice number; miscellaneous data such as customer number, salesman, customer order number, and invoice date; and item information such as stock number, description, quantity, unit price, amounts, and their total.

QUESTIONS

1. What would be the ultimate solution for the recording problem?

2. How do the star wheels recognize the beginning of a new field in the program card?

3. When are the numeric and alphabetic *shift* keys used, with and without program control?

4. Explain the purpose of the reading station.

5. Name four objects that will space backward when the backspace key is depressed.

6. How are a correctly punched card and an error card identified after verification?

PROGRAM PROBLEM

To initiate the requirements for order writing and billing, item cards have been prepunched with stock number, description, unit cost, unit selling price, and stock location. The cards are located adjacent to the keypunch operator. As orders are received, the operator removes one card corresponding to each item order. The card needs only the salesman code, quantity, customer number, and current date punched. Indicate the punches required to prepare a program card for the problem. The format of the order card is as shown in Table 4-1.

Table 4-1   Billing-card Format

Columns	Description
1	Salesman code
17–19	Quantity
20–24	Stock number
25–41	Description
45–50	Unit cost
51–56	Unit selling price
57	Stock location
66–69	Customer number
70–76	Date

5
Classifying and arranging

Documents used in preparation of reports and other data processing products must be arranged in a meaningful sequence in order for the product to be useful. Manual sorting of data is time-consuming and subject to unlimited error. Likewise, manual selection of desired data from a file of records is a slow and inaccurate process.

Documents are normally keypunched in random sequence. Therefore, before any report can be printed, the cards must be in the desired sequence. This can be accomplished accurately and quickly by high-speed sorting machines. The cards can then be subsequently rearranged into other sequences to produce many important products.

For example, sales transaction cards can be classified or arranged into customer-name sequence to produce invoices and statements. Then an analysis of the sales transactions can be made by sorting the cards by product number to determine product popularity and customer buying habits, such as color, make, style, and price. The cards can be sorted into sales district or salesman sequence. For an exception-type report, such as on a particular product or customer, certain cards from the file may be selected by the sorter for processing.

There are several models of sorters available, differing mainly in speed. The IBM 82 sorter operates at 650 cards per minute, the IBM 83 sorter (Fig. 5-1) operates at 1000 cards per minute, and the transistorized IBM 84 sorter operates at 2000 cards per minute. All sorters are alike in operation and are simple to operate. However,

the sorter requires perhaps more concentrative effort to operate than any other machine, especially with voluminous files.

SORTER FUNCTIONS

The sorter can be used for a variety of purposes, the most common being to sort a deck of cards into ascending or descending sequence. *Arranging* is the process of sorting cards in numeric or alphabetic sequence according to any classification punched in them. Thus, many reports can be prepared, all originating from the same cards but each requiring a different sequence. *Classifying* is the process of grouping cards in numeric or alphabetic sequence. For instance, a file may be grouped by account number for summarization by account.

Selection is the function of pulling certain items from a file of cards. This is accomplished by selecting cards punched with specific digits or characters, called *control punches*. As an example, master cards with an X punch in column 80 (also referred to as X-80) and containing customer name, address, and account number, may be separated from sales transaction cards. The transaction cards, containing customer number, item purchased, amount, date, etc., are referred to as detail cards since they are relatively transient. The details would not contain an X in column 80 (also referred to as NX-80). Master

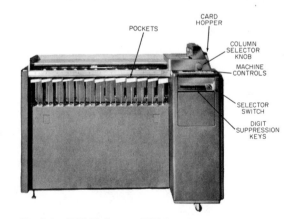

Fig. 5-1　IBM 83 Sorter. (IBM Corp.)

cards, on the other hand, contain data of a permanent nature.

Editing, from a data processing standpoint, means to identify erroneous data. We may distinguish the difference between auditing and editing by defining *auditing* as the process of checking for accuracy. Editing is the process of checking conformance to a particular pattern, that is, checking for the impossible. For example, a *name* field cannot contain numeric information; a *social security* field may not contain alphabetic data or blank columns. The sorter detects errors of this nature and stops or rejects them, depending on the switch setting.

Card counting is possible by a mechanism that registers a 1 for each card that passes through the sorter. A maximum count of 999,999 is registered on a dial that is read for manual transcription. The total is used for control purposes to ensure that the correct number of cards is processed for the job. Another card-counting device contains 14 five-digit counters, one for each pocket and one for totals.

MACHINE OPERATION

The sorter has 13 pockets, one for each of the 12 possible punches in a card column and a reject pocket, which has several uses. Card reading is accomplished by a brush (Fig. 5-2), which can detect the presence of a punched hole. Since the sorter reads only one column of the card at a time, only one brush is necessary and is positioned by the operator to read one of the 80 vertical columns. As the card passes through the machine, it passes over an electric contact roller. While the card is passing over the contact roller, it passes under the reading brush. If a hole is sensed, the brush makes contact with the electric roller (closing the circuit) and a timed electrical impulse passes through the brush. The impulse actuates a chute blade, which directs the card to the appropriate pocket. If the card column being read is blank, no electrical impulse is available, and the card is directed to the reject pocket.

The sorter, like all machines, functions on the basis of timing. The only difference between one punch in a card

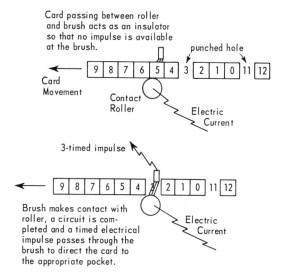

Fig. 5-2   Card-reading schematic.

and another is its position. One punch is distinguished from another by its being at a certain place at a certain time while moving past the reading mechanism. The amount of time taken to pass from a given spot in one card to the same spot in the next card is called a *card cycle.* Cards normally enter the sorter 9-edge first. As the card passes under the brushes, the 9 position of the column being sorted is read, then the 8 position, the 7 position, and so on until the 12 position. In fact, the machine recognizes which digit is punched by the amount of time that elapses from the moment the 9 position passes under the brush until the moment the brush makes contact with the roller and the impulse becomes available.

SORTING PRINCIPLES

Numeric sorting is the arrangement of a field of information which contains only the punched holes 0 to 9. Each column of the field requires one sort, so the cards must be passed through the machine once for each column of numeric information to be sorted. The column selector knob is set to the units column of the field since sorting progresses column by column from right to left across the field. When the *start* key is pressed, the cards begin entering the machine one at a time from the bottom of the stack. Assume that a deck of cards is to be sorted on employee number, columns 54 to 56. The cards are sorted first on column 56. Cards sorted in the 0 pocket contain all employee numbers ending in 0, for example, employee numbers 310, 940, 270, 580, etc. Cards sorted in the 1 pocket contain all the employee numbers with 151, 671, 321, 801, etc. Other cards fall into their respective pockets. For ascending sequence the cards are removed from right to left, stacking the 1s on the 0s, 2s on those, and so forth.

On the second sort, the column selector knob is set to the tens position, or column 55. After the sort is completed, the cards are removed from the pockets in order. The file is now in sequence by the tens and units position of employee number or 01 to 99.

To complete the numeric arrangement, the sorting brush is set to the final column, the hundreds position. Cards falling into the 0 pocket contain employee numbers 001 to 099; pocket 1, employee numbers 100 to 199; pocket 2, employee numbers 200 to 299, and so forth.

Now that we have covered the technique of sorting, let us discuss the *sort-selection* switch. A five-position rotating switch (Fig. 5-3) determines the sorting pattern. The N (numeric) setting causes cards to be directed to the 0 to 9 pockets normally. Cards with errors, such as double-punched cards, fall into the reject pocket if the *edit* switch is ON. So, for our sample of sorting employee number, the *sort-selection* switch is set to N and the *edit* switch turned ON. The Z (zone) setting directs cards with 0, 11, and 12 to their respective pockets. Cards without a zone or any cards with more than one zone fall into the reject pocket. The A1 (alphabetic sort 1) setting sorts the

letters A to I into pockets 1 to 9, respectively. The letters J to R fall into the 11 pocket and the letters S to Z into pocket 0. Cards with numeric digits, as well as multiple-digit punches or multiple-zone punches, fall into the reject pocket. The A2 (alphabetic sort 2) setting sorts the 11 zone (J through R) and 0 zone (S through Z) cards on the digit punches. The error condition is the same as A1. The AN (alphanumeric) setting sorts the numerical digits 0 to 9 to their appropriate pocket, cards with 12 zone (A through I) into the 12 pocket, cards with 11 zone (J through R) into the 11 pocket and cards with 0 zone (S through Z) into the reject pocket. The error condition is the same as A1.

Alphabetic sorting requires two passes through the machine for most cards for each column of alphabetic information to be sorted, because an alphabetic character is recorded by two punches (zone and digit) in the same column. As with numeric, each column of the field, beginning with the units column, must be sorted. On the first pass for each column sorted, the *sort-selection* switch is set to A1. The letters A to I (Fig. 5-4) sort into pockets 1 to 9 and are sorted completely on this pass. The 1 to 9 (A to I) pockets are stacked in order. Now the cards are ready for the second sort on A2. Sort the cards from the 11 pocket (J to R) on switch setting A2, which sorts them into the 1 to 9 pockets. Stack them in order and place behind the A to I cards. Next, sort the 0 zone cards (S to Z) which also sort into the 1 to 9 pockets. Place these behind the other cards and repeat these A1 and A2 sorting procedures for each column, progressing from right to left across the field.

Alphanumeric sorting is accomplished using the AN *sort-selection* switch. This setting follows handling techniques similar to the alphabetic sort. The digits 0 to 9 sort into the 0 to 9 pockets, thus separating the numeric cards from the letters. The 12 zones, 11 zones, and 0 zones sort into the 12 pocket, 11 pocket, and reject pocket, respectively. The digit cards are stacked in order, and the three separate alphabetic groups require only one more sort. To complete the alphabetic sort, sort the 12-zone cards (A to I) on A1; sort the 11 zone cards (J to R) and 0 zone cards (S to Z) on A2 switch setting. For reasons that will be explained later under collating se-

Fig. 5-3   IBM 83 Sorter Machine Controls.

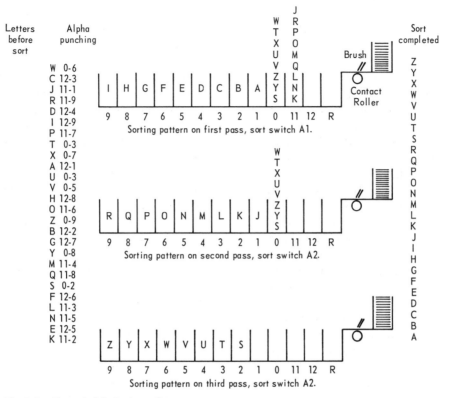

Fig. 5-4 Normal alphabetic sorting.

quence, the alphabetic cards A to Z are placed in front of the numeric 0 to 9 cards after each column is sorted.

Block sorting is a technique used with a large volume of cards. The two major advantages of block sorting are reducing the possibility of error and completing rush jobs by the quickest method. For instance, a sorting job involving 40,000 cards can be separated into segments. If the field is alphabetic, the cards may be sorted first on the leftmost column of the field in order to segment the cards by zones. In so doing, the A to I (12 zone) cards may be sorted on all columns while the J to R (11 zone) and S to Z (0 zone) wait their turn. As the A to I group is sorted, the other two groups may be sorted on other machines. If one group is missorted, only that group must be resorted and the others may continue being processed with different machines. When only one sorter

is available, the A to I group may progress to the next machine for further processing after the sorting is completed. Then the next group can be sorted, passed on to the next machine, and so forth.

Card sorting usually involves more than one field. Unless the problem is defined accurately and the operator understands exactly what report is wanted, the job will most likely be finished incorrectly and require rerunning. This is one reason "electronic brain" is far from being a correct term for data processing machines. Machines cannot think, will process data precisely as instructed by the human programmer, and, in fact, will process incorrect information as rapidly as correct information. As an example, a report showing total sales by salesmen within each sales office as well as totals by districts may be requested vaguely as "by district, by office, by salesman."

In order to eliminate any confusion as to the correct sequence, each field is identified by its importance within the report. *Major sequence* is assigned to district, *intermediate* is assigned to sales office, and *minor* sequence to salesman.

We may associate our names with these terms. Our last name would be given a value of major sequence because it is the most important, our first name would be intermediate since it is next important, and our middle name would be minor because it is of the least importance. We should remember that, unlike the importance of names, importance of data can be changed by the user and that which is of major importance in one report may be of minor importance in another. For example, one report may show totals by sales offices as major and by product as minor in order to compare the sales of each office. Another report may reflect product as major and sales offices as minor in order to compare sales of each product.

Modern business concerns often have occasions when only certain information is needed from an entire file. Let us assume a need has arisen to relocate a portion of the company. Naturally, it would be less costly for the company to move single employees. Management has requested a report on single, male employees, containing such items as name, occupation code, date of birth, withholding exemptions, etc. By using the *digit-suppression* keys (Fig. 5-3), the cards desired to prepare the report may be selected without disturbing the remainder of the personnel file, which is in name sequence. There are 12 *digit-suppression* keys which correspond to the 12 punching positions in a card. When a key is depressed, it causes the reading brush to disregard the punch detected in that column. Since we want to retain the original sequence of the file, we must prevent the cards from sorting into their respective pockets. If single, male employees are coded 5 in the marital status–sex column, the 5-73 (5 punch in column 73) cards will sort to the 5 pocket and all others will fall into the reject pocket if all *digit-suppression* keys are depressed except the 5 key. Thus the cards not required for the report sort to the reject pocket and the sequence remains undisturbed.

Special devices are available that save card handling and time, and extend the application possibilities. The *sort-suppression* switch, when ON, directs all cards into the 12 pocket that otherwise would have sorted to their appropriate pockets. In the example of selection above, the selected cards would have been out of sequence had we desired cards coded 5-73 and 6-73. With the *sort-suppression* switch ON, the cards with a 5 or 6 in column 73 would sort to the 12 pocket and remain in alphabetic sequence by name.

Another special, time-saving feature is the *alphabetic sorting device*. The A1, A2, and AN switch patterns are permanently changed. On an alphabetic sort, the letters, A, C, E, G, I, L, O, R, U, and X fall into pockets 0 to 9, respectively, with the switch set to A1 on the first sort. The remaining letters fall into the 11 and 12 pockets. Without removing the cards in pockets 0 to 9, the switch is set to A2 and the cards from the 12 pocket are placed in the hopper followed by the cards from the 11 pocket. Cards sort to their proper pocket and the column is completely sorted with a minimum of card handling. The letters in pockets 0 to 9 are shown in Fig. 5-5. Similar time is saved on an alphanumeric sort. The digits sort to the proper pocket and are stacked in order. The letters are arranged into pockets 11, 12, and reject in such a fashion to require only one pass altogether. Other special features are also available.

DOCUMENT AND ACCOUNTING CONTROLS

This section concerns the system of checks and balances to ensure that only correct and authorized data enter the accounting operation for processing. The extent of document and accounting controls depends upon the

Fig. 5-5 Pattern for special alphabetic sorting feature.

nature of the application to be processed, as well as the procedures and equipment employed in processing it. Controls are built into the procedure during the planning phase, and, of course, are improved as the need arises. A proper balance between their cost and value is important. The effectiveness of controls may be sacrificed when overcontrol occurs. Only those which satisfy a need should be included.

Controls should be simple and easy to maintain in order to prevent disruption of the workflow. Whenever possible, they should be mechanized. The control operations within data processing should be documented in the machine-processing procedure as to recording of record counts or totals and action to take when an out-of-balance condition is located.

A variety of control techniques will be discussed. Our discussion begins by briefly covering controls outside the data processing department and then covering those used and established within data processing. Controls are included with this chapter because the sorter is widely used as an initial control point.

At the point of receipt or origin, a serial number can be logged and stamped on each individual document. This is particularly important where documents that represent monetary value must be accounted for. Punch cards as documents (for such applications as billing, checks, etc.) are popular because the source data and machine medium are the same, making mechanized control possible for both. The punched serial number allows automatic checking for missing documents.

Signed transmittal slips are used to establish control and transfer responsibility when documents move from one department or location to another. The transmittal slip accompanies a group or batch of documents and includes the number of documents as well as an indication of beginning and ending serial numbers. We may conclude accounting controls outside the data processing department by stating that this agency is responsible for the initiation, authorization, and verification of accounting transaction documents.

Let us begin the techniques of controls in data processing as the documents are received. If the documents are already punched, they may be counted on the sorter and compared to the total on the batch ticket. Where stricter controls are necessary, the serial numbers may be checked automatically by a collating machine for sequence, duplicate numbers, or missing documents. Unpunched documents are verified after keypunching by the method covered in the preceding chapter. This assures that the cards are correct before processing in another operation. The cards are counted immediately after verification and checked against the batch ticket total.

The IBM 108 card proving machine covered in the next chapter is an effective tool for controlling. Cards can be counted, checked for consecutive numbering, and edited for blank columns, double punches, or proper sequence. Control totals (such as dollar amounts or quantities) and hash totals, which are based upon an identification code (such as employee number), may be accumulated for balancing operations during processing. The accumulated totals could be balanced with a total, if known, punched in the last card.

Summarization in punched card form can be proved by combining the detail cards used to prepare the summary data with the newly punched summaries and performing a zero balance operation. *Zero balancing* is accomplished by adding the detail cards for each category and subtracting the corresponding summary card. The result is a zero balance if both are correct. A simpler control can be performed by tallying a final total on the printer during summarization, accumulating the summary cards, and comparing the totals. When the summary cards are to be processed by the computer against information stored within, i.e., random access disk file, or recorded onto magnetic tape, the program (computer instructions) should develop a total from the cards and balance it to the totals processed internally.

During report preparation all transaction items must be calculated accurately and included in the processing. The data themselves are assumed correct since punching, summary operations, etc., are proved as they occur. Crossfooting insures the desired accuracy. *Crossfooting* is the operation of calculating columnar totals in a horizontal spread to prove processing accuracy. For example, the final totals of gross pay should equal the final totals of net pay plus deductions.

Finally, the machines have built-in checks for internal control. The IBM 407 accounting machine automatically stops when the printing mechanism contains data different from that in the counters. Calculators have similar built-in checks. Computers will halt on *parity checks,* which means that information in memory does not agree with data read by the input device or with output data which are ready for punching or printing. Information written on magnetic tape is checked for validity immediately after writing. And the controls appear almost endless.

Our next machine will also be a sorting device and will begin the building-block process of wired programming.

QUESTIONS

1. What is a master card? A detail card?
2. Can a *numeric* field of two positions be arranged in sequence with a single sorting pass? Explain.
3. Assuming 10 percent handling time, how long should it take to sort 9053 cards on a seven-digit *numeric* field?
4. How would all switches be set for selecting digits 5 and 7 without disturbing either file's sequence?
5. What is the first and last column sorted in a minor-to-major sort?
6. Which technique(s) in controlling documents can be performed on the sorter?

6
Statistical machines

The science that deals with the collection of facts or data is known as *statistics*. They are important to both business and government in making vital decisions. And in turn, these decisions affect our lives. Stores sell popular items we prefer based upon sales statistics, the nation's economic pulse is examined based upon employment statistics, seats in Congress are allocated based upon census statistics, and so on.

EDITING MACHINES

Statistical machines, also referred to as card proving or editing machines, perform many tasks in addition to compiling statistics. For example, cards may be edited for consistency of coding before processing by other data processing machines. This gives added assurance that the punch-input data are correct, thereby reducing the possibility of having to rerun the final product because of incorrect data. At the same time, totals can be accumulated, manually recorded, and compared with the final report to ensure that the correct cards were processed.

In appearance, the IBM 108 card proving machine (Fig. 6-1) looks like the sorter, covered in the preceding chapter. The similarity ends with appearance. Although both machines are capable of sorting cards, the 108 must be instructed by control-panel wiring to do so. In fact, the machine has to be wired to perform any operation. This is known as a wired program as opposed to a stored program. A *program* is simply a sequence of

machine instructions to direct the machine step-by-step in the solution of a problem. A *stored program* consists of instructions stored inside the machine, whereas a *wired program* is in the form of instructions specified by the interconnection of wires plugged into a removable control panel.

Printing and summary punching of the results may be accomplished while the machine accumulates totals and compiles the facts. To perform this dual operation the 108 is connected to an output typewriter and card punch. The 108 operates at a speed of 1000 cards per minute. The IBM 867 typewriter and the IBM 534 card punch perform at the rate of 1000 characters per minute.

COMPILING AND EDITING STATISTICS

Before facts can be compiled in a meaningful sequence, there are elementary steps that must be taken. First, we must gather the facts. This can be accomplished through surveys completed by selected individuals, employment forms filled out at the time of hiring, and so forth. Then the facts must be coded to facilitate processing by high-speed machines. An example of coded data is a one-position field containing marital–sex status. Male, unmarried persons can be represented by a 1

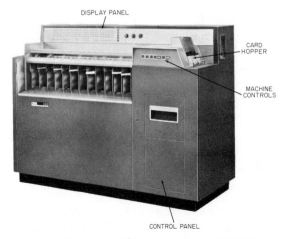

Fig. 6-1   IBM 108 Card Proving Machine. (IBM Corp.)

punched in the field, female unmarried persons by a 2, male married persons by a 3, and female married persons by a 4. As illustrated, two or more facts can be included in a single code. Other facts, such as age, pay grade, salary, occupation, locality, number of dependents, education, rents or owns home, must also be coded. Another advantage gained from coding is that a maximum of facts is recorded in each punched card.

Since the human element enters into coding the facts, as well as into the operation of punching the data onto cards, the facts must be edited to ensure accuracy and consistency. Previously, we defined editing as checking for conformance to a particular pattern, that is, checking for the impossible. For example, marital–sex codes 3 and 4, which represent married persons, can be edited to the field containing age. Those cards punched with an age less than an arbitrary 18 would be rejected to an error pocket. In another error example, the age field is punched as 20, at the same time that the occupation code indicates that the employee is a nuclear physicist. Validity of the *marital–sex* field can be further checked for errors which are codes other than 1 to 4. Likewise, the age field can be checked for incorrect codes not falling within the range of 17 to 65. Nearly every code can be cross-checked to another code. Even a code not related to another can be checked for blank columns or double punches.

After the facts are edited and corrected, we are ready to tabulate them into meaningful statistics to enable comparison, evaluation, and interpretation. As the facts are compiled for printing and punching, the cards may be sorted into 1 of 13 pockets according to categories.

Now that we have discussed what the machine is designed to accomplish, let us begin the basic principles of control-panel wiring.

CONTROLLING MACHINE FUNCTIONS WITH THE CONTROL PANEL

The *control panel* (Fig. 6-2) can be removed from, or inserted into, the machine as needed. The panel has many small holes, called *hubs,* into which you can insert wires

with special tips. Each hub in the panel has a specific purpose. Instructions are given to the machine by plugging wires into the hubs. You must know what each hub is for and then, knowing what you want the machine to do, you can plug the wires into the proper hubs.

When the panel is inserted into the machine, each hub is aligned with a metal contact or *prong*. Each prong is internally wired to cause some machine function, such as reading a card, printing the data punched in the card, and so forth. In order to cause the machine to perform a specific function, a circuit must be completed. External wiring (control-panel wiring) completes the desired circuit. Let us examine Fig. 6-2 with an example. The dotted internal wire labeled A is connected to the reading brush, illustrated in Fig. 5-2. When the brush makes contact with the roller, a timed electrical impulse (referred to as card reading) passes through the brush and internal wiring to prong A. Therefore, the impulse, representing a digit or letter, can be directed to another hub, which will cause a machine action. Prong B is internally connected to cause a chute blade to direct a card into a specific pocket. So our control panel wire completes a circuit, directing the card to the pocket corresponding to the punch read in the card.

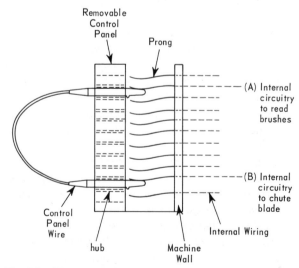

Fig. 6-2 Circuits completed by external wiring in control panel.

Fig. 6-3 Types of entry and exit hubs.

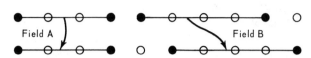

Fig. 6-5 Exit and entry fields connected by one line.

As we have seen, there are two types of hubs (Fig. 6-3). Those which accept impulses are called *entry* hubs, and those which emit impulses are called *exit* hubs. Control panel hubs may be single, or two or more may be internally connected to each other. If they are connected, they are called *common* hubs. *Common* hubs are identified on the face of the panel and diagram (Fig. 6-6) by lines connecting them.

If the *common* hubs are exits, the impulse is available out of all hubs connected by a line. An impulse from two or more sources is received if the *common* hubs are entries. A single external impulse wired into one of the *common* hubs is directed inside the machine to cause a function. That same impulse is available out of the other *common* (connected) hub to perform another function. For example, electricity enters a cooking stove to heat the elements, and also is available from an outlet to operate the toaster or coffee pot.

When it is necessary to connect one *exit* hub to two or more *entry* hubs (or vice versa), *common* hubs may not be available. This is done, instead, through the use of a common connector (Fig. 6-4). An impulse brought into the connecting block is available for the other two terminals in the block. This type of wiring is known as *split wiring* and should be used as a last resort. Given a path, an impulse can flow in any direction. For this reason, a split impulse can cause unwanted machine functions

known as *back circuits.* We shall see their erroneous effects and how to prevent them in Chap. 9.

Paper diagrams (Fig. 6-6) are an exact drawing of the control panel. They are used to keep a permanent record of the control panel setup. To keep the diagram as legible as possible, we have a few simple rules to follow when drawing a diagram. A *name* field containing 15 positions would, of course, require 15 separate wires. But 15 lines on a diagram would present a problem in drawing as well as in reading. To simplify the task, pencil in the leftmost and rightmost hub of the *exit* field and connect these hubs with a horizontal line (Fig. 6-5). Do the same for the *entry* field. Now the two fields are connected by a single line and may represent any number of individual wires in the panel. To identify *entry* and *exit* hubs we shall draw an arrow pointing toward the *entry* hub, that is, showing the direction of the impulse.

The two machines we have dealt with thus far, the keypunch and sorter, were covered thoroughly. However, the 108 and other data processing machines are more versatile, hence more involved. It is not the intent of this book to cover all functions of each machine in depth. One or more functions are covered at length to provide the necessary background to delve further into those areas of greatest importance to the student and his career. With this in mind, let us examine the functions and characteristics of the 108 control panel. Then we shall study an application in detail, involving card selection.

MACHINE FUNCTIONS

The 108 may be wired to sort cards in numeric or alphabetic sequence. The principle for sorting is the same as for the 83 sorter, covered in the last chapter. Also,

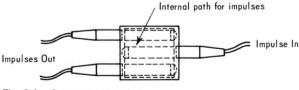

Fig. 6-4 Common connector.

the sequence of a sorted file may be checked for accuracy by the 108 through control panel wiring.

A file of cards may be searched for specific facts or a combination of facts. The selected cards can be directed together into 1 of 13 pockets or to various pockets by groups. Unlike the 83 sorter, the 108 can select multiple-coded columns on a single pass. For instance, all unmarried, male employees skilled as electrical engineers between the ages of 25 and 35 can be selected without disturbing the sequence of the remaining file. In fact, the selected employees can be grouped according to age by selecting cards coded age 25 to pocket 9, cards coded age 26 to pocket 8, cards coded age 27 to pocket 7, and so forth.

Cards selected to specific pockets may be counted and the accumulated totals printed as directed by panel wiring. The machine is able to distinguish the cards of one group from those of another. Therefore, totals are usually printed on a single line for each group of cards. In the above example, for instance, the total of unmarried electrical engineers aged 25 would print on the left margin of the paper, the total of those aged 26 to its right, and so on with the sum of the 11 age-group totals printed as the rightmost amount.

The control panel diagram (Fig. 6-6) appears difficult, if not mystifying, at first glance. We shall see that the panel is quite simple. It is divided into many segments, and many hubs within each segment have the same purpose. Each horizontal row of hubs is labeled with a letter (A-AR) along the left side of the diagram. Each column of hubs is numbered consecutively (1 to 64), beginning at the upper left corner of the diagram. All diagrams are labeled in this manner for referencing and aiding us in locating a specific hub or group of hubs.

As we previously stated, some hubs are exits, meaning that an impulse is available. Other hubs are entries and accept an impulse from the *exit* hubs. The four *sort-exit* hubs (AC, 29 to 32) emit sort impulses and are used to direct cards to a specific pocket. The four *sort-pattern* hubs (AE to AR, 33 to 36) are *entry* hubs to the 12 pockets. Whenever a *sort-pattern* hub is impulsed, a card is sorted to the corresponding pocket. For example, an impulse directed to any of the four 9-hubs (AR, 33 to 36)

results in the card under the reading brushes being sorted to pocket 9. The thirteenth pocket is the reject pocket and automatically accepts cards not selected to one of the other 12 pockets. Now let us see how the *sort* hubs and *sort-pattern* hubs work together in performing a minor operation. The dotted, external control panel wire (X) causes all cards to be directed to pocket 1. Now let us expand this simple operation into a more useful one, that of selecting all records for employees with occupation code 48 (electrical engineer) punched in columns 22 and 23, with marital-sex status code 1 (unmarried male) punched in column 3.

In general, we wire the sort impulse to search for the specific data desired. If the sort impulse locates a record meeting all the specified conditions, the panel wiring directs the card to pocket 5; otherwise, the unwanted records are automatically directed into the reject pocket.

First, let us discuss how card reading differs from the 83 sorter (Fig. 5-2). You will recall that the 83 sorter has a single brush which is manually moved to the column to be sorted. The 108 has two reading stations, each having 80 permanent brushes. Each card is read twice, once as it passes reading station 1 and a second time at reading station 2. We shall be concerned only with reading station 1. The *exit* hubs for these 80 reading brushes are called card reading 1 (J to M, 23 to 42).

The second subject to cover in solving our problem is *selection*. This means making a decision, or, in data processing terminology, a choice limited to electrical impulses. A choice by the machine is made by a device called a selector (S to AB, 1 to 60; AD to AR, 1 to 20). All punch-card machines that operate by control panels have selectors similar to the one we are about to discuss. A selector (Fig. 6-7*a*) has three hubs referred to as *common, normal,* and *transfer*. The *common* hub is connected to either the *normal* or *transfer* hubs. The *transfer* hub derives its name from the fact that when the magnet is energized, the armature is transferred (Fig. 6-7*b*) and the *common* and *transfer* hubs are internally connected. Whenever current is removed from the magnet, the selector returns to normal (Fig. 6-7*a*) and the connection between the *common* and *normal* hubs is restored. Operation of the selector is based upon electromagnetism.

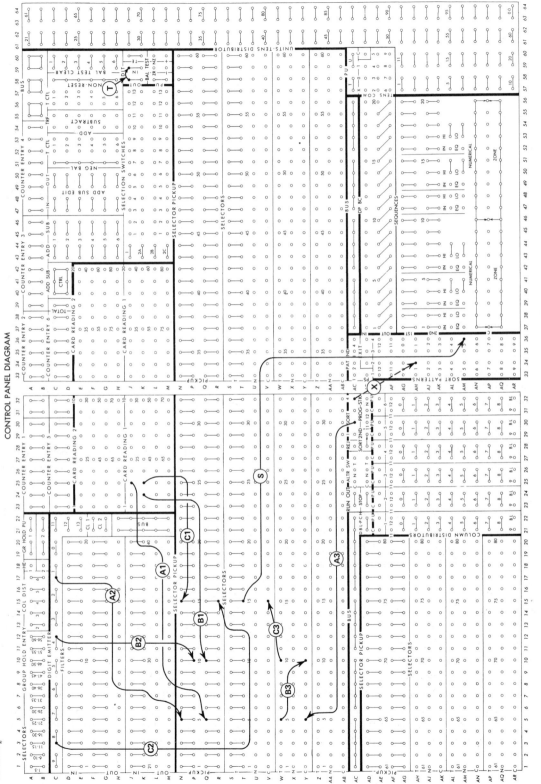

Fig. 6-6 108 wiring diagram for multicolumn selection.

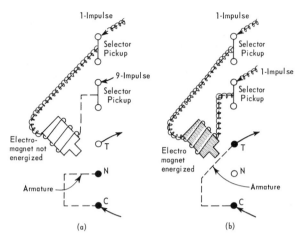

Fig. 6-7 **(a)** Selector normal; **(b)** selector transferred. Both pickup hubs must be impulsed simultaneously before the magnet is energized to transfer the selector.

Each of the 80 selectors has a magnet, which is a piece of iron (called a core) wrapped with wire. Magnetism of the core can be turned on and off by the presence or absence of an electrical impulse. When an impulse is passed through the coil of wire, the magnet becomes magnetized and attracts the armature. This breaks the connection between *normal* and *common* hubs because the armature moves to the *transfer* hub, thus making a connection between *common* and *transfer* hubs. Two *common selector pickup* hubs control transfer of the selector by energizing the magnet. Both *selector pickup* hubs must be impulsed at the same time (Fig. 6-7*b*) to energize the magnet and transfer the selector. The selector automatically returns to normal (Fig. 6-7*a*) before the next card is read.

The third and final subject concerned in solving our problem is the digit emitter (C, 1 to 20). By means of the digit emitter, the machine can manufacture the impulses required. This device merely supplies an impulse corresponding to the reading of each punch in the card. That is, when the 9 row of the card is being read by the brushes, the digit emitter emits a 9 from the *common 9* hub (C, 1 and 2); when the 8 row of the card is being read by the brushes, the *common 8* hub (C, 3 and 4) emits

an 8 impulse, and so on. We use the digit emitter to provide the digits corresponding to the codes we need in our selection problem.

In Fig. 6-6, sort-impulse 2 is wired (A3) to the *common* hub of selector 5. One pickup of selector 5 is wired (A2) from *digit emitter* hub 1 while column 3 is wired (A1) to the other pickup. When a 1 is read at column 3, the selector transfers. This happens because the emitted 1 impulse (A2) and the 1 impulse (A1) read from the card reach the magnet at the same time. Sort-impulse 2 now has a path through the *common* hub by internal circuitry to the *transfer* hub. This means we have a card containing an unmarried–male code, which can be further checked to determine if it has an electrical engineer code. If the selector had not transferred, the sex–status code would have been other than an unmarried male and the sort impulse would end at the *normal* hub (which is not wired). Therefore, the card would fall into the reject pocket.

Note that each of the 80 selectors is arranged in banks of three. This gives each individual selector three sets of *common, normal,* and *transfer* hubs. We wired the second bank of selector 5 at random. Any other bank or selector would have functioned the same.

The selected sort impulse, indicating an unmarried male, passes through selector 5 to the *common* hub (B3) of selector 10. When a 4 impulse (B1) from column 22 and an emitted 4 (B2) arrive at the selector pickup simultaneously, selector 10 transfers. The sort impulse continues through selector 10 to the *common* hub (C3) of selector 15. Again, if the selector had not transferred, the circuit would have been broken and the card automatically directed into the reject pocket.

The sort impulse, having passed two of the three conditions, is now checked for the final condition. If an 8 impulse is read at column 23, it passes to the selector pickup (C1), and an impulse from digit emitter 8 (C2) does likewise. The two impulses arrive at the same time and transfer the selector. The sort impulse has now met all three conditions, namely, a 1 in column 3 (unmarried male) and a 48 in columns 22 and 23 (electrical engineer), and passes through external wiring (S) to sort pattern or pocket 5.

We may summarize our problem by saying that the sort impulse must pass through the *transfer* hubs of the three conditioned selectors. Any wired selector that fails to transfer, breaks the circuit and rejects the card to pocket 13. In addition to the wiring discussed, *edit-out* hubs (T) must be wired to *edit-in* hubs for testing of improper wiring.

Understanding of the above cannot be overemphasized, for this is the basis of most functions in punched card data processing machines. If at first you do not understand, study the chapter a second time and again, if necessary. Later chapters involve selection of printing, addition, subtraction, and so forth.

PERSONNEL STATISTICS

This section concerns various personnel statistical applications that may be processed by the 108 card proving machine. Since the greatest part of a company's income is spent on labor, a statistical study of personnel records by management can result in increased efficiency and production, and a greater return on the labor dollar. A significant factor in achieving these results is understanding personnel turnover.

One such statistical report shows the reason for termination and gives a wealth of information. A count by termination reasons, such as wages, opportunity elsewhere, working conditions, and unsatisfactory work may be compiled by occupation or department. An analysis of the statistics may show a trend of termination in a particular occupation by reason of wages. This calls for a more detailed report of the problem area giving wage rate, length of service, education, length of employment, and so forth. Having the significant facts, management can take corrective action that will assure a more stable organization, higher morale, and elimination of retraining costs.

Selection and placement of employees is often made on the basis of friendship, because the applicant impressed an interviewer, or some other subjective reason. Much guesswork is removed if the person is selected by machine from a number of applicants. However, precise occupation requirements and qualifications must be ob-

tained from the department manager or foreman. Once known, this information is obtained from each applicant, coded, and punched onto a card. The 108 can then divide the applicants by groups according to those who best fit the job specifications. For example, the first group would include those who filled all of the requirements, the next group, those who filled all of the requirements except one, and so on.

Numerous other statistical reports are prepared from personnel records to keep management informed on the status of their employees. The seniority of employees can be compiled by department showing the number with less than 1 year, those with 1 to 5 years, those with 6 to 10 years, and so forth. These statistics forecast retirement and the need for replacements. Another report by occupation gives the number of employees by age groups. This can be especially desirable in establishing requirements for future applicants. The effectiveness of one occupation category may be traced to youthful employees, another occupation category may show the opposite.

Other reports are compiled concerning education, special training, handicapped employees, sex, military status, late and absent status, employee suggestions, and many more. Statistical reports are profitably used by a successful company because they give answers to management's questions.

QUESTIONS

1. How many decisions are available from all of the selectors?
2. Can a *common entry* hub function both as an *entry* and *exit* hub? Explain.
3. How does the field shown in Fig. 6-5 differ from a field wired on the control panel?
4. What is the function of the *sort exit* and *sort pattern* hubs?
5. How would you change the wiring in Fig. 6-6 to select married, male electrical engineers?
6. What is the need for statistical machines?
7. Explain the operation of a selector.
8. What is meant by the term "selected impulse"?

7
The card as a document-recording medium

The punched card is a familiar and popular document with both business and consumer. Income tax returns, car registrations, installment loans, payroll time tickets, and many other documents are often designed on punched cards. Simplicity of the card permits companies to pre-

pare other documents such as checks, bills, invoices, statements, and purchase orders with high-speed data processing machines. This eliminates many manual operations and results in time and dollar savings, which are passed on to the customer. For example, manual preparation of a mailing envelope and statement is eliminated when the punched card is used as a mailing document. The same punched card can also be fed directly into the machines with a minimum of manual handling after the statement is presented for payment. A stub from the card is retained by the customer as a receipt.

However, printing on the card by the keypunch (Fig. 3-2) is unsuitable for customers unfamiliar with data processing. There are several machines capable of printing on the card. The IBM 557 interpreter (Fig. 7-1) eliminates the difficulty in reading information printed by the keypunch by arranging the fields in an easily read format. For example, the fields containing name, street address, and city and state can be printed on three separate lines in the center of a check with the amount printed at the extreme right.

INTERPRETER FUNCTIONS

The 557 interprets numeric or alphabetic punches and prints the corresponding numerals or letters horizontally on the card as directed by control panel wiring. A print position dial located on the face of the machine is manually turned to select one of 25 possible printing lines. The 557 translates and prints up to 60 characters on each printed line at 100 cards per minute. The printed characters are larger than those printed by the keypunch because only 60 characters are printed on each line instead of 80.

To print more than 60 characters, a second line is used by passing the cards through the machine a second time. On some interpreters this requires changing the control panel wiring to accommodate the format for the second printing line. The 557 control panel has two printing or card-format setups. After the cards have been

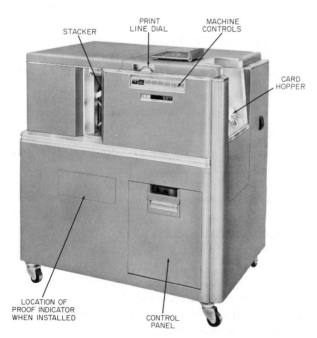

STACKER
PRINT LINE DIAL
MACHINE CONTROLS
CARD HOPPER
LOCATION OF PROOF INDICATOR WHEN INSTALLED
CONTROL PANEL

Fig. 7-1 IBM 557 Interpreter. (IBM Corp.)

printed on the first line, the machine operator flips a switch located on the machine that activates the second format wired on the control panel.

Information can be printed on the card from punches in that card or from another card. Printing data from another card is especially effective when regular payment transaction cards are posted to loan installment history cards (Fig. 7-2). This operation is performed by combining detail cards (payment transactions) behind master cards (premium history record) according to corresponding account numbers. In another example, master name and address cards are combined with statement cards, and name and address are posted from the master card to the detail card. The statement card is then ready for mailing to the customer.

Selective stackers (Fig. 7-3) may be installed to permit separating master and detail cards after printing. This feature eliminates the need to separate the cards by the sorter. Other operations, such as selecting master cards without corresponding detail cards, may also be performed. Another feature, controlled by panel wiring, permits the printing mechanism to print repetitive informa-

tion on all cards. For example, the advertising slogan "Spring Time Is Tune-up Time" can be printed on all statements for a business repairing automobiles.

Proofreading is the operation of checking for incorrect printing. A factor in customer satisfaction is the timely and accurate processing of an account. Every possible measure should be taken to ensure accuracy. Proofreading provides for a second reading of the card, a comparison of the two results, and suppression of printing on the card in error. Similar action occurs for printing. An error in any position read or printed lights the proof indicator located under the stacker pocket (Fig. 7-1). Check protection is ensured by printing asterisks to the left of the amount whenever the number of positions in the amount is less than the maximum size of the field. For example, a four-position total in a seven-position field is printed as $***35.90.

Several other devices are available that increase the flexibility of this versatile printing machine. We shall be concerned with the basic functions of printing, elimination of control punches, and controlling the printing of zeros.

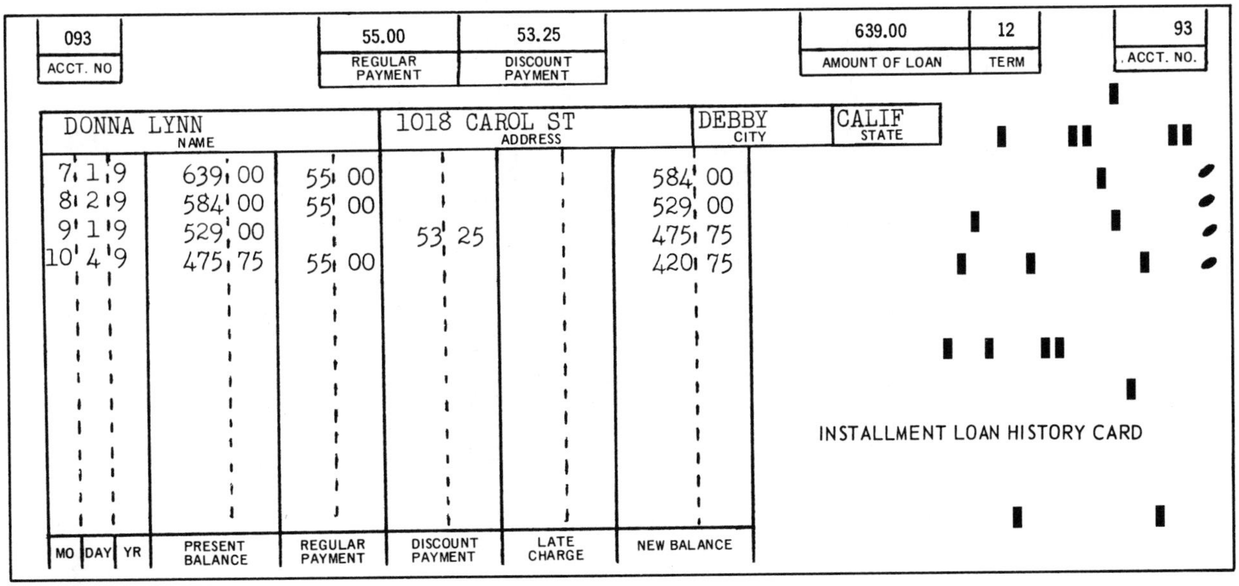

Fig. 7-2 Installment loan history card printed by 557 Interpreter.

CARD READING AND PRINTING

The basic operation of the interpreter is to read information punched in a card and print that information on the same card. Printing is done by means of 60 typewheels, each containing 10 numbers, 26 alphabetic letters, and 11 special characters, such as the dollar symbol ($).

Fundamentally, printing is caused by an external wire that completes a circuit between the reading brushes and the printing device. Electrical impulses which result from sensing holes in the card (Fig. 7-3) travel by internal wiring to the control panel where the operations of the machine are controlled by means of external wiring. Wires plugged into the *print-entry* hubs continue traveling by internal wiring to the print wheels. In Fig. 7-4, the 80 *exit common* hubs for card reading are located in rows D to L, columns 1 to 20. The 60 *entry* hubs to the print wheels are located at rows M to P, columns 1 to 20. A second set of *entry* hubs to the print wheels is located below these. Either may be used and permits two different card or print formats to be wired on the same control panel.

Let us discuss the panel wiring necessary to print the top line on the card in Fig. 7-2. The name and address are not punched in the card and are printed from a master name card in another operation. The posted ledger entries are likewise not punched and are printed monthly from regular payment transaction cards.

To print the fields for discount payment (A), account number (B1 and B2), regular payment (C), term of the loan (D), and the amount of loan (E), we simply wire from the hubs corresponding to the known columns in the card to the hubs corresponding to the desired printing location. As the card is read, the electrical impulses travel through internal circuitry to the 80 *interpret-reading* hubs. Our external wiring continues the impulses to print entry 2 where internal circuitry again provides a path to the 60 print wheels. Note that we have wired account number to print in two different locations by use of the *common* hubs. Each of the two hubs located at rows Q and R, column 21, is called an X switch. Switches are identified on the control panel by two hubs connected by a line with an arrow. This switch (F) must be wired ON for the operation of basic printing.

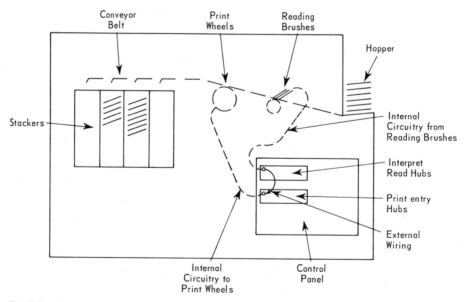

Fig. 7-3 Internal and external wiring schematic.

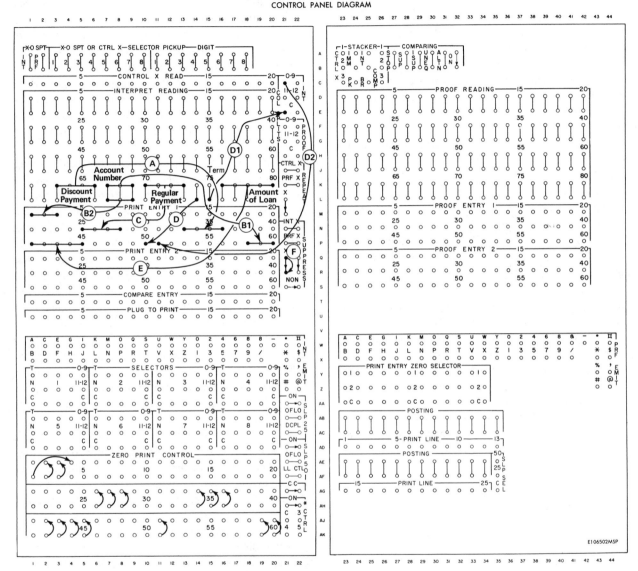

Fig. 7-4 Normal printing, 557 Interpreter.

CONTROL OF PRINTING

The X-control punch in column 75 of the installment loan history card is a code that identifies customers who have had previous loans. Its purpose is to permit selection of X-75 or NX-75 cards in order to prepare reports desired by management. However, the X punch poses a problem to the interpreter. The machine does not recognize it as a control punch. Instead, the interpreter combines the X-control punch with the numeric punch, resulting in the printing of an alphabetic character. In the illustration (Fig. 7-2), the month in the *term* field (length of the loan) would print as 1K instead of 12. Therefore, we must wire the control panel to print the numeric information instead of the alphabetic character. The device to solve our problem is called a column split.

The *column split* (Fig. 7-5) is a selector and operates similarly to the one covered in the preceding chapter. As the name implies, the device separates the 0 to 9 punches from the 11 and 12 punches. Like the selector in Fig. 6-7, the column split has three hubs, labeled *common*, 0 to 9, and 11 and 12. The main difference between the column split and the selector is that the column split is controlled automatically. You will recall that we can break the common and normal internal connection in the selector by directing an impulse to the selector pickup, resulting in a common and transfer connection.

Cards are fed into the interpreter 12-edge first. At 12-time (when the 12 punches are read by the reading

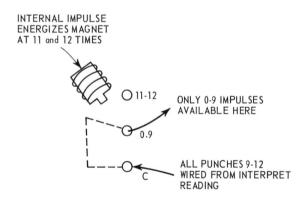

Fig. 7-5 Column split at digit time.

INTERNAL IMPULSE
ENERGIZES MAGNET
AT 11 and 12 TIMES

○ 11-12   ONLY 0-9 IMPULSES
           AVAILABLE HERE

○ 0.9

○ C   ALL PUNCHES 9-12
           WIRED FROM INTERPRET
           READING

brushes), the magnet (Fig. 7-5) is energized by an internal impulse and the armature is attracted to the magnet, thus making a common and 11-and-12 internal connection. The magnet remains energized during 11-time. The impulse to the magnet is removed before 0-time and the armature returns to the normal (0 to 9) position. Therefore, when the magnet is not energized, a connection between common and 0 to 9 exists. Now that we know how the column split operates, let us follow the panel wiring (D1 and D2) to prevent the control-X impulse from reaching the *print-entry* hubs.

As an X-75 card passes the reading brushes, the magnet is energized at 12-time. The X impulse from reading-brush 75 passes through internal circuitry to the *interpret-reading* hubs. Column 75 is externally wired (D1) to the *common* hub of the column split. The X impulse continues internally through the column split to the 11 and 12 hub. This hub is not wired; therefore, the impulse is nullified. Before digit (0 to 9) time, the magnet is dropped out (deenergized), restoring the 0 to 9 and common connection. At 2-time the 2 impulse passes internally from the reading brush to the *interpret-reading* hubs and externally to the *common* hub of the column split. The 2 impulse continues internally through the column split to the 0 to 9 hubs whereby an external wire (D2) furnishes a path to print position 51. Therefore, we have eliminated the X impulse and printed only the numeric formation.

The 557 has eight 5-position selectors (Y to AD, 1 to 20) that permit selection of the information to be printed. Depending upon a control punch, information may be printed in one of two locations from one field punched in the card. For instance, the monthly payment transaction card, used to update the loan history card (Fig. 7-2), could have the payment punched in one field, with an X punch to distinguish between regular payments and discount payments. The *payment* field would be wired to the *common* hubs of a selector and the regular payment (NX condition) wired from the *normal* hubs to print. The discount payment (X conditions) would be wired from the *transfer* hubs to print in another location. The opposite is also possible, that is, to select from one of two possible fields punched in a card to print in one location.

We have completed a study of a second type of selector and discovered a similarity. Because of this and other similarities, a misunderstanding exists, namely, that all data processing machines are basically the same. Machines are different and have characteristics of their own. However, a building-block principle of learning is possible because knowledge of the machines is reinforced from one machine to another. Studying a basic machine-theory curriculum and one or more individual machine courses lays the groundwork for the operator or programmer to learn other machines with less effort. As you have already recognized, this book is also based upon a building-block principle. Hence, an understanding of subsequent machines yet to be covered should be easier even though they are more complex than the ones discussed thus far.

CONTROLLING THE PRINTING OF ZEROS

The meaningfulness of a zero depends upon its position within a number and often upon the number itself. The first zero of social security number 039-44-8143 has significance, whereas the first zero of dollar amount 04650 has no significance. The *amount* field should be printed as $46.50; the control panel must be wired to print the low-order (units position) zero, since it has significance, and to eliminate printing of the high-order (leftmost position) zero, since it has no significance.

The hubs that control the printing of zeros are located at rows AE to AK, columns 1 to 20. There are two *zero-print* hubs for each print position. Let us discuss their positioning to better understand how the control panel is wired. The lower hub in the first position (Fig. 7-6) is the lower hub of print position 1, and the upper hub in the second position is the upper hub of print position 1, and so on. Therefore, the first set of diagonal *zero-print* hubs corresponds to print-entry position 1, the second set corresponds to print-entry position 2, and so forth.

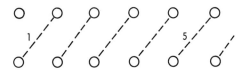

Fig. 7-6   Zero-print-control hubs.

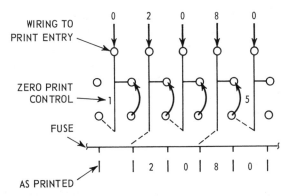

Fig. 7-7   Zero-print schematic, printing zeros to right of significant digits only.

Printing occurs automatically for the digits 1 to 9 and any alphabetic character. This is possible because the digits 1 to 9 transfer the zero-print contacts as illustrated in Fig. 7-7. Zeros by themselves do not transfer the contacts. If the print contacts do not transfer, data for that position cannot reach the fuse and consequently does not print. Therefore, a path to the fuse must be provided for zeros, resulting in external control by panel wiring for the printing of zeros. This is accomplished by wiring the *zero-print-control* hubs for each position of all numeric fields. For example, in Fig. 7-7 the upper of hub 1 is externally wired to the lower of hub 2, the upper of hub 2 is externally wired to the lower of hub 3, and so on. The significant digits in Fig. 7-7 have a path directly to the fuse. The zeros in print positions 3 and 5 have an indirect path to the fuse by control panel wiring.

It is important to be able to follow the path of an impulse both internally and externally. You can gain this understanding by following the path of the zero impulse from position 5 through the external zero-print-control wire to position 4 and internally through the transferred contact points of position 4 to the fuse.

The insignificant zero in position 1 does not have a path to the fuse, so it does not print. It cannot reach the fuse line by way of lower hub 1 since the print contacts are not transferred. Neither can it reach the fuse by the external wire between hub 1 and 2 because the digit 2 has transferred the print contact.

In addition to normal zero-print control, we can make

zeros to the left of a significant digit print as illustrated by account number in Fig. 7-4. It is also possible to print a field of all zeros. For instance, in dollar amounts, it is a general practice to print .00 whenever a zero amount is encountered. The zero-print wiring for the six fields printed at the top of the Loan Installment Card (Fig. 7-2) is shown in Fig. 7-4.

QUESTIONS

1. What selector wiring is necessary to print in a single location on the card from one of two possible fields punched in the card?

2. To print a card 80-80, that is to print all 80 columns in the same format they are punched, how would you wire the control panel?

3. Illustrate the wiring required to print only the numeric data punched in column 37 and to combine the control X punch in column 37 with the numeric code punched in column 80.

4. In Fig. 7-7, what wiring is needed to cause the zero in print position 1 to print?

5. What does 9-time mean?

6. Explain the path of an electrical impulse from the reading brush to the print wheels?

7. What causes the middle zero (position 3) in Fig. 7-7 to print?

8
Mechanized filing means

Filing and locating records is a major problem in modern business. Each phase of business has its own requirements for record keeping of sales, inventory, purchases, credit, shipments, payroll, taxes, production, and so on. Complete and accurate documentation is necessary if the company is to meet its obligations to its customers and stockholders. It is necessary also for tax and social security requirements.

PROBLEMS IN RECORD KEEPING

At first, businesses keep their records and important transactions in a book that usually requires a separate page for each category of information. As the business grows, so does the problem of filing. Record keeping progresses from one book to a number of books and soon to several filing cabinets. A filing clerk is eventually required, then several are needed to prevent lagging too far behind the actual transactions. An even bigger problem is now coming into the picture, that of correct filing and accessibility. Consequently, the filing system is in constant turmoil in search for improvement.

Locating information is a costly and time-consuming process. If the data have to be listed, the report will probably be out of date and, perhaps, useless by the time it is written. A fast means of filing and locating information is required. This is only one of the ways data processing can assist in producing a profit.

The most common filing system is a cabinet with several drawers. However, different-sized documents are difficult to file. To easily locate information when needed, the documents must be numbered, requiring another manual operation. It is now obvious that manual methods are unfeasible for a company that requires a number of clerks to handle filing.

REQUIREMENTS OF FILING

Since we have discussed the problems in filing, let us consider some requirements of a punched-card filing system. The card format, covered in Chaps. 3 and 4, must be designed to provide complete and accurate data. After the cards are punched, they must be arranged for filing. This is made possible by the sorter. If cross-indexing is desired, a duplicate file can be readily created and each deck arranged in a different sequence. An example of cross-indexing is two files of a company's customers, one in account-number sequence and the other in alphabetic sequence by name.

A good filing system permits moving data into and out of the files easily. As we shall see, high-speed data processing machines meet both requirements. Another criterion of good file maintenance is the ability to compile *selected* information for report preparation. The machine covered in this chapter can select particular documents, groups of documents, or certain documents in a group, and arrange them into the desired sequence. Most important, a good system permits locating and removing data on short notice, regardless of sequence. Consequently, management decisions can be founded on factual information made available at the proper time.

The volume of transactions determines the magnitude of the filing problem. The filing system is designed to accommodate every pertinent detail, adding up to a large mass of data. Space to store files is expensive, and sometimes not even available. An idea of the savings gained by using punched cards instead of original documents is seen from the following fact. Approximately 25 filing cabinets of data in source-document form can be condensed into punch-card form requiring only one cabinet. This is possible because a single cabinet, designed to store 120,000 punch cards, will contain the equivalent of nearly 10 million items of information.

A filing system must be flexible and accurate. Mechanized filing is virtually 100 percent accurate and documents can be located at speeds of several hundred per minute. Documents must be filed according to some important classification, such as account number. However, management may desire certain items unrelated to the sequence. This is possible by mechanized filing. The only requirement is that someone instruct the machine how to locate the item at random. We have covered the many facets of filing. Now let us cover the machine, called a *collator,* that solves the filing problem and many other problems.

COLLATOR FUNCTIONS

The four basic functions performed on the collator are combining two files of cards into one file, checking the sequence of cards in a file, matching two files of cards, and selecting specific cards from a file. During these operations, cards may be edited or checked for accuracy of punching.

There are several types of collators, each capable of performing the basic functions. The main differences are speed and the ability to process either numeric data or numeric and alphabetic data. The IBM 88 collator (Fig. 8-1) has been chosen for illustration. It is rated at a speed of 650 to 1300 cards per minute and processes numeric information. Cards are fed from opposite ends of the 88 collator and are stacked in five pockets, according to the grouping desired. The primary feed hopper accepts cards nine-edge first, and the secondary feed hopper accepts them 12-edge first.

The function of *sequence checking* verifies the sequence, ascending or descending, of a file. Since each feed has two sets of reading brushes (Fig. 8-3), each card is compared with the one ahead to determine if it is higher, lower, or equal to the preceding card. Sequence checking can be performed as an independent function, or in combination with one of the other operations. The control panel is wired to stop the machine and turn on an *error* light when an error in sequence is detected.

Merging is the operation of combining two files of cards (Fig. 8-2) that are already in numeric or alphabetic

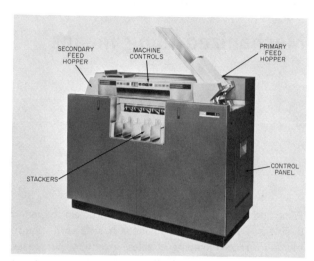

Fig. 8-1　IBM 88 Collator. (IBM Corp.)

sequence. The merging operation involves comparing a card in one file with a card in the other file to determine which card should be selected first to the pocket containing the combined file. If the comparison is low, the low card is selected to the pocket, and another card is fed into its place for comparing. Two cards of equal rank may be selected to the pocket at the same time. Otherwise, merging is simply a process of selecting the lower of two cards being compared.

Matching is similar to merging, except that the two files containing matched cards are stacked in two separate pockets. The unmatched cards from each file are stacked in third and fourth pockets. The operation of matching can be altered to *match-merging* by selecting the matching cards from both files to pocket 3, and the unmatched cards to pockets 1 and 5.

Selection is the term used for the operation of withdrawing cards from a file according to conditions wired on the control panel. For example, it is possible to select the first card or last card of each group, all cards with a given number, or cards punched with digits between two control numbers, such as 499 and 600. Both feeds may be used in this operation by sending part of the file through the primary feed and the remainder of the file through the secondary feed. Selection may be combined with other operations, or performed by itself.

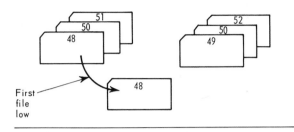

First file low

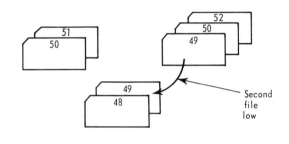

Second file low

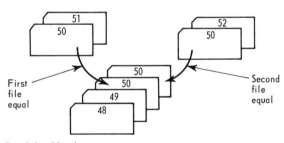

First file equal

Second file equal

Fig. 8-2   Merging.

PRINCIPLES OF COLLATING

The first step in solving a problem, before wiring the 88 collator, is to understand the relationship between the control panel (Fig. 8-5) and the internal schematic (Fig. 8-3). Each problem should be analyzed using the internal schematic by studying the various conditions that may arise as cards are fed through the machine. For instance, an out-of-sequence card is identified whenever a number in unit 1 is lower than the number in unit 2 of the sequence units. In the primary feed of Fig. 8-3, the card punched 32 is lower than the preceding card. Therefore, the collator recognizes the error card one feed cycle before it arrives at the eject station. However, if the card

in the eject position had been punched 36 instead of 34, the collator would still have recognized the card punched 32 as an error. By analysis of the three cards, 36, 32, 35, it is apparent that the card punched 36 is out of sequence.

The schematic diagram shows the path of the cards from the primary and secondary hoppers to the pockets. The five pockets are normally wired to direct *unselected* primary cards to pocket 1, *selected* primary cards to pocket 2, *combined* cards from both feed hoppers to pocket 3, *selected* secondary cards to pocket 4, and *unselected* secondary cards to pocket 5.

Let us now identify certain *exit* and *entry* hubs on the control panel that correspond to the schematic.

Cards fed through the primary unit are read first by 80 primary sequence–read brushes (L to P, 23 to 42). The cards are read next by 80 primary read brushes (F to J, 23 to 42). Data from cards passing the primary sequence–read brushes are normally stored through control panel wiring in primary sequence unit 1 (K, 23 to 44). Data are usually stored in primary sequence unit 2 (C, 23 to 44) from cards passing the primary read brushes. Thus, the primary sequence unit has two entries, sequence-entry 1 and sequence-entry 2. Each entry has 22 positions. A number read into any sequence-unit-1 position is compared with a number read into the corresponding sequence-unit-2 position. The result of the comparison may be high, equal, or low. One of the HI, EQ, or LO selectors (Q to S, 30 to 35) automatically transfers for each card read, depending on the comparison. For example, if the number in primary unit 1 is lower than the number in primary unit 2, the LO selector transfers. These selectors can be used to control machine operations, such as stopping the machine when an out-of-sequence condition is detected.

The secondary sequence units function as described above, and for this reason, we shall not describe them. You can locate the *secondary* hubs on the left half of the control panel and relate them to the schematic. We will specifically locate the hubs as needed.

The comparing unit (Fig. 8-3) has two entries labeled primary and secondary. Each entry has 22 positions for storing numbers. A number read at secondary read (F to J, 1 to 20) is normally wired to the secondary comparing unit (D and E, 1 to 22). This number is compared with a

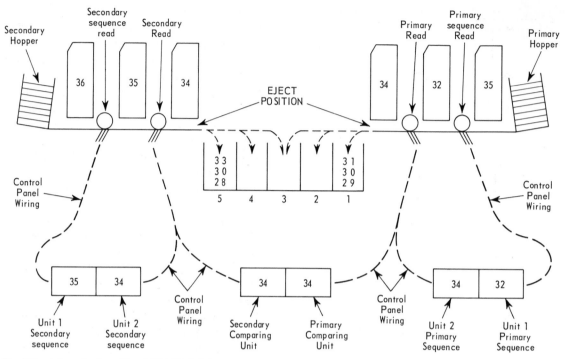

Fig. 8-3 Internal schematic of IBM 88 Collator.

number stored in the primary comparing unit (D and E, 23 to 44) from the primary read brushes (F to J, 23 to 42). The result of the comparison will be a low secondary, equal, or low primary condition. One of the LS, EQ, or LP selectors (Q to S, 17 to 28) transfers automatically for each card read, depending on the comparison. For example, if both numbers in the secondary and primary comparing units are equal, the EQ selectors (Q to S, 19 and 20 and Q to S, 25 and 26) transfer, while the LP and LS selectors remain normal.

The EQ selectors would be transferred as the cards stand in our illustration (Fig. 8-3) because the comparing unit contains equal numbers. Therefore, an impulse could be wired through the transferred side of the EQ selectors to merge the matching cards into pocket 3. An impulse may be wired through the *normal* or *transfer* hubs to control other machine operations, such as matching or match-merging.

The LO, EQ, HI test for the three sets of comparing or memory units begins at the left position and progresses

to the right. For this reason, major, intermediate, and minor fields (covered in Chap. 5) must be wired in a particular pattern. The major field, such as last name, is wired to the left; the intermediate field, such as first initial, is wired next; and the minor field, such as middle initial, is wired to the right.

Although we have not considered collating alphabetic information, it is appropriate at this time to explain the reason for placing numeric cards behind alphabetic cards during sorting, as explained in Chap. 5. The alphanumeric collator, as well as computers covered in later chapters, is designed to sequence check in the order of (low to high) blanks, letters A to Z, and numbers 0 to 9.

APPLICATIONS

Suppose such a large number of cards must be removed from the files as to be manually unfeasible. We have a history file of sales cards in major sequence by customer number and minor sequence by date of purchase. Management has requested a report showing the last purchase for each customer to determine the effectiveness of the sales program. Customers who have no record of recent purchases will be identified and contacted by salesmen. Our problem, obviously, is to select the last card of each group or customer number. This is accomplished by wiring customer number from primary sequence–read to primary sequence unit 1 (Fig. 8-3), and primary read to primary sequence unit 2. Whenever a new customer number is recognized, the HI selector transfers, permitting the wiring of an impulse through the *transferred* hubs of the selector to select the last card of each group. A similar application is selecting the first card of a group.

Another application is the selection of zero-balance cards. Suppose our accounts receivable file of customers' current purchases and total-to-end-of-preceding-month summary cards are summarized periodically. In most cases, the new balance-forward card is a positive amount since the customer has a revolving account. However, in some instances, the customer pays the balance of his account. This results in a zero-balance card when the file is summarized. The zero-balance cards may be removed by the collator, resulting in a reduction in the volume of cards that must pass through various machines in subsequent processing.

Searching the file for specific items is a worthwhile application. Management may desire to analyze the sales of a new product. The file of sales cards is unlikely to be in product sequence. This certain product, say product number 09345, must be located with a minimum of machine hours. Of course, we could select the 09345 items by the sorter, but this would disturb the sequence of the file. The collator finds the items by use of a finder card containing the punched product code 09345. This card is read into the secondary comparing unit, which is controlled to prevent data from other cards reading in and erasing the 09345 product number. In other words, 09345 is permanently stored for comparing with data from each sales card passing through the machine. Primary read is wired to the primary comparing unit, which is controlled to clear and accept new information whenever a new card is read. Thus, an equal condition

means a card containing product number 09345 is at the primary eject position and ready for selection.

Let us cover more specifically an application by control panel wiring. Check reconciliation (Fig. 8-4) can be performed by a matching operation. Most of the checks for a pay period should have been cashed and returned from the bank after one week. A duplicate reconciliation card is kept for each check. By matching the current file of canceled checks against the reconciliation file, the payroll department can determine which checks have not cleared the bank. The reconciliation file is placed in the primary feed and the canceled checks in the secondary feed. As the cards pass the primary and secondary brushes, a comparison of the two files is made. Figure 8-5 is the control panel wiring necessary to perform the operation. The check number in the canceled checks is wired (A) to the secondary comparing unit. The corresponding field of the reconciliation file is wired (B) to the primary comparing unit.

The two files must be in check-number sequence for an effective matching operation; therefore, we shall sequence check both files. The check number punched in the canceled check is wired (A1) to secondary sequence entry 2 and to (A2) secondary sequence entry 1. The check number punched in the reconciliation file is likewise wired (B1) to primary sequence entry 2 and to (B2) primary sequence entry 1. This completes the positional wiring that provides a path for the information in the card to the comparing or memory units. The remainder of wiring is control wiring, that is, wiring to control card feeding, selecting, and so forth.

The *SEQ N* (N-ON, F-OFF) switch is wired (D1) to cause the machine to stop on an out-of-sequence condition, that is, the secondary sequence unit 1 being lower than unit 2. The *SEQ N* switch is wired ON (D2) to stop the machine whenever an error is detected in the primary side. The *SEQ F* switch is wired OFF for all other operations.

The *SECDY READ IN* (F and G, 21 and 22) and *PRI READ IN* (F and G, 43 and 44) switches cause the associated comparing unit to clear an old reading on each corresponding card-feed cycle so that a new number can be read in. These switches can be selectively operated, or not wired when it is necessary to control

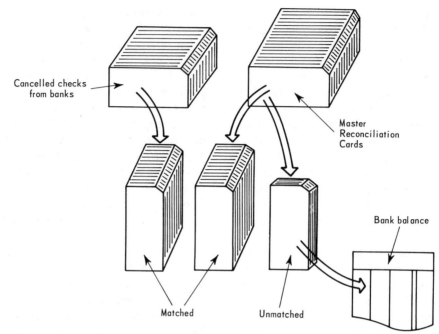

Cancelled checks
from banks

Master
Reconciliation
Cards

Bank balance

Matched

Unmatched

Fig. 8-4 Check reconciliation.

storage of numbers or to hold a previous reading without restoring. Since our problem calls for comparing each card in the secondary, we wire (E1) to read in a new number for each secondary feed. The primary comparing unit is wired (E2) to read in a new number for each primary feed. The primary and secondary sequence units now restore and read in automatically with each primary and secondary feed cycle.

Our next control wiring is to control selection of cards (Fig. 8-6) to specific stackers. The *secondary stacker* hubs (Q to S, 5 to 7) control selection of secondary cards to pocket 3 (merged cards) and pocket 4 (selected secondaries). The *PKT CTRL* hubs emit impulses that may be selectively wired to direct cards to the proper pocket. If pocket 3 or 4 does not receive an impulse, the secondary card automatically stacks in stacker 5. The *primary stacker* hubs (Q to S, 38 to 40) control selection of primary cards to pocket 2 (selected primaries) and pocket 3 (merged cards). If pocket 2 or 3 does not receive an impulse, the primary card automatically stacks in pocket 1.

Whenever a canceled check matches a reconciliation card, the EQ selector (Q to S, 19 and 20) transfers, allowing the PKT CTRL (F1) impulse to direct the canceled check to pocket 4. The PKT CTRL (F2) impulse emits at the same time and selects the corresponding reconciliation card to pocket 2. If the EQ selector does not transfer, the PKT CTRL impulse cannot reach the pocket hubs; therefore, the card selects to pocket 1 or 5, depending on the comparison.

The *SECD FEED* (T, 13 to 16) and *PRI FEED* (T, 29 to 32) hubs are entries to control card feeding, our final control wiring. Selection to the proper pocket (Fig. 8-6) cannot function without card feeding. On an equal condition the EQ selector transfers, permitting an all-cycles impulse to reach the (G1) *SECDY FEED* hubs and (G2) *PRI FEED* hubs. If the comparing unit is not equal, the LS selector or LP selector transfers, permitting a secondary feed (H) or a primary feed (I).

There are many variations of matching operations in addition to the above problem. For instance, there may be multiple-card groups in the primary or secondary

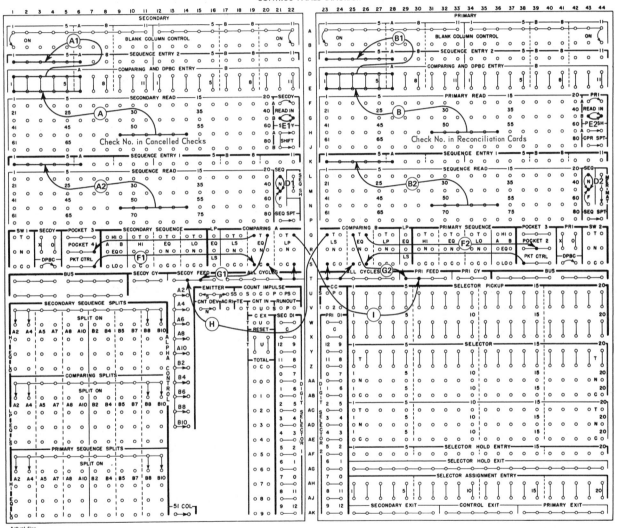

Fig. 8-5 IBM 88 Collator wiring for matching.

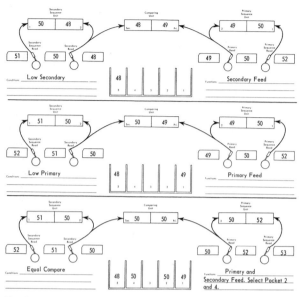

Fig. 8-6 Schematic for matching.

feed, with the job calling for multiple-card groups of one file to be filed in front of corresponding groups in the other file. In this case, the wiring in Fig. 8-5 would not suffice. Each problem must be analyzed by the schematic (Fig. 8-6) and solved on its own merits.

ACCOUNTS PAYABLE

Transactions involving purchased products and services create a company liability. Each liability must be paid and the payment charged against the operation that made the liability necessary. In order for the company to operate profitably and efficiently, complete and accurate records of all transactions must be kept. The difference between profit and loss is based upon decisions made by management. Detailed record keeping provides answers to management's questions through analysis of payments, discounts, and statistical studies of vendors and their products.

Accounts payable has two broad objectives, disbursement and distribution. *Disbursement* is the recording of liabilities from the time they occur until they are paid.

Distribution is an accounting means of breaking down transaction payments by categories for analysis, such as the amount of the purchase, what it was spent for, and the reasons for the purchase. We will describe the disbursement phase of accounts payable.

Disbursement is divided into four phases, establishing liability, validating the liability, posting the liability, and satisfying the payment. Let us cover each individually.

Establishing liability involves a request and authority to purchase. A common request is to replenish items sold by the company that have reached a reorder point. The request is usually on a preprinted punched-card form and contains such information as part number, quantity, date required, order number, signature of requestor, date, and so forth. The card may be written by mark sensing (Fig. 9-4) the numbers. This method speeds up the operation by eliminating keypunching, since the mark-sensed numbers can be read and punched by the reproducing punch, covered in the next chapter. The purchase order is prepared from the punched card by the 407 accounting machine or computer. At the time the order is written, on-order cards are prepared for the accounts payable file. These cards are filed in an open-order file until the materials are delivered.

Validating the liability is done by acknowledging receipt of the goods in an undamaged condition, in the proper quantity, and of the type ordered. The packing list received in the shipment, if not in punched-card form, is punched after it is received verified from the warehouse. When the invoice is received from the vendor, it is punched and compared by the collator with the purchase request card and the packing-list card. The matching transactions are now approved for payment. We can say that validation, to a certain extent, is controlled by the collator.

Posting the liability may be in the form of one card for each item received or one card with the total due, less any discount. The latter is a simple means of posting the liability and processing other reports, such as an invoice register. This report provides an audit trail and a permanent record of indebtedness, making it possible to review any transactions without reference to the original documents. It is desirable to maintain a record of liabilities for each vendor. One method is posting to ledger cards. The file contains one card for each vendor. The accounts payable card can be posted to the vendor ledger card by the 557 interpreter as illustrated in Fig. 7-2.

It is important to pay each obligation promptly. The company is interested in a sound credit reputation, as well as in discounts resulting from early or prompt payment. A good business practice is to send a remittance statement with the check. A remittance statement is simply an explanation to the vendor of the obligations covered by the payment. Check forms and statement-of-remittance forms are often attached to allow both to pass through the printing machine at the same time. This method has the advantage of printing the check and remittance in a single processing step. The accounts payable cards are merged with the corresponding vendor name-and-address cards by the collator for this operation. In the same operation a summary card is punched for each check written. These cards become the reconciliation file and are matched against canceled checks received from the bank to determine outstanding checks.

QUESTIONS

1. What is the major reason for feeding cards in one feed 12-edge first and 9-edge first in the other feed?

2. Based upon the numbers stored in the memory units of Fig. 8-3, which selectors on the control panel will transfer for secondary sequence unit, comparing unit, and primary sequence unit?

3. Assuming that two fields instead of one are to be matched in Fig. 8-5, how will the fields be positioned to enter the memory units if the check number is the *minor* field?

4. In an operation of selecting zero-balance cards, exactly how will the machine know which card contains a field of zeros?

5. What wiring causes the cards in Fig. 8-5 to stack in pockets 1 and 5?

6. In Fig. 8-6, what condition will cause the primary to feed a card? The secondary?

7. What purpose does the wire labeled EI serve in Fig. 8-5?

PROBLEM

There is an alternate method to control card feeding for the matching operation in Fig. 8-5. Using fewer wires than the example, illustrate the control wiring to perform the functions specified in Fig. 8-6.

9
Automatic punches

In business today, at least 90 percent of the information used has been recorded previously. Since most significant data are used repeatedly, maximum efficiency is achieved by recording the source data only once. To eliminate re-transcribing data manually, the automatic punch was invented.

REPETITION

A new employee's name, social security number, and other pertinent data are recorded at the time of hiring. These same data are used over and over to prepare the company payroll, reports for the Federal government, and numerous other record-keeping tasks. The employee's pay check, written every pay period, is based on compu-tations resulting from the hours worked and includes in-formation recorded at the time of hiring. The hours worked are normally recorded manually, but can be mechanized to a large extent through mark sensing, explained later in this chapter.

There are various automatic punches, each specifically designed to solve the problems of handling repetitive in-formation and constant data. The IBM 514 reproducing punch (Fig. 9-1), which performs operations at 100 cards per minute, has been chosen for illustration due to its simplicity. The characteristics and capabilities of other automatic punches are briefly discussed at the end of this chapter.

REPRODUCER FUNCTIONS

The basic function is reproducing punched information from one card onto another card. The data in the source card can be reproduced in their entirety or in part, and the new card can be arranged in the format desired (Fig. 9-2).

Comparing is the operation of verifying data in the original card against data punched in the new card. Two files that should be identical can also be verified by the reproducer, even though punching is not involved.

Gangpunching is copying information from a master card onto succeeding detail cards requiring the same data (Fig. 9-2). Interspersed gangpunching (Fig. 9-3) is the operation of punching constant data onto groups of cards from a master card preceding each group. Recall from Chap. 5 that an X-control punch distinguishes a master card from the detail card.

Summary punching is the automatic preparation of one total card to replace a group of transaction cards. The summary card contains identifying data, such as account number or employee number, and the totals accumulated by the accounting machine. For example, summarization of daily time attendance cards at the end of the pay period would result in one card for each employee, containing employee number and total num-

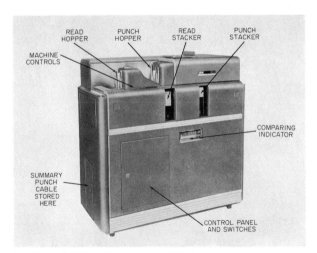

READ HOPPER · PUNCH HOPPER · READ STACKER · PUNCH STACKER

MACHINE CONTROLS

COMPARING INDICATOR

SUMMARY PUNCH CABLE STORED HERE

CONTROL PANEL AND SWITCHES

Fig. 9-1 IBM 514 Reproducer. (IBM Corp.)

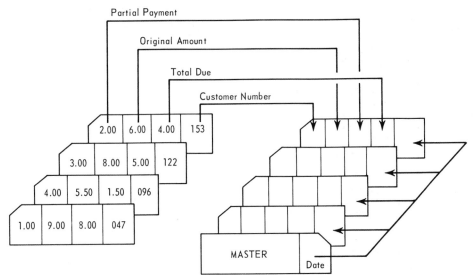

Fig. 9-2 Reproducing and gangpunching.

ber of hours. Summary punching is accomplished by connecting the reproducer and accounting machine by a connector cable. Summarization is used primarily to carry balance totals forward to the next period and to reduce card volume. The latter technique alleviates peak work load and speeds report preparation. Other automatic punches are connected to statistical machines or calculators for punching the results.

Mark sensing is an electronic method for converting pencil marks on cards (Fig. 9-4) into punches in the card.

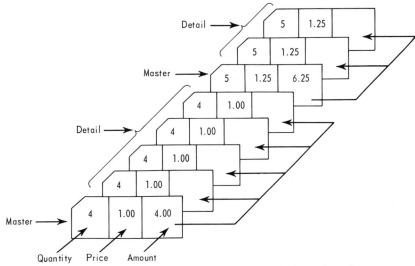

Fig. 9-3 Intersperse gangpunching amount in lieu of calculating each card.

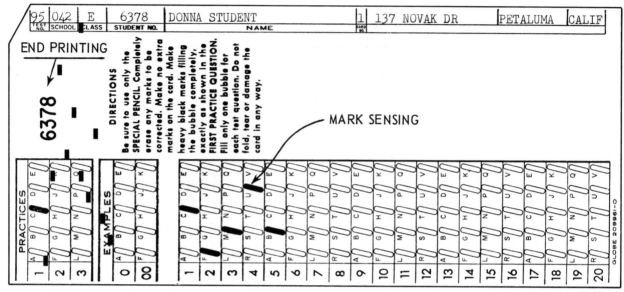

Fig. 9-4 Mark-sensed grade card with student number end-printed.

For example, as remittances are received in an accounts receivable application, a special block is marked when received in full. When partial payments are received the exact amount is mark sensed on the card. After the day's business, the mark-sensed cards are read and punched with the amount received, thus eliminating manual keypunching.

Although there are other functions, we have covered the most common ones. The next pages cover the control panel, wiring principles, and an application.

MACHINE LOGIC

The two feed units (Fig. 9-5) are referred to as the read unit and the punch unit. They may be used separately or together. When both units are in use, the cards move in synchronism. That is, the reproducing, comparing, and punch brushes are simultaneously reading row 12 of the cards as the punch magnets punch row 12.

In order to understand the principles of wiring, we must understand the relationship between the card-feed schematic and the reproducer diagram (Fig. 9-6). To summarize the relationship, the internal wiring from the functional units terminates at the control panel. External wires are plugged into the hubs of the panel to complete a circuit. For instance, information read from the card is carried by internal circuitry to the control panel where external wires must direct the impulses to punch the desired columns.

Cards fed in the read unit first pass five read-X brushes, to be explained later. The next station contains 80 reproducing brushes, which are located on the panel at rows A to D. The last station is the 80 comparing brushes located at rows AG to AK.

Cards fed in the punch unit first pass six punch-X brushes, which are covered later in this chapter. Next is the punching station. The *entry* hubs for the 80 punch magnets are located at rows K to N. The 80 punch brushes are located at rows Q to T. Since all the brushes in the read and punch units read impulses, the corresponding hubs on the wiring panel are exits.

The control panel *entry* hubs to the left comparing magnets are located at rows AC to AF. Entries to the right comparing magnets are located at rows Y to AB. Rows AA, AB, AE, and AF are associated with mark sensing and summary punching when these operations are being performed. Otherwise, they serve as the last 40 positions of the comparing unit. Since we have correlated the control panel with the reproducer schematic, let us discuss the wiring in relation to an application.

PRINCIPLES OF WIRING

One phase in an accounts receivable system is rebilling the customer for his outstanding balance after he makes partial payments. Recall that earlier the partial payment was mark sensed on the card. The mark-sensed amount is punched and the balance due calculated and punched. Now a statement card must be prepared for

mailing which includes account number, original amount, partial payment, total due, and date. Figure 9-6 shows the wiring necessary to punch the delinquent statement.

The source cards are placed in the read hopper and the statement cards in the punch hopper. As each card passes the reproducing brushes (Fig. 9-5), the customer account number (A1) and partial payment (C1) are read and transmitted through panel wiring to the punch magnets for offset reproducing. The corresponding statement card under the punch magnets is reproduced at this same time. Likewise, the original amount (B1) and total due (D1) are straight reproduced. The first source card and the newly punched statement card move to the next stations. The second source card and blank statement card move to the reproducing brushes and punch magnets respectively.

Since we have completed the first punch cycle, you ob-

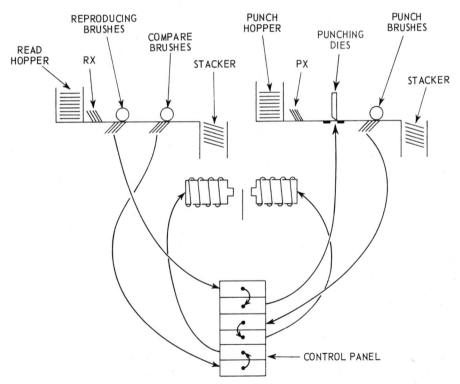

Fig. 9-5 Schematic of read and punch units.

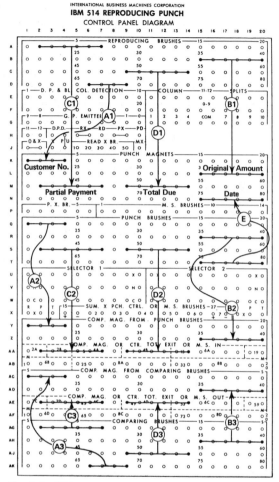

Fig. 9-6 Wiring to reproduce a statement card.

viously noted that date was not punched. Because comparing occurs simultaneously as the following card is being punched, gangpunching date can commence with the second punch cycle. We must manually punch date in the first statement card. Since this card is under the punch brushes at the same time the following card is under the punch magnets, date can be read by the punch brushes and relayed by panel wiring (E) to the punch magnets. Date is thus punched in each card from the preceding one.

To verify the reproduced data, the original card is compared with the new card immediately after punching. The new data are read at the punch brushes and wired to the comparing magnets (A2, B2, C2, D2). Note that the wiring for the new card corresponds to the new format. The original data are read at the comparing brushes and wired to the opposite comparing magnets (A3, B3, C3, D3). Any comparing positions may be used for verification as long as the two magnets correspond.

Now let us examine closer the method of comparing. There are 80 sets of magnets, each wrapped with wire. When an impulse is passed through the coil of wire, the magnet becomes magnetized. When the current is removed, the magnet is turned off. The armature remains centered when both magnets are off or both are magnetized. If only one of the magnets becomes magnetized, the armature is attracted to it, indicating an error in punching.

As an example, an A (12 and 1 punch) is read at the reproducing brushes and is directed by panel wiring to the punch magnets. For illustration purposes, suppose that only the 12 is punched. As the 12 at the comparing brushes is compared with the 12 at the punch brushes, both magnets are magnetized simultaneously, resulting in the armature remaining centered. After 12-time, both magnets are turned off when the current is removed. At 1-time, the comparing brush magnetizes the left magnet. However, since the 1 erroneously was not punched, current does not reach the right magnet from the punch brushes. Therefore, the armature is attracted to the left magnet. This, in turn, stops the machine, and the comparing indicator, located under the stacker pockets, indicates the magnet in error.

Let us next discuss how to control card reading, punching, and selection. The function of RX (read X) and PX (punch X) brushes (Fig. 9-5) is to recognize X or no-X cards in the read or punch unit. For example, as the first master card in Fig. 9-3 passes the punch brushes, the price extension is punched in the first detail. The first detail now serves for punching the second detail passing the punching station and so forth. When the second master reaches the punching station, it would receive the price extension punches (double punching the second master) from the last detail of the preceding group unless we prevented it.

The *common* hubs labeled PX (row H) (Fig. 9-6) suspend punching one card cycle when impulsed from PX brush (row P) or read-X brush (row J). Therefore, a single wire from PX brush, which senses the X master card, to the *PX* hub suspends punching as the master card passes the punch station.

Our last reproducer function is that of *emitting*. Frequently we want to punch repetitive information, such as date, onto the new card. Because the original cards do not contain the desired information, we must manufacture the impulses required. A device to solve this problem is called an emitter. The emitter provides 12 impulses just like those obtained from a punched card, that is, the 12 to 9 punches. For instance, the 1 hub emits as the 1 row of the card passes under the punch magnets, the 2 hub emits at 2-time, and so on. The *exit* hubs for the 12 impulses are located at row G, 1 to 10 and row H, 1 and 2.

Suppose our problem illustrated in Fig. 9-7 called for the word MAY to be punched in columns 14 to 16. We simply combine the 11 and 4 (letter M) impulses with a common connector (Fig. 6-4), and plug the wire into hub 14 of the punch magnets. The 12 and 1 (letter A) impulse, and the 0 and 8 (letter Y) impulses would be wired to columns 15 and 16, respectively. However, care must be exercised when combining impulses so as not to create a back circuit. A *back circuit* is an impulse that

passes in the wrong direction and causes incorrect operations. This occurs because an impulse, once given a path, can flow in any direction. For example, emitting FEB into columns 10 to 12 would result in multiple punches in all three columns. Since the 12 punch must be combined with a 6 to produce the F, with a 5 to produce the E, and with a 2 to produce the B, the 12 impulse has a path to all three columns, resulting in an erroneous machine action.

The IBM 519 document originating machine performs the same functions as the 514 reproducer. In addition, cards can be *end printed* (Fig. 9-4) in bold letters. This is especially effective when cards must be physically handled by employees unfamiliar with punched cards. Cards may be printed with easily recognized digits representing part numbers, employee numbers, discount deadline dates, and so on. This machine also edits cards for blank columns or double punches. An example is editing the *money amount* field in a check for missing punches. A 7 missing in the fifth position of the *money* field would mean an error of $700.00. Another feature of this machine, three entries to the punch magnets, gives extra versatility for expanded applications.

The IBM 528 accumulating reproducer has the same features as the IBM 514 reproducer, plus the capability to read and accumulate totals at 200 cards per minute, with the summary results punched at 100 cards per minute. The accumulating function makes this machine ideal for summarizing new balance cards. For example, a master inventory card file can be updated by filing issue and receipt cards with the master file and creating a new deck by summarization.

ACCOUNTS RECEIVABLE

This section concerns accounting for money owed to a company by its customers for merchandise sold or services rendered on a credit basis. Mechanization of accounts receivable files facilitates accounting, collecting money owed, minimizing losses from bad debts, and maintaining good customer relations through prompt and

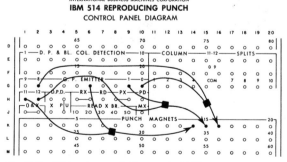

Fig. 9-7 Wiring to punch the word "MAY".

accurate record keeping. To accomplish this:

Customer accounts must be established.

Records must be kept of all transactions affecting the accounts.

Credit must be screened.

Trial balances must be prepared periodically.

Customer statements must be prepared.

Provision for determination and follow-up of late payments must be made.

Analysis and information reports for the credit and other departments must be prepared.

Once applications are approved by the credit department, a master card is established containing account number, name, address, salesman, location, and other pertinent data. Whenever possible, items are coded to facilitate machine processing and positive identification.

Transactions such as payments, charges for merchandise sold or services rendered, and credit memos for reversing or adjusting invoices in case of returns are processed by recording the charge or credit to the customer's account. One method of recording transactions is the balance-forward approach. A balance card file is maintained containing the balance-forward summary card reflecting the status of the accounts at the end of the previous period, plus subsequent invoice transaction cards. Payments are recorded by punching a cash credit card for each payment and merging the card into the file. The accounts receivable file, containing a balance-forward card and current transaction debit and credit cards, then represents the amount owed. To reduce the volume of the file, it is summarized at statement preparation time.

Screening additional credit and approval of new purchases are based on the exception philosophy. Accounts that have exceeded the credit limit and that have a record of partial payments or delinquency are mechanically extracted periodically. They are presented to the credit department for analysis. This approach is made for applications involving small purchases, whereas applications involving large purchases may require the credit department to screen each purchase order.

Trial balances are necessary periodically to determine if the totals of all individual accounts are in balance. This is done by listing and accumulating the accounts receivable file on the accounting machine or computer. If the file is not in balance, the error can be found by sorting the original transactions by date and a comparison made by daily control totals.

Preparation of customer statements can be accomplished in several ways. The balance-forward statement is prepared by merging the customer master address file into the accounts receivable card file and listing it on a printing machine to show the previous balance, dates, invoice number for each charge or credit for the current period, and the total amount due. The open-item statement shows all unpaid items and the total balance. This accounts receivable method works by applying payments to individual purchases instead of to the outstanding balance. The summary statement is gaining popularity in modern business due to its money-saving simplicity. This type of statement is printed on a punch card suitable for mailing. The name and address are printed on one side by the IBM 557 interpreter, and the opening balance, total of the current month's purchases, payments made, and the ending balance are printed on the reverse side of the statement.

Determination of delinquent or questionable accounts can be controlled by furnishing the credit department with outstanding balances which show purchases appreciably exceeding payments for the past 30, 60, and 90 days; a listing of customers with delinquent payments; and a listing of customers with recurring partial payments. Once delinquent accounts are located, mechanized collection follow-up can occur through automatic preparation of reminder notices or collection letters.

The credit department may request reports on paying habits by locality or season or other reports pertinent to controlling credit. One such report often requested is a listing of accounts with partial payments for the current period. The partial payment cards are identified by an X punch. If the cards are selected by the sorter, they must be merged back with the accounts receivable file after the listing is prepared. To save time, the entire accounts receivable file is fed through the 514 reproducer to duplicate only the partial-payment cards.

QUESTIONS

1. At the start of an operation the comparing indicator comes on and points to an entire field as being in error. The card is checked and found correct. How do you account for this?

2. What dual functions do the comparing magnets serve?

3. Name the three sets of 80 reading brushes and list their functions.

4. What happens if the machine fails to read the X-punched master card during an intersperse gang-punching operation?

5. Name the hubs on the panel used for reproducing. Name the hubs used for gangpunching.

6. Explain the consequence of punching MAR instead of MAY in Fig. 9-7. Using the column split, eliminate the back circuit and punch MAR correctly.

10
Programming the electronic calculator

The need for calculation is recorded throughout history. The ancient abacus has been widely used for thousands of years in the Orient and Russia. The Romans used still another calculating device called the *tally*. These simple devices were effective until the seventeenth century,

when the growth of education and scientific curiosity demanded more and faster calculations. Mechanical calculators, beginning with John Napier's multiplying rods and Blaise Pascal's adding machine, have been continually improved ever since. Modern business resulted in the development of the electronic calculator.

The IBM 604 electronic calculator (Fig. 10-1) reads data from punched cards, does a precise set of calculations, and punches the results in the same card or a following card. Computations are performed by the 604 in a fraction of a second and the results are punched by the IBM 521 card read punch at 100 cards per minute. Punching and reading are accomplished at twice this speed, or 200 cards per minute, by the IBM 541 card read punch. This is a tremendous improvement over manual methods. The multiplication of two 6-digit numbers 1000 times requires about 24 hours using the pencil-and-paper method or about 10 hours using a desk calculator. The

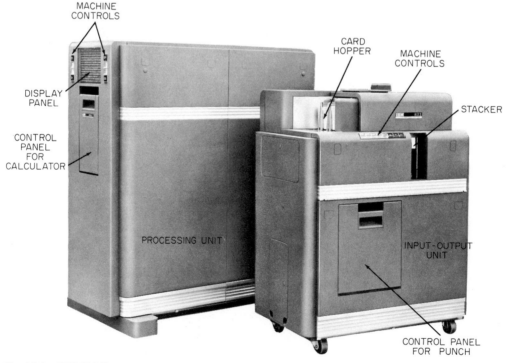

Fig. 10-1   IBM 604 Electronic Calculator. (IBM Corp.)

IBM 604, coupled with the IBM 541, can perform the same calculations in 5 minutes.

Faster and larger calculators are available in the 600 series. The IBM 608 and IBM 609 are built with transistors instead of vacuum tubes. Transistors have the advantages of requiring less space, using less electricity, and not dissipating heat. The IBM 609 uses the binary system and magnetic core storage, explained in Chap. 15.

Before we go further, let us discuss three requirements for calculation. First, the information must be in a form readable by the calculator. Input, therefore, can be punched cards. Second, the device must be able to perform the basic mathematical operations, that of addition, subtraction, multiplication, and division. Three basic functions are executed in a logical sequence for each card. However, flexibility is a must. For instance, certain cards may require variations in computation. In a payroll operation normal pay is computed for regular hours whereas overtime pay is computed at another rate. Third, the results of the computation must be recorded in a usable form. The output is punched in the card.

WIRED PROGRAMMING

Our problems thus far have involved machine operations that occurred during card reading. The machines in this and the following chapters perform operations both during card-read operations (referred to as card cycles) and between card-read operations (referred to as program cycles or program steps). *Program steps* are a series of machine cycles that begin immediately after a card cycle. After the program steps are completed, another card cycle occurs and the process is repeated. You will recall that a program is a series of steps, or set of instructions, arranged and performed in a prescribed sequence to produce the planned results.

The 604 goes through a series of 60 program steps. On any given program step a storage or memory unit can be instructed to read out and add the contents to data in a counter, and a counter can be instructed to read out and store the result in memory or reset (clear to zeros). You may question why the machine does not compute all

numbers at the same time. Let us explain by discussing the method we use in manual computation.

Add visually the figures 63, 79, and 85. Chances are that you added in steps instead of deriving the final answer at one time. You probably combined 3 and 9 for a partial answer and added this to 5 for a total in the units column of 17. Then you added the 1 you carried to the 6, added that total to 7, and that answer to 8 for a column total of 22 or a final answer of 227.

The calculator performs addition in a similar manner. When the card is read, the factors 63, 79, and 85 are stored in separate memory units. On program step 1, the storage unit containing 63 is read out and added into an electronic counter. The storage unit containing 79 is read out on program step 2 and added to the counter, forming a partial answer of 142. On program step 3, the storage unit containing 85 is likewise read out and added to the counter. The final answer of 227 is developed in three program steps. All problems are solved in a similar way by simple, but fast, step-by-step operations.

CALCULATOR FUNCTIONS

All computations are based upon addition, regardless of the type of machine. Subtraction, multiplication, and division are accomplished by a modified form of addition. We shall discuss each, beginning with addition.

The 604 electronic calculator derives its name from the fact that its arithmetic unit, storage units, and other components are composed of electronic tubes. You will recall from Chap. 3 that information is represented in the machine by the presence or absence of electronic impulses. Numbers are represented (Fig. 10-2) by four vacuum tubes, each having a value of 1, 2, 4, or 8. When any tube is on (electronic impulse applied), it represents the value assigned to it. When the electronic impulse is removed, the tube is said to be off and its value is zero. The combined values of the tubes that are on that represent one decimal position are the equivalent of the number being represented.

Prior to reading a card containing factor 57036, an instruction caused the counter to reset or turn to all

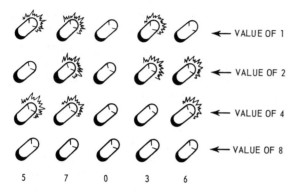

VALUE OF 1

VALUE OF 2

VALUE OF 4

VALUE OF 8

5   7   0   3   6

Fig. 10-2 Electronic counter.

zeros. The instruction to add factor 57036 in the counter (Fig. 10-2) results in electronic impulses turning on the 4 tube and 2 tube in the units position. The 1 and 2 tubes are turned on in the tens position, all tubes remain off in the hundreds position, and so on. This method of combining different values to achieve desired numbers is called *binary-coded decimal,* as opposed to the binary system covered in Chap. 14. Binary-coded decimal means that each decimal digit in a number is represented in binary.

Other factors in the same card are retained in storage until the first addition is completed. The second factor, 912, is instructed to add to the contents of the counter. The unit's position is added first by combining the 2 impulses with the 6 value in the counter so that the 8 tube in the units position is turned on, and tubes 2 and 4 are turned off. The 1 impulse is added to the 3 value in the tens position, resulting in tubes 1 and 2 being turned off and tube 4 turned on. The 9 impulse is added to the zero value in the hundreds position, turning on tubes 1 and 8. Values in the two high-order positions are unaffected. The counter now stands at 57948.

The third factor, a minus 401, is read out of storage and must be subtracted from the counter. We previously stated that all machines are limited to addition. In order to subtract by means of addition, we complement the number to be subtracted and add the minuend to the complemented subtrahend. The complement of any number is the value that must be added to it to raise it to the

largest number in the system, which in the case of base ten or decimal is 9. The resulting 1-carry from the high-order position is automatically re-added to the unit's position as illustrated below.

Manual method	Machine method
57948	57948
−401	−00401
57547	99598
	① 57546
	→1
	57547

Multiplication is performed in the IBM 604 by a process of addition and shifting. The multiplier is stored in a designated multiplier unit. Multiplication begins with the high-order position of the multiplier and moves to the right. The machine adds the multiplicand to itself the number of times indicated by the high-order digit in the multiplier, shifts one position to the right, and repeats the process for each number in the multiplier. For instance, this is how a three-digit number is multiplied:

725	
×123	
72500	100
07250	10
07250	10
00725	1
00725	1
00725	1
89175	123

Division is accomplished by the 604 in essentially the same way we divide manually. The main difference is that division by calculators is performed by a combination of subtractions using our new rules for subtraction. The entire divisor is subtracted from the high-order positions of the dividends repeatedly until the remainder is less than the divisor. Then the entire operation is shifted one position to the right and the process is repeated. The operation stops when the remainder is less than the divisor. The quotient is developed in a separate counter by adding 1 each time a subtraction is completed, as illustrated by the following example.

$526 \div 25 =$

```
            526
            749
      ①     275              10
          → 1
            ───
            276
            749
      ①     025              10
          → 1
            ───
            026
            974
      ①     000               1
          → 1
            ───
            1 (remainder)     21 (quotient)
```

Calculation may be accomplished by two methods, crossfooting and summary punching. *Crossfooting* is the operation of accumulating several factors from one or more cards to obtain a total or series of totals. For instance, gross pay may be accumulated by adding regular pay and overtime pay, and net pay derived by subtracting all deductions from gross pay. *Summary punching* is the accumulation of data from each card of a group and punching that information, along with identifying information, into a separate card called a summary card. As an example, weekly earnings cards are merged with the last pay period's year-to-date summaries, new totals for individual fields are accumulated, and a new year-to-date summary card is punched for each employee.

Whenever the sequence of program steps is altered as the result of a decision made by the machine, the process is called *branching*. Branching can be programmed as the result of control punches in a card or a decision made during calculation. As an example, 4.4 percent must be deducted for FICA (Federal Insurance Contribution Act, commonly called Social Security) from the earnings of employees who are subject to this tax. In our example the calculation would be $\$151.00 \times 0.044 = \$6.644$, rounded off to \$6.64 weekly. Because only a certain amount of an employee's wage is subject to this tax, the program must have provisions for elimination of FICA deductions after each employee has contributed his share. This is possible by subtracting the FICA limit from the total YTD FICA and the weekly FICA amount.

As arithmetically illustrated below, it is possible to arrive at one of three conclusions: that all FICA should be deducted, that some of FICA scould be deducted, or that none of FICA should be deducted.

Example

YTD FICA	\$132.80	\$285.52	\$290.40
Weekley FICA	6.64	6.64	6.64
Total	139.44	292.16	297.04
Maximum FICA	−290.40	−290.40	−290.40
Result	−150.96	+ 1.76	+ 6.64

If the answer is negative, all of the calculated FICA must be deducted. However, to resolve the question of whether some or none should be deducted, additional program steps are required. The solution is provided by subtracting the calculated FICA from the last result.

Result	1.76	6.64
Weekly FICA	−6.64	−6.64
FICA deduction	−4.88	+0.00

A zero amount means none and a negative amount means some. The final deduction is made by taking the value with the negative sign and making it a positive amount. The program logic for the above problem is graphically shown in Fig. 10-3.

PLANNING THE OPERATION

The solution to a problem is divided into many simple operations. We must provide the machine with precise instructions telling it what to do and in what sequence. First, we must define and analyze the problem. Next, we plan the sequence of instructions that the machine must go through in order to do the job.

There are two devices that assist in planning the job—a program flowchart and planning chart. A flowchart, (Fig. 10-3) is a pictorial representation showing the sequence of instructions. It is used as an aid in determining program sequence in the preliminary work required for

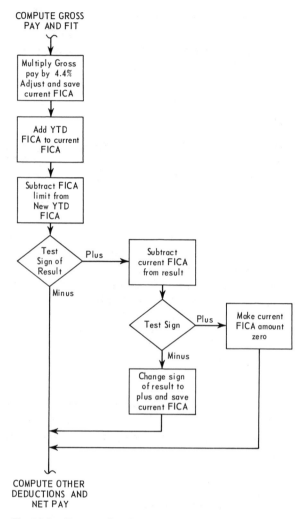

COMPUTE GROSS PAY AND FIT

Multiply Gross pay by 4.4% Adjust and save current FICA

Add YTD FICA to current FICA

Subtract FICA limit from New YTD FICA

Test Sign of Result

Plus — Subtract current FICA from result

Minus

Test Sign

Plus — Make current FICA amount zero

Minus

Change sign of result to plus and save current FICA

COMPUTE OTHER DEDUCTIONS AND NET PAY

Fig. 10-3 Program flowchart.

planning the application. The *planning chart* (Fig. 10-4) is prepared to determine the most logical use of the storage units before any attempt is made at control panel wiring. A minimum of wiring errors can be expected when you translate the program steps from the planning chart into machine instructions.

A segment of a program involving a payroll application is shown in Fig. 10-3. The FICA calculation is graphically illustrated by a subroutine. A *subroutine* is part of a pro-

gram containing a series of program steps that deviate from the main program to accomplish alternate calculations.

The planning chart (Fig. 10-4) is used to record where the input factors are stored when the card is read, what happens to the data during the program steps, and how the output is handled during the punch cycles. It is designed with a vertical arrangement of the program steps, and a horizontal arrangement of the units into which factors may be entered. Information entering and departing storage or the counter can be charted on the line corresponding to the program cycle.

The first and last columns on the planning chart identify the factors read from the card, 20 program steps, and the results to be punched. *Factor storage* represents four memory units, two of them having three positions and two having five positions. Information may be held in these units until needed for calculation. The MULT QUOT column is used to store the multiplier or quotient. The next column represents a 13-position counter which is used to develop answers for problems involving addition, subtraction, multiplication, and division. Information cannot be read into the counter on the read cycle. General storage is divided into four separate units, two of them having three positions and two having five positions. These units provide additional working storage.

The low-order position of the five units is used for sign control only and cannot be used for storage of numbers. Punching can occur from the counter and general storage units, but is not possible from factor storage or the multiplier-quotient unit. This should be kept in mind when storing factors that are to be punched. The space allotted for each program step for factor storage, multiplier-quotient, counter, and general storage is divided into two sections. The upper section is used to write in symbols or words which identify a factor. The lower section reflects the number of positions each unit contains or the actual figures resulting from the manual calculation of a representative problem.

Now that we have described the planning chart, let us discuss an application of it. The first step in a payroll problem is to calculate gross pay. This is determined by adding the hours worked each day and multiplying the

604 ELECTRONIC CALCULATING PUNCH

PLANNING CHART

PLICATION __Calculate Gross Pay__   PROBLEM __(A + B + C + D + E) R = P__

PROG. NO.	FACTOR STORAGE				MULT. QUOT.	COUNTER	GENERAL STORAGE				PROG. NO.
	ASSIGNMENT 6·4 8·6						ASSIGNMENT 6·4 8·6				
	1	2	3	4			1	2	3	4	
READ	RI A 08	RI B 08	RI C 07		RI R 275		RI D 08	RI E 10			READ
1	RO A					+ A 08					1
2		RO B				+ B 16					2
3			RO C			+ C 23					3
4						+ D 31	RO D				4
5						+ E 41		RO E			5
6						R O & R (factor H) 00				RI H 41	6
7						H x R = P 11275				RO H	7
PCH						Gross Pay 11275				Tot Hours 41	PCH

Fig. 10-4 Planning chart.

weekly total by the hourly rate. The problem involves several factors; discussion will be simpler if we assign letters for each.

Hours worked Monday	A
Hours worked Tuesday	B
Hours worked Wednesday	C
Hours worked Thursday	D
Hours worked Friday	E
Total hours worked	T
Hourly rate	R
Gross pay	P

The problem can now be stated as the formula $TR = P$, where $T = A + B + C + D + E$.

We mentioned earlier that program steps occur between card cycles, that is, after the card is completely read and before the next card is read. All known factors, therefore, must be read from the card and retained in working storage until needed for calculation. This is shown by writing factor A into FS1 (factor storage 1), factor B into FS2, and factor C into FS3. Since there are five fields and only four factor storage units, let us write factor D in GS1 (general storage 1) and factor E in GS2. Factor R is entered into a special 5-position storage unit labeled MULT QUOT. The multiplier must be entered in this unit for multiplication operations.

On program step 1, factor A is read out of FS1 and added to the counter. Factor B is read out of FS2 on program step 2 and added to the counter, resulting in the accumulation of factors A and B, and so on. Each of the factors is accumulated *step-by-step* and the multiplicand (factor H) is fully developed on step 5.

Before going further, let us discuss three requirements for multiplication. First, the multiplier must be stored in the MULT QUOT unit so the machine can analyze and process each position individually. Second, the multiplicand must be in storage, and third, the two factors must be multiplied. As stated earlier, the product is developed by repeated addition. In order to satisfy requirement three, the multiplicand must be moved to a storage unit since the counter is used to develop the product. Program step 6 transfers factor H to GS4 and clears the counter. Factor H is read out and multiplied by factor R on program step 7, and the product (factor P) is devel-

oped in the counter. Total hours are punched from GS4, and gross pay is punched from the counter. In the next section, we shall wire the panel based upon the planning chart.

PAYROLL APPLICATION

Before wiring the control panel to calculate gross pay, we must understand certain characteristics of the calculator. Three basic functions of any calculating device are to read, compute, and write. The 604 electronic calculator consists of two units interconnected by cable. The input-output unit that performs the read and write function is the 521 card read punch. Factors are read by the 521, relayed to the 604 for calculation, and the result is transferred back to the 521 for punching.

The 521 has three card stations. A first-reading station is used to enter factors into the storage units and to control selection. Next is the punching station. Between these two stations, there are 230 electronic cycles available for calculation. One program step normally equals one electronic cycle; however, multiplication and division operations require several cycles, depending upon the size of the number. The third station is second reading and is used for operations involving gangpunching, recalculation, and editing for blank or double-punched columns.

The display panel on the 604 (Fig. 10-1) consists of lights and switches to control machine operations and to indicate the status of conditions affecting operations. The small neon lights indicate the factors stored and the functions performed on any given program step. The purpose of the display panel is to aid in locating control-panel errors during program testing. The neon lights representing values are arranged in groups of four, as indicated in Fig. 10-2.

There are two control panels on the 604 calculator. One is located in the 521 card read punch and is used to control input-output operations. The other control panel is located in the 604 unit and is used to supply instructions for calculation.

We shall begin our problem with the 521 control panel.

In the course of wiring both control panels, you should follow Fig. 10-4 because all wiring is based upon the planning chart. The read step (Fig. 10-5) permits the storage of five fields, containing the hours worked, as the card passes the first reading station. The hours worked on Monday are wired (A) to FS1, those on Tuesday are wired (B) to FS2, those on Wednesday are wired (C) to FS3, those on Thursday are wired (D) to GS1, and those on Friday are wired (E) to GS2. This positional wiring provides a path from the reading brushes to the storage units. However, information is not stored unless read-in (R and S and X and Y, 15 to 18) is impulsed. When

PUNCH PANEL (521 - 541)

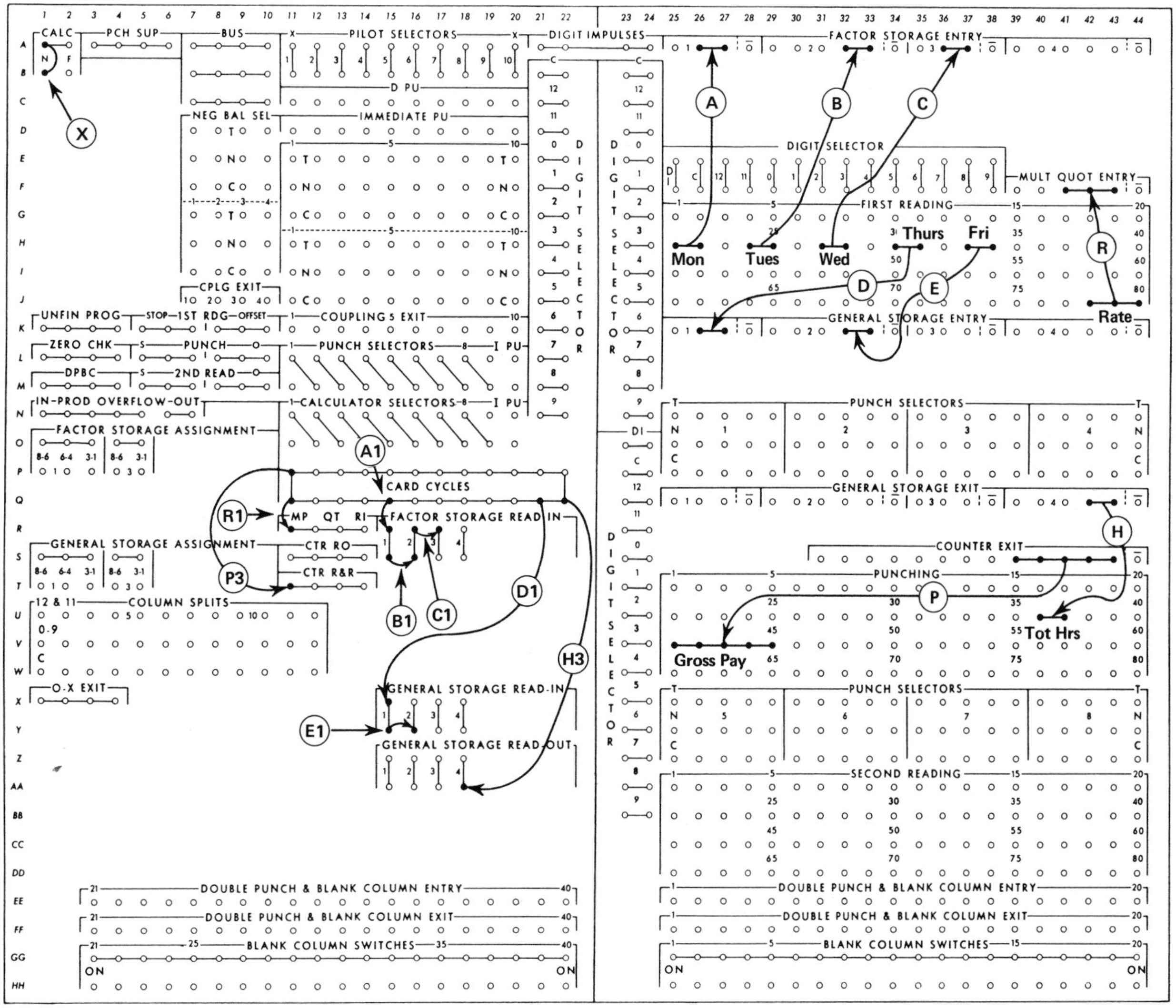

Fig. 10-5 IBM 521 Input-Output Control Panel. (IBM Corp.)

a storage unit is impulsed to read in, it clears out the previous contents by resetting to zero before new information enters. Each of the wired factor-storage units is wired to store the hours for Monday (A1), Tuesday (B1), and Wednesday (C1) on each card-feed cycle. Likewise, general storage accepts the hours for Thursday (D1) and Friday (E1).

Hourly rate (R) is stored in the MULT QUOT unit. The rate must go into this unit because it is the multiplier. The *control* hubs are wired (R1) to clear any previous multiplier and to accept a new reading on every card cycle.

This completes the positional and control wiring necessary to store the factors as they are read from the card. Immediately after all punches in the card have been read, the 604 begins calculating at program step 1 (Fig. 10-6). All computations are completed before the card arrives at the punching station and before the following card arrives at the first-reading station.

The first factor is added to the counter on program step 1. This is accomplished by wiring program step 1 to FS1 readout (A2) and read-in plus (A3). Impulsing read-in plus causes the counter to add the contents (factor A) of factor storage 1. Each program step (A to Y, 1 to 8, and Y to HH, 19 to 22) has three independent exits and a *SUP* hub. When *SUP* hub is impulsed, that program step is suppressed. The *program steps* are electronic cycles which occur successively. In other words, when program step 1 is active, steps 2 to 60 are inactive. Then program step 2 is active and steps 1 and 3 to 60 are inactive. During each step the machine can be controlled to perform a specific part of a required calculation.

Transferring information from one unit to another unit is possible because all units are internally wired together. Data are read out of a unit only when the corresponding *readout* hub is impulsed. The information enters the desired unit by impulsing the *read-in* hub of the corresponding unit. Both the *readout* and *read-in* hubs must be impulsed on the same program step in order to transfer the data. If a unit has not been impulsed to read in, data stored within remains unaffected. Information in a unit clears out when the corresponding *read-in* hub is impulsed, but when readout is impulsed, an exact copy of the contents is transferred and the data in the storage

unit are unaffected. Therefore, read-in is destructive and readout is nondestructive.

Continuing with the wiring, factor B is read out of FS2 by impulsing FS2 *readout* hub from (B2), program step 2. The hours are added to the counter containing factor A by impulsing (B3) *counter read-in plus* hub. Factor C is added to the counter by wires C2 and C3, factor D by wires D2 and D3, and factor E by wires E2 and E3.

As we previously stated, the counter is used to develop the product during multiplication; therefore, the multiplicand standing in the counter must be moved to another storage unit. Two things must be considered before deciding in which unit to store factor H. First, we have no further use for the storage units containing factors A to E. At first glance it would appear that factor H could be stored in any working storage area. However, you will recall that *only* general storage can be used for punching, and since total hours must be punched in the card, factor storage is ruled out. So why not general storage 2? It is true that factor H would replace the contents in GS2 and this meets the requirements for multiplication. However, the same general storage unit cannot be used for both input and output operations. GS2 is used for storing input from a card and cannot be used for punching results because punching the results of a calculation occurs at the same time that the following card is being read at reading station 1.

Factor H is transferred from the counter (H1) and read in (H2) general storage unit 4. Unlike storage units which clear whenever new information is read in, the counter must be reset (H1) or cleared to all zeros. If only the *counter readout* hubs (Q and R, 14 to 17) had been impulsed, an incorrect product would have been accumulated during the multiplication step since the counter was not cleared of the total hours worked.

Program step 7 impulses the multiplicand in GS4 to read out (P1) and the machine is instructed to multiply (P2). When the *multiply plus* hub is impulsed, the multiplicand is repetitively added in the counter the number of times specified by the MULT QUOT unit. We have completed the calculation and the results need only to be written.

Punching the results is controlled by the 521 control

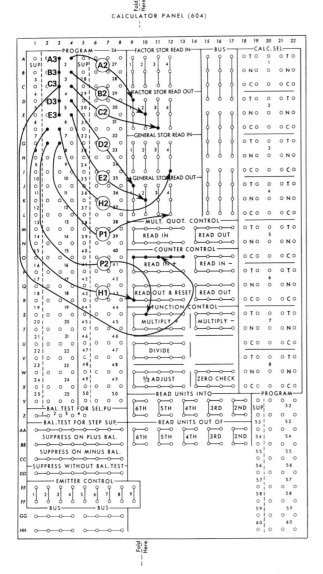

Fig. 10-6 Programming the IBM 604 Electronic Calculator to crossfoot.

storage 4 as the card passes the punching station. Wire P3 reads out the information for punching and resets the counter. As the card is being punched, a new card is being read and the process of calculation is repeated on the new factors. The $CALC$ (calculate) switch is wired ON (X) whenever the calculator and read-punch units are used together.

Payroll accounting involves one of the most frequently performed computations in business. We have covered only a simple aspect of this important application, that of computing gross pay; overtime pay was not considered. Various taxes are required by federal and state laws, and become an involved part of a company's payroll operation. These and other deductions are normally included in master cards and must be considered in planning and wiring the application. It is quite apparent that payroll calculation is complex.

There are many hubs, such as those used for selection, lining up decimals, adjusting products, branching, and testing for positive or negative results, that were not used in our problem. Nevertheless, we have been exposed to programming logic, our basic subject for the remaining chapters.

QUESTIONS

1. A calculating device is capable of performing three basic functions. Which two functions are controlled by the IBM 521 unit?
2. In Fig. 10-4, could factor H have been stored in factor storage unit 4 or general storage unit 2 on program step 6? Why?
3. How many columns can be stored from a card being read?
4. What is the difference between card cycles and program cycles?
5. Why is the binary-coded decimal system used in machines instead of the decimal?
6. What is the 9s complement of the number 2468013579?
7. How many symbols in Fig. 10-3 are branch symbols? Name them.

panel (Fig. 10-5). Total hours are wired (H) from GS4 exit to punch-in positions 36 and 37. Gross pay is wired (P) from counter exit to punch-in positions 41 to 45. Wire H3 instructs the machine to punch the contents of general

8.   The subroutine in Fig. 10-3 contains how many symbols?

9.   What is the primary function of the 604 control panel? The 521 control panel?

10.   In Fig. 10-6 why is program step 6 necessary?

11.   In Fig. 10-5 there are *counter-exit* hubs but no *counter-entry* hubs. How do you account for this?

12.   Name two purposes for the wire labeled A1 in Fig. 10-5.

13.   If wire H2 on program step 6 is inadvertently omitted, how will the multiplied product be affected? The results punched in the card?

11
The accounting machine

The heart of a punched-card data processing system is the accounting machine, which turns out a printed finished product. These products may be in the form of printed reports, such as payroll registers; document forms, such as statements; or punched cards, such as checks. In addition, an accounting machine can tabulate data from a card file, print the subtotals and final totals in predetermined locations on continuous paper forms, and punch the summarized information onto summary cards.

There are several types of accounting machines. The most widely used is the IBM 407 accounting machine (Fig. 11-1). It can read, compare, select, add, and subtract at the rate of 150 cards per minute, and print at the rate of 18,000 characters a minute. The processed data may be punched by connecting the 514 reproducer to the accounting machine. Improved models have been designed with additional storage and the capability to multiply and divide.

Although not so common, the accounting machine continues to be used for printing output by some computers. The printing speed of the 407 is slow in comparison with computer speeds, but this disadvantage may be offset since the accounting machine can be used independently. This is especially true in scientific applications where a vast amount of calculation is performed and the amount of output is small.

MACHINE FUNCTIONS

The basic function of printing is accomplished by 120 print wheels. An entire line can thus be printed at one time. Each print wheel contains the numbers 0 to 9, the letters A to Z, and 11 special characters. Printing is accomplished by one of three methods. *Detail printing* (Figs. 11-2 and 11-3) is the operation of printing a portion or all of the information from each card passing through the machine. The line may be printed in a sequence different from the format punched in the card. Additional information, such as headings or column identification, and punctuation, such as dollar signs or decimals, can be printed even though not punched in the card. *Group printing* (Fig. 11-4) is used in preparation of summarized or tabulated reports. This method of printing involves entering amounts from each card directly into counters without printing. At the end of each group of cards, totals are printed with identifying information. *Multiple-line printing* is the operation of printing data from a single card on two or more lines. For instance, name and address punched in a master card can be printed on three separate lines on shipping labels.

The three types of printing can be performed in the same report run. Further, printing may be selected; that is, a choice can be made between different fields punched in a card or between several printing locations. In fact, the techniques of printing usually are limited only by the imagination of the technician wiring the control panel.

Accumulation of totals is performed by adding or sub-

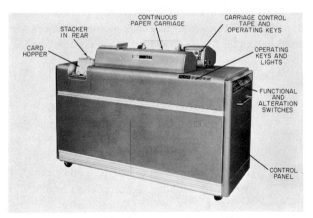

Fig. 11-1   IBM 407 Accounting Machine. (IBM Corp.)

CONTINUOUS PAPER CARRIAGE

CARRIAGE CONTROL TAPE AND OPERATING KEYS

STACKER IN REAR

CARD HOPPER

OPERATING KEYS AND LIGHTS

FUNCTIONAL AND ALTERATION SWITCHES

CONTROL PANEL

DATE	NAME	PROD #	SALES AMT	PROD TOT	SLSM TOT	QTN
JAN 30	C R WILLIAMS	39607	39.60			10
JAN 30	C R WILLIAMS	39607	138.60			35
JAN 30	C R WILLIAMS	39607	27.72			7
				$205.92		52
JAN 30	C R WILLIAMS	41630	42.50			5
JAN 30	C R WILLIAMS	41630	93.50			11
				$136.00	$341.92	16
JAN 30	E R YORK	21605	153.00			12
JAN 30	E R YORK	21605	510.00			40
JAN 30	E R YORK	21605	127.50			10
JAN 30	E R YORK	21605	51.00			4
				$841.50	$841.50	66
		TOTAL	$1,183.42			
JAN 31	W E SIMON	39607	277.20			75
JAN 31	W E SIMON	39607	138.60			35
JAN 31	W E SIMON	39607	162.36			41
JAN 31	W E SIMON	39607	27.72			7
JAN 31	W E SIMON	39607	39.60			10
				$645.48		168
JAN 31	W E SIMON	39608	591.50			13

Fig. 11-2 Sales report showing minor totals by product, intermediate totals by salesman, and major totals by day.

tracting amounts punched in cards. The arithmetic operations are performed in counters according to instructions given by control panel wiring. There are 28 individual counters for accumulating subtotals and final totals. The different levels of totals (Fig. 11-2) are called minor, intermediate, and major. A sales report indicating totals by product, by salesman, by day is an example. The totals by product are identified as minor, by salesman as intermediate, and by day as major. As soon as all transactions for a given product have been accumulated, the total is printed. The contents of the minor counter are cleared and transferred to another counter for accumulating the intermediate total. Similarly, total sales by salesmen are printed as soon as all of the transactions for a given day have been accumulated. The contents of the intermediate counter are cleared and transferred to another counter for accumulating the major total, and so forth.

Besides accumulating totals by columns, the accounting machine has the capability of crossfooting amounts punched in a single card or a series of cards. For example, $A + B + C - D = T$. This term refers to accumulating amounts printed horizontally across the page, as opposed to accumulating columns of figures.

Two types of programming are performed by the IBM 407. One type is crossfooting, accomplished similarly to the problem cited earlier on the 604 calculator, involving calculation of total man-hours worked. That is, the factors are stored as the card is read at the reading station, and are added one-by-one on successive program steps.

The second type of programming is called *program control*. Program control enables the machine to distinguish the cards of one group from those of another so that individual group totals can be printed. The three classifications of program control are minor, intermediate, and major. When a difference between minor groups is detected by the comparing unit, contents of the minor counter are printed on program step 1, sometimes called a *minor-total cycle*. When a change in intermediate groups is distinguished, contents of the minor counter for the last minor group accumulated are printed on program step 1, and contents of the intermediate counter are printed on program step 2, sometimes called an *intermediate-total cycle*.

Summary punching, accomplished by connecting the 514 reproducer to the accounting machine, is the preparation of one total card to replace a group of detail cards. In the sales report (Fig. 11-2), we could create a minor summary card for each group of identical products sold by each salesman. During preparation of the sales report, minor totals by product are transferred through the cable and punched in summary cards. The primary purpose of summary punching is to reduce card volume and accelerate the preparation of other reports, or to create balance-forward cards. Normally, all data to be punched is controlled by the wired panel in the accounting machine.

The IBM 407 has 64 positions of storage. The memory units are used for storing information, such as company name and address, to be printed on form or sheet headings. Information for summary punching may be stored, or columnar heading information can be stored and printed at the top of each new sheet.

Forms control is defined as the control of spacing between lines, skipping to a new page when one form is filled, printing totals on predetermined lines, and so forth. A tape-controlled mechanism controls the spacing and positioning of continuous forms at high speed while documents or reports are being printed. An invoice contains two sections, the head and the body. The *head* of the invoice contains the name and address of the cus-

tomer, ship-to address, invoice number, and date. The *body* of the invoice contains the date an item was ordered, item number and description, quantity ordered, the unit price, the item amount, and the invoice total. The forms-control carriage takes into consideration the printing of one line or many lines per customer, printing the final total of the invoice in the proper block, and other skipping or spacing requirements.

INVENTORY CONTROL APPLICATION

Our problem on the IBM 407 is the preparation of an Inventory Transaction Report (Fig. 11-3). The Stock Status Summary (Fig. 11-4) is a tabulated report containing the same information. With minor alterations, the same control panel could be used to produce both reports. Before wiring the control panel, let us gain a brief insight into the use of these two reports. Sales may be lost as a result of insufficient stock. On the other hand, the company desires not to overstock. Excessive stocks reduce the company's profit through extra overhead and storage cost, and tie up company capital when it could be used elsewhere.

In order for management to effectively control the inventory problem, the answers to certain questions must be provided. We shall cover these questions and relate them to our reports. The basic question to any inventory application is: What is the quantity on hand? Three records contain the information to answer this question. A balance-forward summary card from the previous report provides the opening balance and descriptive information, such as stock number, description, stock room location, unit cost, etc. Provisions are made to record all inventory transactions that will adjust the opening balance. This record is actually the on-hand quantity from the last report.

Although there are many types of transactions, such as adjustments, we will be concerned with only two, receipts and issues. Since there are obviously several cards making up this report, each different transaction card must be coded. The accounting machine recognizes the type of transaction and performs a routine to increase

STOCK NUMBER	DESCRIPTION	UNIT COST	DOCUMENT NUMBER	TRANS CODE	TRANS DATE	OPENING BALANCE	TRANSACTION		ON HAND	PLANNING	
							RECEIPTS	ISSUES		ON ORDER	AVAILABLE
31051	DRESS 1 PC BROWN	13.75		1	15 MAY	49					
31051	DRESS 1 PC BROWN	13.75	09045	2	23 MAY		35				
31051	DRESS 1 PC BROWN	13.75	23141	3	20 MAY			49			
31051	DRESS 1 PC BROWN	13.75	71563	4	28 MAY				35	105	140
31052	DRESS 1 PC RED	13.75		1	15 MAY	93					
31052	DRESS 1 PC RED	13.75	23641	3	26 MAY			23			
31052	DRESS 1 PC RED	13.75	23750	3	30 MAY			14	56		56
31054	DRESS 1 PC BLUE	13.75		1	15 MAY	61					
31054	DRESS 1 PC BLUE	13.75	10133	2	16 MAY		15				
31054	DRESS 1 PC BLUE	13.75	09556	2	30 MAY		15				
31054	DRESS 1 PC BLUE	13.75	24100	3	21 MAY			70	21		21
31061	DRESS 2 PC GREEN	21.30		1	15 MAY	37					
31061	DRESS 2 PC GREEN	21.30	11304	2	27 MAY		25		62		62
31064	DRESS 2 PC YELLOW	21.30		1	15 MAY	55					
31064	DRESS 2 PC YELLOW	21.30	24169	3	17 MAY			15			
31064	DRESS 2 PC YELLOW	21.30	24250	3	18 MAY			40			
31064	DRESS 2 PC YELLOW	21.30	70411	4	18 MAY				40	40	40
31130	SUIT WOOL GRAY	37.16		1	15 MAY	26					
31130	SUIT WOOL GRAY	37.16	23190	3	21 MAY			5			
31130	SUIT WOOL GRAY	37.16	23195	3	22 MAY			7			
31130	SUIT WOOL GRAY	37.16	71355	4	22 MAY				13	15	28
31297	SLACKS TIGHT PINK	9.00		1	15 MAY	178					
31297	SLACKS TIGHT PINK	9.00	09643	2	29 MAY		80				
31297	SLACKS TIGHT PINK	9.00	24512	3	18 MAY			105			
31297	SLACKS TIGHT PINK	9.00	70480	4	19 MAY				153	30	183

Fig. 11·3   Inventory Transaction Report prepared by IBM 407 Accounting Machine.

| STOCK NUMBER | DESCRIPTION | UNIT COST | DATE | OPENING BALANCE | TRANSACTION | | ON HAND | PLANNING | |
					RECEIPTS	ISSUES		ON ORDER	AVAILABLE
31051	DRESS 1 PC BROWN	13.75	1 JUN	49	35	49	35	105	140
31052	DRESS 1 PC RED	13.75	1 JUN	93		37	56		56
31054	DRESS 1 PC BLUE	13.75	1 JUN	61	30	70	21		21
31061	DRESS 2 PC GREEN	21.30	1 JUN	37	25		62		62
31064	DRESS 2 PC YELLOW	21.30	1 JUN	55		55		40	40
31130	SUIT WOOL GRAY	37.16	1 JUN	26		12	13	15	28
31297	SLACKS TIGHT PINK	9.00	1 JUN	178	80	105	153	30	183

Fig. 11-4 Stock Status Report prepared by IBM 407 Accounting Machine.

or decrease the corresponding inventory balance. *Receipt* transactions are simply shipments from the vendor that increase the opening balance. *Issue* transactions are sales to customers and decrease the opening balance. Now we can say the on-hand total is computed by adding receipt transactions to the opening balance and subtracting issue transactions.

Before we can effectively control overstocking of inventory, we must answer another question: What is on order? This answer is essential since any decision to order additional inventory must be based upon the knowledge of any open orders. The planned available inventory, then, is obtained by adding on-hand to on-order quantities.

We are concerned only with a portion of the complete inventory application. Other provisions must be made to automatically order new stock when a reorder point is reached, keep track of open orders, make adjustments for overshipments and undershipments, run reports on fast-moving and slow-moving items, and so forth.

WIRING THE INVENTORY PROBLEM

A *planning chart* (Fig. 11-5) is used to wire our 407 control panel problem. Since there are many operations that must occur at precisely the right time, the machine seldom works correctly the first time, due to incorrect panel wiring. A minimum of *debugging,* that is, correcting deficiencies in wiring or programming, is necessary

when the problem is properly analyzed and planned. Let us begin our discussion of the wiring in Fig. 11-7 by briefly covering the entire problem. This will enable us to tackle the problem in detail and still keep in mind what we expect the machine to do.

Positional wiring generally is concentrated on the left side of the control panel and control wiring on the right side. Positional wiring provides a path from the *card-reading exit* hubs to *entry* hubs used for printing, punching, comparing, counters, storage, and so forth. Control wiring provides for control of entry, exit, adding, subtracting, and other functions.

In the upper left portion of the panel, stock number is wired to the comparing unit (C to F, 1 to 30). When a difference in stock number is detected, program start is initiated, causing a series of program steps that are used to compute the on-hand and available quantities. This is different from the 604 calculator which automatically performed 60 program steps after each card had been read.

In the middle left area of the panel, each field (wires labeled A to F) in the card is printed by wiring *second reading* (*exit* hubs for the reading brushes) to *normal print* (*entry* hubs to the print wheels). Four separate cards contain the information needed to prepare the Inventory Transaction Report. The *quantity* field representing opening balance, receipts, issues, and on-order transactions is punched in the same columns of each card. A different control punch in each card identifies the type of transaction; therefore, the quantity must be

CARD COLUMNS	43–47	15–30	31–35	36–40	1	7–11	56–59	56–59	56–59	56–59	56–59	
PRINT POSITION	1–5	8–23	27–31	34–38	41	44–48	51–54	57–60	63–66		76–79	
COLUMN HEADING	Stock number	Description	Unit cost	Document number	Trans. code	Trans. date	Opening balance	Receipts	Issues	On hand	On order	Available
COUNTERS							8D	6B	6C	Compute in 8D	8F	Compute in 8F
PRINT COUNTERS										69–73		82–86
SELECTORS — NO.							1 T	1 N	10 T		13 T	
SELECTORS — PU							1 cc 1		3 cc 1		4 cc 1	
PROGRAM STEP 1							+Rec	RO&R 6B				
PROGRAM STEP 2							−Iss		RO&R 6C			
PROGRAM STEP 3							RO&R 8D			Print		
PROGRAM STEP 4											RO&R 8F	+ On hand
PROGRAM STEP 5												Print
STORAGE — UNIT												
STORAGE — IN												
STORAGE — OUT												
SUMM PUNCH COL												

Fig. 11-5   IBM 407 Accounting Machine planning chart for Inventory Transaction Report.

printed in the appropriate column (wires labeled G, H, I, and K) through selection. Quantity is also wired into four counters (wires labeled 5) in order to compute on-hand and available quantities.

You will recall that it is unnecessary to provide positional wiring for moving data from one storage unit or counter to another in the 604 calculator because all units are internally connected. The counters on the accounting machine are provided in 3, 4, 6, and 8 positions. If the need arises for a 10-position counter, a 4- and 6-position counter can be coupled. For this reason, the counters are not internally connected, and positional wiring from one counter to another must be externally wired. Counter entries are connected to provide a path from second reading to each of the four counter entries. Like previous machines we have covered, information does not enter the counter from positional wiring alone. Control wiring must instruct the counter when to add or subtract. For example, a quantity from an open-balance card flows through all four wired counters. But it adds only in the opening-balance counter because the corresponding *counter-plus control* hub receives an impulse. When it is necessary to add information from one counter to another in order to compute on-hand and available quantities, a path (wires labeled 6) must be provided by connecting counter exits.

Machines have many built-in checks. In one, information entering a counter is checked against the information set up by the print wheels to be printed. When a difference exists, the machine stops. For this reason all data wired to print from the counter must reach the print wheels through counter control print (AZ to BB, 1 to 40).

In the upper right area of the control panel, we find the wiring to control the printing of *opening balance, receipts, issues,* and *on-order* fields. The wires labeled G1, I1, and K1 identify the type of transaction being read while the wires labeled G2, I2, and K2 control the co-selectors used in conjunction with selective printing.

The *control* hubs for each of the 28 counters are located in the right center section of the panel (S to AO, 53 to 80). Impulsing these hubs causes the corresponding counter to add or subtract as the card is read at second reading. If a counter is to add from every card, the *plus entry* hub must be impulsed every card-feed cycle. If only certain cards are being added, the impulse must be selected to reach the *counter-plus* hubs only for the particular cards being added. Located at AP to AW, 53 to 72, the program steps control counters to read out, reset, and so on. They perform basically the same functions as those in the 604 calculator, covered in the preceding chapter. There are 70 program steps; however, the number of steps available depends upon how the control panel is wired. The zero-print control unit (BG to BL, 41 to 80) is wired for normal zero print, that is, to print only significant zeros. Now that we have broadly covered the wiring, let us cover the problem in detail.

PRINTING

Basically, printing is accomplished by wiring from one of two sets of *second-reading* hubs (AC to AF or G and H, 1 to 40) to one of two sets of *print-entry* hubs (S to U or V to X, 1 to 40). Like most machines covered previously, the 407 has two reading stations. The 80 *first-reading* hubs are wired principally to control operations as the card passes the next station, second reading. The 80 *second-reading* hubs are used for printing and entering information into the counters (AG to AN, 1 to 42) and storage (O to R, 1 to 32). The unique reading mechanism (Fig. 11-6) permits the card to be reread as often as desired. This is possible because each station has 960 reading brushes, 12 for each row in the card and 80 sets of 12 for each column in the card. After the card has been read once, the machine can be instructed to reread the card if necessary.

Each of 120 print wheels has a corresponding *normal print-entry* and *transfer print-entry* hub. Only one set of the *print-entry* hubs is active at the same time. When a *print-entry* hub is impulsed from a *second-reading* hub, directly or through selectors, the print wheel prints the numeric, alphabetic, or special character that is punched in that column of the card. The print entries are also wired from storage exit (Y to AB, 1 to 32) and the emitter (S to V, 41 to 52). The emitter provides 47 machine-manufactured characters for printing and punching. For

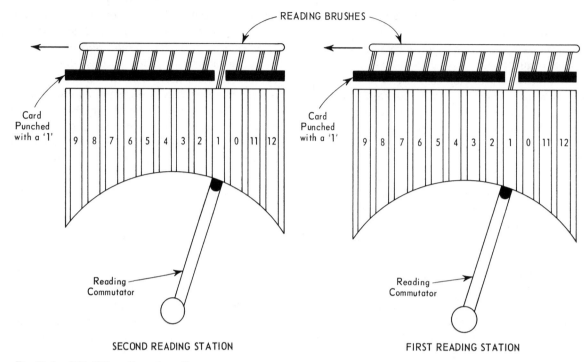

Fig. 11-6   IBM 407 reading schematic.

instance, the word TOTAL may be printed adjacent to all amounts on total lines. The comma, decimal, and dollar symbols may also be printed where needed for *money* fields, etc.

In our problem (Fig. 11-7), we wire stock number (A), description (B), unit cost (C), document number (D), type of transaction (E), and document date (F) in normal print. Detail printing for the Inventory Transaction Report (Fig. 11-3) occurs automatically. However, if we desire to tabulate the report as illustrated by the Stock Status Summary Report (Fig. 11-4), group printing can be accomplished by wiring the *list-off* switch (E and F, 80). Spacing is controlled by the hubs located at K and L, 73 to 77. The inventory register is single-spaced by connecting (12) the *common-exit* hub to the hub below, labeled 1. Wire 12a permits double spacing between different stock items.

Quantity is punched in the same columns of all four types of cards and, therefore, must be selectively printed. Selective printing is accomplished by two methods. By using the *alteration* switches, one control panel can be used for several different reports. In essence, two or more jobs are wired on the same control panel and the wiring to process a particular report is made active by manually turning the switches OFF or ON. Changing from detail printing to group printing is only one such use. Located on the side of the machine (Fig. 11-1), the switches are set before beginning the job and may not be changed during the operation.

Another method of selective printing is controlled by selectors. Unlike alteration switches, selectors make a choice during the operation based upon a type of card, a decision made by the machine, or some other condition. There are various types of selectors in the accounting machine, each designed for a specific purpose.

SELECTION

Digit selectors (A to M, 41 to 52) provide a medium of controlling machine functions based upon the presence

IBM 407, 408, 409 ACCOUNTING MACHINES, CONTROL PANEL DIAGRAM

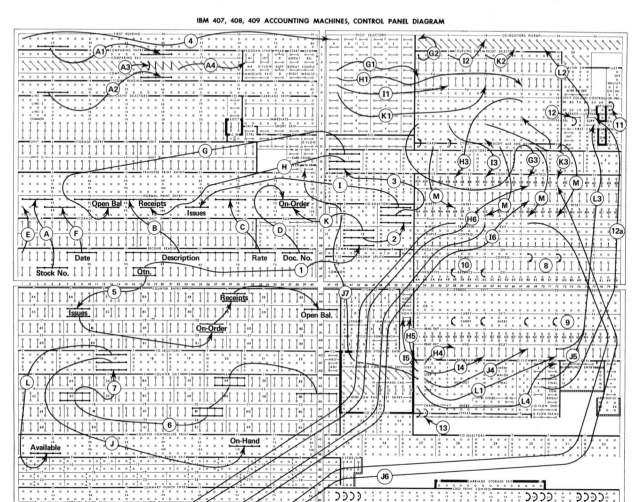

Fig. 11-7 Wired program for Inventory Transaction Report.

of a specific digit. Each digit selector consists of a pair of C (common) hubs and 12 pairs of hubs corresponding to the 12 punching positions in a column of the card. On every card-feed cycle, the C hub is internally connected successively to the 9 hub, 8 hub, 7 hub, and so on. Cards are fed into the machine 9-edge first. In Chap. 7, we studied a similar selector called the column split (Fig. 7-5). The column split provides an internal connection between the *common* and 0 to 9 hubs allowing

digits only to be selected, or between the *common* and 11 and 12 hubs to permit selection of control punches. Instead of having only two hubs that connect in turn to the *common* hub, the digit selector has 12. Before describing the use of digit selectors in our problem, we must tie in two other types of selectors, co-selectors and pilot selectors.

Each of the 32 co-selectors (beginning at P to R, 41 to 80) has five positions, each position having a C (common),

N (normal), and a *T* (transfer) hub. Each co-selector has a *common pickup* hub (A and B, 53 to 80). When the *pickup* hub is impulsed, the co-selector transfers (Fig. 11-8), providing a connection between the *C* and *T* hubs. For our purpose, the co-selector remains transferred for the same length of time as the pickup impulse. When there is no impulse at the *pickup* hub, the co-selector is in a normal condition (Fig. 11-9), providing a connection between the *C* and *N* hubs. Co-selectors normally operate in conjunction with pilot selectors or program steps.

Pilot selectors (Fig. 11-10) are the most flexible selectors we have studied thus far. Each of the 20 two-position pilot selectors (I to N, 53 to 72) can be used independently or in conjunction with co-selectors. They operate the same as other selectors except for timing. Each pilot selector has three *pickup* hubs labeled *X-PU*, *D-PU*, and *I-PU*. The *immediate PU* hub accepts any impulse and transfers the selector immediately.

The *X-PU* hub accepts only X (11) or 12 impulses. When a distinguishing punch is wired to the *X-pickup* hub, the corresponding pilot selector transfers on the

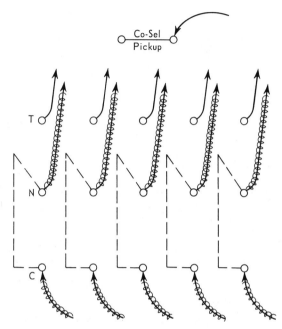

Fig. 11-9 Co-selector in normal state.

following machine cycle, which is normally a card-feed cycle. This means if a card containing an X impulse is wired to the *X-PU* hub from first reading, all punches of any column for that card introduced into the *C* hub of the corresponding selector are available at the *T* hub when the card passes second reading. A digit can also be used as a distinguishing punch to pick up a pilot selector. The column containing the digit is wired to the *D-PU* (digit-pickup) hub. If more than one digit is punched in the column wired to the D-pickup, a digit selector must be used to separate the distinguishing digit from all others in the column. Each pilot selector has a *coupling exit* hub (C, 53 to 72). This hub emits an impulse when the corresponding pilot selector is transferred and is normally connected to a co-selector pickup for the purpose of expanding the pilot selector beyond two positions.

Now that we have completed the study of selectors, let us continue with another segment of our control panel problem (Fig. 11-7), that of selectively printing the *quantity* field. Columns 56 to 59, containing quantity, are wired (1) to the common of co-selector 13. The planning

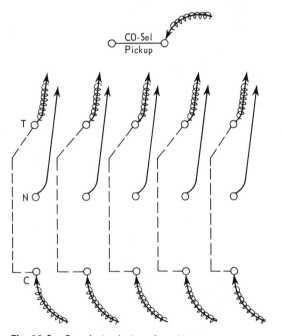

Fig. 11-8 Co-selector in transferred state.

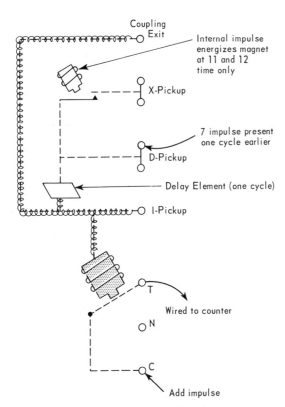

Coupling Exit

Internal impulse energizes magnet at 11 and 12 time only

X-Pickup

7 impulse present one cycle earlier

D-Pickup

Delay Element (one cycle)

I-Pickup

T

Wired to counter

N

C

Add impulse

Fig. 11-10 Pilot selector in transferred state.

chart (Fig. 11-5) indicates that the co-selector transfers whenever there is a 4 punched in column 1, representing an on-order card. If the first card is an opening balance transaction, the co-selector is normal. Therefore, the quantity information passes through wires labeled 2 to the common of co-selector 10. Again, the planning chart indicates co-selector 10 transfers for an issue card or a 3 in column-1 card. This being the case, co-selector 10 is normal and quantity continues through the *normal* hubs (3) to the common of co-selector 1. The planning chart shows co-selector 1 to transfer for an opening-balance card containing a 1 punch in column 1. Therefore, the wires labeled G provide a path for opening balance to print in positions 51 to 54. Before explaining the remaining positional wiring, let us cover the control wiring for co-selector 1.

In order to transfer the co-selector in time to print opening balance, the co-selector pickup must be impulsed before the card is read at second reading. Column 1 is wired (4) from first reading to the common of digit-selector A. This gives the co-selector time to transfer before the card is read at second reading. Keep in mind that this also permits the cards to be compared twice, once with the card ahead while at first reading and again with the following card while at second reading. At 1-time, there is a connection between common and the 1 hub of the digit selector. The 1 impulse from first reading passes internally through the digit selector and wire labeled G1 to the D pickup of pilot-selector 1. The corresponding *coupling exit* hub (C, 53) emits an impulse that passes through wire G2 to co-selector pickup 1, transferring co-selector 1 as the controlling card passes the next station, second reading. To summarize selective printing for the *opening balance* field, the card is recognized at first reading, pilot-selector 1 transfers co-selector 1 on the following card cycle, and as the card passes second reading, quantity is read through the normal side of co-selectors 13 and 10, and through the transfer side of co-selector 1 to print.

Now that we have followed the wiring to print the *quantity* field for an opening balance card, let us continue with a card containing a 2 in column 1 (receipts transaction). The *quantity* field is wired (1) to the common of co-selector 13. Co-selector 13 transfers on a 4 in column-1 condition, so the information passes through the *normal* hubs (2) to the common of co-selector 10. The receipts data passes through the normal side (3) of co-selector 10 also because the selector transfers only for a 3 in column-1 condition. Co-selector 1 is normal at this time because it transfers for a 1 in column-1 condition; therefore, the *receipts* field prints (H) in print positions 57 to 60.

Now let us discuss the printing for an issue transaction. The *quantity* field is wired (1) to the common of co-selector 13. Co-selector 13 is normal and the information continues (2) to the common of co-selector 10. The *issues* field prints (I) in positions 63 to 66 as co-selector 10 transfers for a 3 in column-1 condition. To see why co-selector 10 transferred, let us go back one card cycle when the issues card is being read at reading station 1 (Fig. 11-6). A 3 in column 1 is recognized and the impulse travels through wire 4 to the *common* hub of digit-selector A. At 3-time, the impulse is available from the 3 hub and passes through wire I1 to pilot-selector-5 pickup. Pilot-selector 5 transfers on the following card cycle. The coupling exit emits at that time and the impulse flows (I2) to co-selector pickup 10 causing co-selector 10 to transfer before the card is read at second reading. In other words, just before the 9 row of the *quantity* field is read at second reading, co-selector 10 transfers, providing a path to print positions 63 to 66.

In explanation of the last transaction, a 4-timed impulse is read at first reading and travels through external wiring to the *common* hub of digit-selector A. Since the 4 hub of digit-selector A is connected to the *common* hub at 4-time, the impulse continues its path (K1) to pilot-selector 10 pickup causing the selector to transfer on the following card cycle. The *coupling exit* hub emits (K2) and picks up co-selector 13. The co-selector transfers in time to provide a path through the transferred points of selector 13 for quantity to print (K) in positions 76 to 79. Therefore, the wiring for co-selectors 10 and 1 is nullified as a result of the *normal* hubs in co-selector 13 being disconnected from the *common* hubs. This completes positional and control wiring to print the necessary information from each card. The remaining two fields, *on-hand* and *available,* are computed and printed from counters.

WIRING THE COUNTERS

We begin our discussion of special programming by adding the quantity into the appropriate counter as the card passes second reading. Quantity is wired (5) from second reading to counter 6C (issues) and further connected to counter 8F (on-order), counter 6B (receipts), and counter 8D (opening balance). The sequence in which the counters are connected is of no consequence since the data are available to all four counters and enter the counter only when instructed by control wiring.

During program steps, totals are moved from one counter exit to another for accumulation. A path is provided by positional wiring (6) for this purpose. Notice that the wiring between counters is increased to five positions to allow for *overflow*. This is a term used to identify a result that exceeds the size of the longest field. In our example the execution of an *add* instruction involving two 4-position addends may result in a 5-position sum. If the result developed in the counter is larger than the field wired to counter-control print, the machine stops when the counter is instructed to read out and print. For reasons that will be explained later, the two computed *on-hand* and *available* fields are wired (7) through a selector to print.

The positional wiring described above is only part of the operation to enter information into the appropriate counter. A card-cycles impulse (0, 53 to 72) is normally wired to plus entry (S and T, 53 to 80), causing the card to add into the counter as it is read at second reading. We should mention at this time that during detail printing, information read from the card is setup first in the print wheels. The information is then read back from the print wheels and entered in the counter. In this manner, data added in this counter always agree with the information printed.

However, this can cause ill effects in some cases. Let us examine Fig. 11-7 closer. The *quantity* field is selectively printed so that quantity prints under the appropriate column. But are there other ways of quantity to print in the wrong column at card-cycle time? Look at wire J connecting counter exits to counter-control print. To prevent quantity from printing in the on-hand column, which is a computed total, a card-cycles impulse (wire M) is wired to the *direct-entry* hubs (W and X, 53 to 80) of each counter being used. This suppresses the printing of quantity in the on-hand positions 69 to 73 by permitting data to add directly into the counter instead of from the print wheels.

A control punch determines which counter the card should add into. The card-cycles impulse must be selected to reach the appropriate *plus* hubs for the particular card being added. This is possible by wiring the card-cycles impulse through a pilot selector controlled by the identifying punch to plus entry. A card-cycles impulse is wired to the *common* hub of pilot-selector 1 and from the *transferred* hub (G3) to counter-8D-plus entry. Pilot-selector-1 pickup is impulsed from first reading (4) through hub 1 (G1) of a digit selector. If a 1 impulse is present, the pilot selector transfers and the card-cycles impulse has a path (G3) to counter-8D-plus entry. If the impulse is absent, the selector is normal, thus breaking the circuit and preventing counter 8D from adding.

Each counter has several other hubs that affect entering information into a counter. We shall discuss each as needed. The *negative-balance-control* hubs (AD to AE, 53 to 80) are used to convert complementary results. Since subtraction is accomplished by adding the 9s complement of the figure being subtracted, the result must be recomplemented before printing. For example, a minus amount of 0456 enters the counter as 9543; therefore, any minus results must be recomplemented when the counter is read out. The *negative-balance*-ON hubs (AC, 53 to 80) emit an impulse when the counter turns negative. Certain machine operations can be conditioned from these hubs on a negative balance. In our problem, we use them to impulse (8) the *negative-balance-control* hubs so that complement totals will print as true figures.

The *CI-carry–exit C-carry–entry* hubs provide a path by external panel wiring for an internal 1-carry to the unit's position as illustrated below. A significant fact is that all counters reset to 9 rather than zero, thus leaving 9s standing in every counter position whenever the counter is reset (cleared) or contains a zero balance.

When two or more counters are coupled (connected) to increase capacity, the *CI* and *C* hubs provide a path for the internal 1-carry from the high-order position of the leftmost counter to the low-order position of the rightmost counter. In our problem, each counter is wired (9) to prevent the shortage that would result from addition and subtraction. Before tackling any new hubs, let us finish the wiring into the counter at card-read time for the remaining counters.

Pilot-selector 5 pickup is wired (I1) to transfer for a 3 in column-1 condition. When a 3 card is detected, counter 6C adds as a result of pilot-selector 5 transferring, thus permitting the impulse of the card cycle to reach the

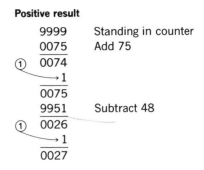

Positive result

9999	Standing in counter
0075	Add 75
0074	
0075	
9951	Subtract 48
0026	
0027	

Negative result

0035	Standing in counter
9650	Subtract 349
9685	
0071	Add 71
9756	
9971	Subtract 28
9727	
9728	Complement of 271

counter-plus hubs. *CI* and *C* hubs are wired normally. The *negative-balance*-OFF hubs (AF, 53 to 80) emit whenever a counter contains a zero balance and can be used to pick up selectors for controlling machine operations. Since a zero balance is indicated by all 9s in the counter, negative-balance OFF is wired (10) to negative-balance control so that the total will print as zeros. Recall that the purpose of negative-balance control is to convert complementary results, and all 9s are the complement of a zero amount.

Pilot-selector 10 controls entry into the on-order counter. The selector is impulsed (K1) to transfer whenever a 4 is recognized at first reading. If the selector is normal, quantity is not entered in the counter. If the selector is transferred, the quantity is added. *Negative-balance-control* (8) and *CI* and *C* hubs (9) are wired normally. Pilot-selector 15 is picked up on a 2-in-column-1 condition at first reading. If the pickup receives an impulse, the selector transfers on the following card cycle and the receipts quantity is added into counter 6B as the card passes second reading. A general rule for wiring *negative-balance-control* is to wire the hubs ON whenever a negative total is possible. Since the contents of counter 8D are transferred to counter 8F, *negative-balance-control* (8) is wired ON. The *CI* and *C* hubs (9) are wired normally.

PROGRAMMING

Thus far, we have printed the fields punched in the card and entered the quantity into the counters. Each card in a group is processed in the manner mentioned until a control break occurs. This simply means the last card of the group has been processed at second reading and the first card of the following group is at first reading. The control break is distinguished by the comparing unit (C to F, 1 to 30). When a control break occurs, the inventory application calls for a series of program steps to compute the on-hand and available totals for each stock number.

Each position of the comparing unit consists of two comparing entries and two *comparing-exit* hubs. Comparison is accomplished by wiring the *stock-number* field from first reading to one row of the comparing entries (A1) and from second reading to the other row of comparing entries (A2). During each card cycle, the readings to both sides of the comparing entries are compared. If the two readings for all wired comparing positions are identical, a comparing-exit impulse is not available. If the two readings for any comparing position are not identical, a comparing-exit impulse is available from the two common *comparing-exit* hubs.

For example, stock number 31297 compared against stock number 41297 results in a difference in comparing-position 17 only. For this reason, the comparing exits must be wired (A3) together. The comparing-exit impulse from position 17 travels through external wiring (A3) to program start (A4).

When program start is impulsed, a series of program steps (AP to AT, 53 to 72) is taken. Normally, 3 program steps (minor, intermediate, and major) are taken, but as many steps as needed may be activated by wiring (11) the *SPL PRG* (special programming) switch ON. When these two hubs are connected, the minor, intermediate, and major program steps lose their identity and instead

become program steps 1, 2, 3, 4, 5, 6, 7, etc. The program steps are taken in succession and are internally connected to the *channel-entry* hubs (AV, 53 to 68) for each program step.

Each vertical row of *program* hubs has a corresponding *channel-entry* hub. Unless the *channel-entry* hub is impulsed, the *program-exit* hubs above them are inactive. The *all-cycles* hubs (AW, 53 to 68) emit impulses every machine cycle. Machine cycles are different from card cycles, which emit each time a card passes a reading station. Machine cycles emit every cycle to include those between card cycles, such as program steps. When all cycles are wired (13) directly to channel entry, five program steps are activated. To provide additional needed program impulses, two vertical rows are wired. Although not used in our problem, the all-cycles impulse may be selectively wired to channel entry to permit one channel for steps 1 to 5, a second channel for steps 6 to 10, a third channel for steps 11 to 15, and so on.

The *planning chart* (Fig. 11-5) signifies that the receipts counter is added to opening-balance counter on program-step 1. Counter 6B is instructed (H4) to RO&R (read out and reset) on program-step 1. As previously stated, a counter does not add unless the contents reach the print wheels through *counter-control-print* hubs. Selector 17 is normal on program-step 1; therefore, this condition is met through wire J. However, the *NON P* (nonprint) hub must also be impulsed (H5) to prevent the information from printing in the *on-hand* field. Otherwise, overprinting, thus an unreadable *on-hand* field, would result when the *on-hand* field is printed on step 3. Now that we have read out the counter containing the receipts amount, we must impulse the plus entry of counter 8D.

Whenever *readout* and *reset* hubs are impulsed, the corresponding *plus transfer* hubs (Y, 53 to 80) or *minus transfer* hubs (Z, 53 to 80) emit. This provides an impulse at the proper time to add the contents of counter 6B into counter 8D. We cannot wire directly into counter 8D because a back circuit results when 8D is impulsed by a card-cycles impulse as the cards pass second reading. To eliminate the back circuit, the *plus transfer-exit* hub of counter 6B is wired to *filter-entry* hub 6 and from *filter-exit* hub 6 to the *plus entry* hub (H6) of counter 8D. The purpose of the filter is to permit passage of an impulse in only one direction—into entry and out of exit. Counter 8D now contains the opening-balance totals plus the issues totals.

The planning chart (Fig. 11-5) designates that the issues counter is subtracted on program-step 2 from the counter containing an accumulation of opening balance and issue totals. Counter 6C is impulsed (I4) to RO&R on program-step 2. The issues amount is prevented from printing in the on-hand field by impulsing the *NON P* hub (I5). At the same time the *plus transfer* hubs of 6C emit an impulse (I6) that travels through *filter* hub 13 to the *minus entry* hubs of counter 8D. The on-hand amount has been computed in counter 8D.

Program-step 3 emits an all-cycles impulse (J4) to RO&R counter 8D. Nonprint is not impulsed; the on-hand amount wired (7) to the *common* of selector 17 prints (J) in positions 69 to 73 through the *normal* hubs of co-selector 17. Selection prevents the on-hand amount from printing in the available field also. Wire J7 picks up the 120 transfer-print positions, thus disconnecting normal-print positions from the print wheels. Without this wire, information in counter 8D has a path from counter entry (wire 5) through selectors 1, 10, and 13 to normal print as counter 8D is transferred (wire J6) to counter 8F. Spacing (12) occurs for each line printed; therefore, the third program step is wired (J5) to the *SUPP* (space suppress) hub to permit the crossfooted total to print on the last printed line. When RO&R is impulsed, the *plus transfer* hub of counter 8D emits and the impulse flows (J6) through *filter* hub 20 to the *plus entry* hub of counter 8F. The available total, computed in counter 8F, is finalized except for printing.

The total to print in the available column is RO&R (L1). The contents of counter 8F travel through wires labeled 6 and 7 to the *common* of co-selector 17. In order to print the amount in positions 81 to 86, co-selector pickup 17 is impulsed (L2) on program-step 4 to transfer immediately. Also, program-step 4 is wired (12a) to hub labeled *extra,* which causes an extra space between different stock numbers (Fig. 11-3). Note that selector 17 is picked up by the *common* hub (K, 76 and 77) which has been impulsed from program-step 4. The contents of counter

8F continues their path through the transferred side of the co-selector (L) to print. Space suppression is wired (L3) from program-step 4 via *common* hub of counter 8F to permit printing on the same line as the on-hand total. Minor-program stop is wired (L4) to halt program progression beyond step 4. The machine then begins processing the first card of the next group which is now at second reading. In other words, it begins printing the data punched in the card and entering the information into the appropriate counter. The entire cycle is repeated until the next control break causes another series of program steps.

The accounting machine prints only significant digits 1 to 9 and any letter or special character. In order to print zeros, the impulse wired to print entry must be able to reach the fuse. Each print entry has a pair of *zero-print-control* hubs (BG to BL, 41 to 80) diagonally arranged, as illustrated in Fig. 7-6. The zero-print control for the IBM 407 is wired the same as the IBM 557 interpreter. Therefore, you should review the zero-print control in Chap. 7 and particularly Fig. 7-7. We have wired (14) each of the numeric fields in our problem for normal zero-print control.

CONTROL PANEL DIAGRAM SUMMARY

Program start is initiated by a change in stock number (wire labeled A4). All fields for normal printing are wired from second reading to normal print (wires labeled A to F). Quantity is selectively printed through selectors 1, 10, and 13 (wires labeled G, H, I, and K). Quantity is entered into counters 6B, 6C, 8D, and 8F (wires labeled 5). All four counters are connected to provide a path for rolling the contents from one counter to another (wires labeled 6). Fields J and L are selectively wired to counter-control print. The pilot selectors are wired to control the co-selectors for selectively printing fields G, H, I, and K. Card-cycles impulses are wired through pilot selectors so as to enter quantity into the appropriate counter. *On-hand* and *available* fields are computed on four program steps (AP to AW, 53 to 72). And last, each field containing zeros is wired for normal zero-print control (14).

Chapter 11 has encompassed all of the machine functions covered in previous chapters. We included selection similar to the 108 card proving machine, printing as performed by the 557 interpreter, comparing similar to the 514 reproducer and 88 collator, and programming as in the 604 electronic calculator. Our problem (Fig. 11-7) appears quite complicated. In fact, the problem *is* complex when considered in its entirety. However, when studied in segments, an understanding in depth is not beyond comprehension. We briefly covered the wiring at the beginning in order to understand the major facets of the problem as related to the control panel. Next, we covered the problem in detail, and last, we summarized the wiring. You will probably find that restudying is in order for a complete understanding.

QUESTIONS

1. Name six functions of the accounting machine. Name two or more subfunctions or uses of each.
2. What type printing is employed in Fig. 11-3? In Fig. 11-4? What two basic questions are answered by these reports?
3. How do you account for the quantity entering only one counter in Fig. 11-7 since the counter entries and exits are connected?
4. What is the purpose for the *pilot-selector-coupling-exit* hub? When does the hub emit?
5. In Fig. 11-7 three of the four wired pilot selectors are used to transfer co-selectors. Why is the coupling exit for the fourth pilot selector not wired?
6. Why must the counter exits be wired to counter-control print instead of normal print?
7. What is the reason for wiring fields J and L through co-selector 17 in Fig. 11-7?
8. Name four uses for negative-balance control.
9. How would you change the zero-print-control wiring in Fig. 11-7 to print insignificant zeros for document number?
10. Normally, only three program steps are available. Identify them and explain how the number of program steps may be expanded.
11. In Fig. 11-7, wires H6, I6, and J6 are wired through filters to prevent back circuits. Which *counter* hubs would be affected by the resulting back circuit if filtering were eliminated?
12. What is the purpose of the *CI* and *C* hubs?
13. How could the same card-cycles impulse in Fig. 11-7 be wired in all four pilot selectors to control adding into the counters?
14. When do the *plus transfer-exit* hubs emit?
15. There is a back circuit in Fig. 11-7. Locate it and explain the resulting error in relation to the printed report.

12
Flowcharting

Possessing a data processing department by no means assures a company a profitable operation. In fact, a few data processing installations fail to justify even their existence. Estimates of the proportion of unprofitable data processing operations have run considerably higher than 50 percent. These operations may be suffering from a "trial and error" method of reaching their objectives. Getting a program debugged and working is all that counts to some data processing managers, but this philosophy is painfully expensive.

The success of a data processing operation depends largely upon processing methods and procedures. The development of documentation is built around both functions. We have found use for two types of pictorial documentation, control panel diagrams and planning charts, as effective tools in improving procedures and processing methods. Another such tool is the flowchart.

INTRODUCTION TO FLOWCHARTING

The *flowchart,* consisting of symbols connected by lines, assists in analysis and solution of data processing problems and analysis of the machine method by which the requirements of processing are met. Most data processing applications involve many alternatives and exceptions, making them difficult to state verbally or in written form. So, the data processing technician turns to two types of flowcharts in translating the different operations into step-by-step machine instructions.

The broadest use of the flowchart is to convey information. After a procedure and program are written, thoroughly tested, and proved correct, the flowchart becomes a permanent part of procedure documentation. It enables the operator to easily visualize and process the information, using the required machines in the intended sequence. For the programmer attempting to improve the program or processing procedure, the flowchart provides a means of rethinking and analyzing each machine instruction to find a shortcut. The sequence in which operations are to be executed should be precisely stated and presented so that they are easy to visualize and follow. The two types of flowcharts are the systems flowchart and the program flowchart.

A *systems flowchart* (Fig. 12-1) is a pictorial representation of the machine processing of information from source documents (input) to the desired final product (output). In other words, this type flowchart describes the flow of data through all machines comprising the data processing system. Such a picture gives primary emphasis to the sequence of machines to be used and the special handling necessary in a given step.

A *program flowchart* (Fig. 12-2) (sometimes called a *block diagram*) describes what takes place within a wired or stored program. This type of flowchart is a means of representing a logical sequence of machine instructions which a computer would take in processing data. Emphasis is on the internally stored instructions and the sequence in which they are programmed.

Each manufacturer of data processing machines provides a flowchart template made of plastic and consisting of cutout symbols necessary for drawing both systems and program flowcharts. Unfortunately, the use of symbols is not standard. This is of little concern, however, as long as there is uniformity within a data processing installation.

SYSTEMS FLOWCHART

The symbols (Fig. 12-3) represent major data processing functions, such as sorting, collating, and processing of data by the accounting machine or computer. In a systems flowchart, an entire processing phase or step,

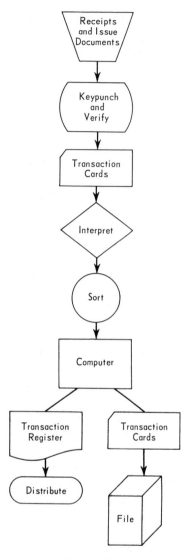

Fig. 12-1 Systems flowchart.

Otherwise, the flowchart becomes cluttered with details and the overall picture is lost.

The flowchart does not contain sufficient detail to enable a data processing operator to set up the machines and carry a job through to completion. Narrative instructions for each symbol, referring to columns to be sorted and switch settings, are written to supplement the flowchart. These procedure steps are described in detail to enable the operator to perform the entire job with little or no supervision.

In order for one symbol to have a meaningful relationship to other symbols, they must be connected by lines and arrows to indicate the direction of flow. The symbols are usually drawn from top to bottom, giving primary

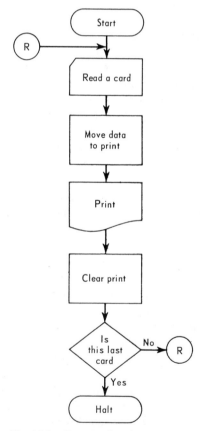

Fig. 12-2 Program flowchart.

such as a program run, is represented by a single processing symbol. They are so designed as to be visually meaningful; however, comments placed within each symbol add specific meaning. The systems flowchart is a simple picture showing the flow of work, and the comments within each symbol should be brief and clear.

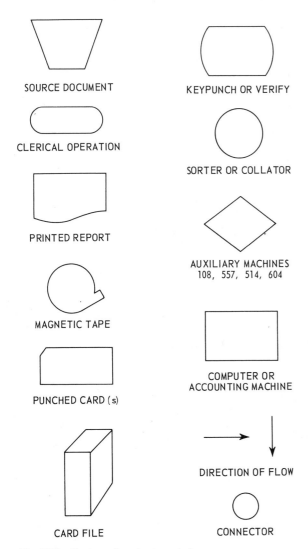

SOURCE DOCUMENT

CLERICAL OPERATION

PRINTED REPORT

MAGNETIC TAPE

PUNCHED CARD (s)

CARD FILE

KEYPUNCH OR VERIFY

SORTER OR COLLATOR

AUXILIARY MACHINES
108, 557, 514, 604

COMPUTER OR
ACCOUNTING MACHINE

DIRECTION OF FLOW

CONNECTOR

Fig. 12-3 Systems flowchart symbols.

consideration to neatness and uniformity. When the normal direction is opposed, the tendency should be from left to right whenever possible.

Figure 12-4 demonstrates a method of incorporating four types of transactions involved in preparing the Inventory Transaction Report discussed in the previous chapter. A detailed study of this flowchart will greatly assist you in working your first problem.

Problem 1

To exercise your knowledge of data processing machine functions, draw a flowchart for a billing operation based upon the given facts. In so doing, you will fit the machines together as a system and develop an understanding of the work flow. The problem involves preparation of pre-billing cards and subsequent processing to the billing stage for a small utility company. Of course, there are many variations among utility companies such as cycle billing, length of billing period, collection practices, and types of reports. However, our objective is not a sophisticated application, but merely a simplified flowchart to test our understanding of how the various punched-card machines are linked together to form a data processing system.

In choosing this problem, prime consideration was given to an application widely familiar to most students. You should write a brief narrative, as illustrated in Fig. 12-4, to describe the function performed by each symbol. To assist you in approaching the problem in a logical manner, let us consider several facets in a utility billing application.

1. Instead of keypunching each customer's billing card monthly, certain information is available from existing files. The account number, meter number, rate, route number, billing day, etc., are punched in the previous month's billing file. Therefore, a partial billing card may be prepared by reproducing data from the prior month's billing card in a prebilling card.

2. Two basic items, previous and present meter readings, are necessary to mechanically produce a billing card. Since the previous reading is the same as the present reading in last month's billing card, this information is reproduced into the prebilling card at the same time that other fixed data are reproduced from the prior month's billing card. The present reading must be recorded by physically reading each meter. One method is to record the meter reading and keypunch the information in each prebilling card. A faster and more economical means is to furnish the man reading the meters with the prebilling cards. He mark senses the information read from the meter onto each card, and this information

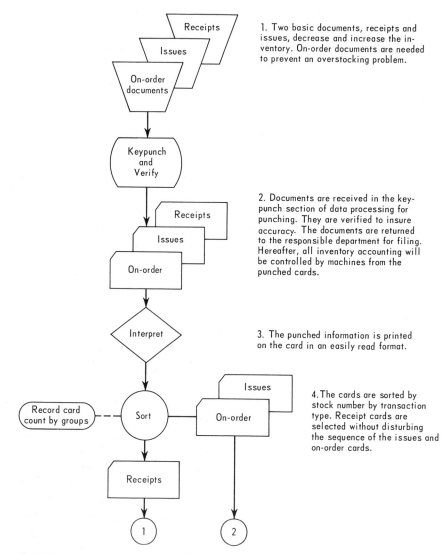

1. Two basic documents, receipts and issues, decrease and increase the inventory. On-order documents are needed to prevent an overstocking problem.

2. Documents are received in the keypunch section of data processing for punching. They are verified to insure accuracy. The documents are returned to the responsible department for filing. Hereafter, all inventory accounting will be controlled by machines from the punched cards.

3. The punched information is printed on the card in an easily read format.

4. The cards are sorted by stock number by transaction type. Receipt cards are selected without disturbing the sequence of the issues and on-order cards.

Fig. 12-4   Systems flowchart of Inventory Transaction Report.

is automatically punched in the card by a 514 reproducer.

3.   If the mark-sense approach is taken, do not forget accounting controls. For instance, the same number of cards given each meter reader must be returned at the end of the day, assuring that no cards are lost. When the cards are returned to the data processing department for punching the mark-sensed meter reading, billing date

and reading date may be gangpunched into the cards during the same operation.

4.   After the prebilling cards from the previous month's billing cards are reproduced, closed account cards must be selected and destroyed. New account cards must be filed into the prebilling deck.

5.   The cards are ready for calculation upon return

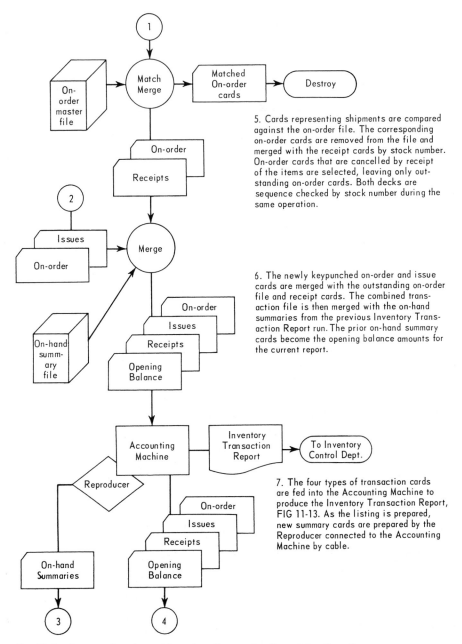

5. Cards representing shipments are compared against the on-order file. The corresponding on-order cards are removed from the file and merged with the receipt cards by stock number. On-order cards that are cancelled by receipt of the items are selected, leaving only outstanding on-order cards. Both decks are sequence checked by stock number during the same operation.

6. The newly keypunched on-order and issue cards are merged with the outstanding on-order file and receipt cards. The combined transaction file is then merged with the on-hand summaries from the previous Inventory Transaction Report run. The prior on-hand summary cards become the opening balance amounts for the current report.

7. The four types of transaction cards are fed into the Accounting Machine to produce the Inventory Transaction Report, FIG 11-13. As the listing is prepared, new summary cards are prepared by the Reproducer connected to the Accounting Machine by cable.

Fig. 12-4 Systems flowchart of Inventory Transaction Report (continued).

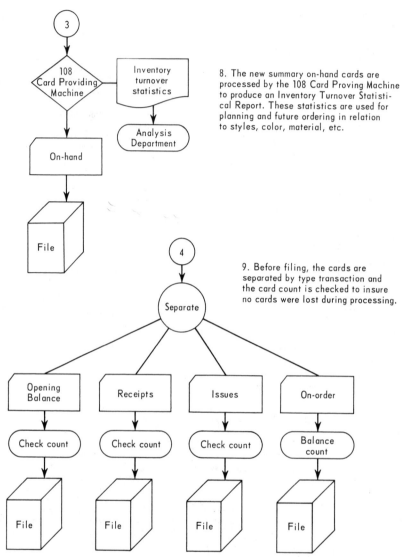

8. The new summary on-hand cards are processed by the 108 Card Proving Machine to produce an Inventory Turnover Statistical Report. These statistics are used for planning and future ordering in relation to styles, color, material, etc.

9. Before filing, the cards are separated by type transaction and the card count is checked to insure no cards were lost during processing.

Fig. 12-4 Systems flowchart of Inventory Transaction Report (continued).

from being read and being punched with mark-sensed information. The cards are calculated for units consumed (current reading minus prior reading), and the result is multiplied by the rate. Each extended field is punched in the card.

6. The billing card is now prepared, but is not suitable for mailing to the customer. In any case, if this were done, there would be no record of billing and follow-up. The billing work card is reproduced as a perforated billing form including a stub, which is torn off and retained by the customer as a receipt.

7. A customer name-and-address master file is essential since other billing data fill most of the card. These cards are merged with the billing cards by account

number; the customer name and address are read by the 557 interpreter and printed on the following corresponding billing card. Do not forget that the prebilling cards must be interpreted before given to the meter reader.

The flowcharting techniques just discussed dealt with punched-card machines and the flow of data from one machine to the next. The next topic involves flowcharting of program instructions to be used in subsequent computer programming chapters. In other words, this type of flowcharting deals with internal processing by a computer system.

PROGRAM FLOWCHART

As previously defined, a program flowchart is a diagram of a set of machine instructions which causes a computer to process data and to produce specific results. The data available for input and the desired output are known; the program flowchart consists of bridging the gap between, using the necessary machine processing.

As pointed out when planning the problem for the 604 electronic calculator and 407 accounting machine, planning or programming is an extremely important phase of putting an application into operation. A well-planned application results in efficiency by holding debugging and computer-testing time to a minimum. More important, the next project or assignment can be started on time instead of days or weeks later. Optimum planning more than compensates for the effort and time expended.

The program flowchart symbols (Fig. 12-5) give us a means of presenting instructions so that they are easy to visualize and follow during the developmental stages of programming.

A control panel is wired to perform functions in the proper sequence and at the proper time. In a stored program, the instructions are punched onto cards and stored in memory. Let us take the example illustrated in Fig. 12-2. The application calls for a detail listing, which involves reading a card and printing the data.

The *read-a-card* symbol contains an instruction to cause the input device (card reader) to feed a card past the reading brushes and place the contents into memory.

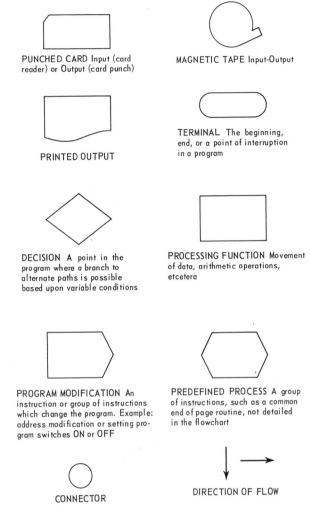

PUNCHED CARD Input (card reader) or Output (card punch)

MAGNETIC TAPE Input-Output

PRINTED OUTPUT

TERMINAL The beginning, end, or a point of interruption in a program

DECISION A point in the program where a branch to alternate paths is possible based upon variable conditions

PROCESSING FUNCTION Movement of data, arithmetic operations, etcetera

PROGRAM MODIFICATION An instruction or group of instructions which change the program. Example: address modification or setting program switches ON or OFF

PREDEFINED PROCESS A group of instructions, such as a common end of page routine, not detailed in the flowchart

CONNECTOR

DIRECTION OF FLOW

Fig. 12-5 Program flowchart symbols.

Processing other than printing is not called for; therefore, in the next symbol data are transferred to a predetermined location for printing. Next, a symbol contains a *print* instruction which causes the printer to write a line. The print area is cleared to properly store the next record. At this point, we have completed the processing for the first card.

Seemingly, another identical set of instructions must process the second card, and so on. This is fortunately unnecessary, for if instructions could be followed only sequentially, a complete program would be necessary for each card in the file. To conserve memory, we cause the program to repeat itself. Eventually, repeating the program must be stopped. This is accomplished by inserting an instruction in a decision symbol to test for the last card. If the last card has not entered the card reader, the program repeats itself. When the last card has been processed, the computer is instructed to halt. This tech-

nique of repeating a given set of instructions is called a *loop*.

Let us consider another program flowchart (Fig. 12-6), one for totaling the salary of all employees earning less than $100 per week. Before we discuss the various symbols and their purposes, study the flowchart thoroughly. The first card is read and the salary is compared against a stored constant of 10000. If the answer to the decision symbol is NO, the program branches to read another card and no further processing for that card takes place. If YES, the program continues with the next sequential instruction—adding salary to a counter. The last-card decision is made, and the program repeats the loop if there are cards left in the feed hopper of the card reader. If the answer is YES, the program continues. The contents of the counter are moved to the print area, the accumulated total is printed, and the computer halts.

This problem demonstrates the necessity for flowcharting and the consequent errors that may be foreseen by analyzing the instructions on paper as the computer will execute them. If you detected the error, you are ahead of the game. The program gives the desired final result *only* if the last card contains a salary *less* than $100. If the last card contains a salary of more than $100, the program branches to read another card based upon the flowchart logic and prevents the accumulated total from printing. As you can see, all paths that the program may take must be tested.

Problem 2

Before we discuss more involved problems, an exercise in program logic will permit you to think in terms the computer must use to solve a problem. Draw a flowchart to print the average salary of all employees in the file. The logical approach is to consider what you must do for each card in the file in order to compute and print the average.

DEVELOPING A FLOWCHART

The first task in solving a problem is related to the subject of system analysis or procedure design. This

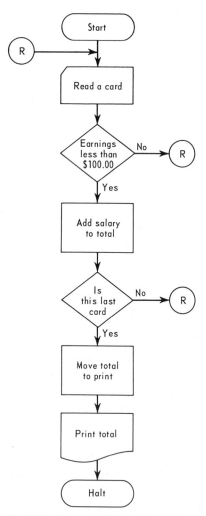

Fig. 12-6 Program flowchart to tabulate gross pay.

phase is begun with problem definition, i.e., determining what is to be done. In a payroll application, the number of hours each employee works must be determined before his gross pay is computed.

In an earlier phase of payroll accounting, prepunched cards were furnished each employee for the purpose of recording the time worked. These cards are punched with employee number and are designed for mark sensing the hours and minutes worked. Called *time attendance cards*, they are verified by the foreman and sent to the data processing department on a daily basis. Certain processing, such as editing and punching the mark-sensed hours, is performed on the cards. Errors are returned to each foreman promptly for correction.

On the last day of the pay period, all time attendance cards are batched and the payroll is begun. Before outlining the sequence of operations required to compute gross pay, certain characteristics of the data must be considered. The master file, maintained on magnetic tape, is needed only to get the pay rate for each employee. Of course, our problem must be kept on a simplified level. In a complete payroll application, other information would be needed from the master tape.

The master tape contains a record for each employee, and each record on the tape is in employee-number sequence. This means that the first record on the tape is the smallest number in the file, the record of the employee with the next higher number follows, and so on. In order to compute the gross pay for each employee, we must locate his pay rate on the tape. With the tape in employee-number sequence, this is not difficult, since the first record needed is located at the beginning of the tape and the next employee record is located by reading only one more record instead of having to search the entire tape.

To sum up what is to be done, we must produce a listing showing name, employee number, total hours worked, pay rate, and gross pay. The hours worked are recorded in time attendance cards, one for each day. Each card must be compared by employee number to accumulate the correct number of hours for each employee; then the hours are added into a counter and multiplied by pay rate. Employee number in the cards must be compared to the tape to ensure that the proper pay rate is used. The employee name and rate are not punched in the card; therefore, they must be extracted from the tape and stored in the computer memory until needed at print time. We must determine the amount of the entire payroll, so the total salary of each employee is accumulated in another counter for a final total. One last requirement is that since the cards are matched by a *control* field, they must have previously been sorted and sequence checked.

The next step is to decide how to do the problem with the computer. This is expressed in a flowchart (Fig. 12-7) by showing the sequence of operations necessary to produce the desired results. With the master and detail files in the same sequence, we get the pay rate from the magnetic tape and the hours from the cards. The best way, as we shall see, is to store the tape data first. Therefore, the first step is to read a record from the master tape file.

Each record read or written on magnetic tape is checked for accuracy. If an error in writing or reading is detected, an indicator is automatically turned ON. This indicator can and should be examined during tape operations. Let us assume that an error is detected during an attempt to read a tape record. We test the read-write indicator immediately after a *tape read* instruction. If the indicator is OFF, the program is to continue; if the indicator is ON, the program is controlled to branch to a tape error subroutine. As previously defined, a subroutine is a set of instructions that deviates from the main program. Expressed another way, a subroutine can be thought of as a small program within a larger program.

An error recovery routine, in general, is a series of instructions causing the tape to backspace one record and attempt another reading. We begin by giving the number of attempts the computer should attempt to read the record. This is accomplished by counting each time the program repeats the tape error loop. The program logic backspaces the tape over the record in error, another attempt is made to read the record, and the read-write indicator is again tested. If the read is good, the program branches back to the main program or to the point of interruption. If the indicator is still ON, indicating

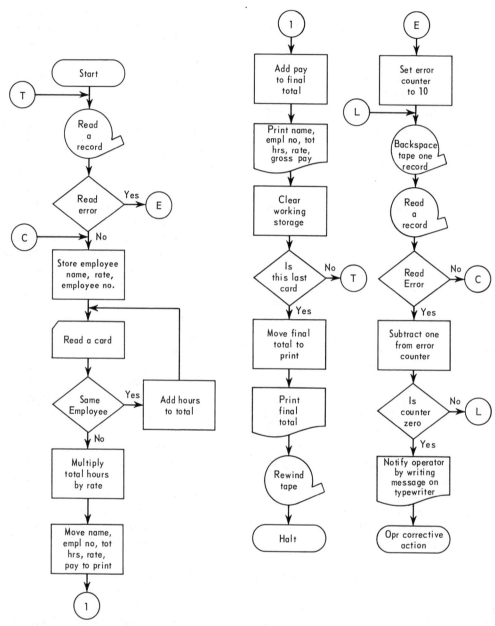

Fig. 12-7 Program flowchart to compute gross pay.

another bad read, 1 is subtracted from a count set up to keep track of the reading attempts. We next determine if the computer has attempted to read the record the number of times we specify. In our example, we try 10 times. If the computer has not reread the record 10 times, the error loop is repeated. Otherwise, if the error persists, the program prints a message on the console typewriter for the machine operator and halts the computer.

Returning to the main program, if the tape record is correctly read, we extract employee name, pay rate, and employee number from the tape and store them in the computer memory. A transaction card is read by the card reader and the contents are transferred into memory. In order to use the correct pay rate with each employee's transactions, we must compare employee number of the card against the employee number stored from the previous tape record. If the compare is equal, the hours worked are added to a counter and another card is read. In this manner, the hours in all cards for the same employee are accumulated.

When a card with a different employee number is detected, no further processing for that card takes place at that time. Instead, the program must continue the computation process for the last employee, that is, multiplying total hours by pay rate and moving the intended data to print. Recall that we decided an overall total would be useful; consequently, we must accumulate each employee's total pay in another counter. At this point, we have the required output in the print area of memory. We now instruct the computer to print, transferring the information from the print area to the printing device. To prepare for processing the next employee, working storage, such as counters, is cleared.

A test to determine if all cards have been processed is made. Two paths are possible from the decision. If there are additional cards waiting processing, the program branches to read the next record on tape and the program is repeated. If the last card has passed the reading brushes in the card reader, the program continues with end-of-job processing. This entails moving the final total to the print area, which has previously been cleared, and printing the amount. The magnetic tape is rewound to the beginning so the operator may remove the tape reel for filing. Processing of the entire file has been completed, so the computer is instructed to halt.

We have discussed the processing requirements for a typical computer application. However, the problem has been greatly simplified for presentation. For instance, we did not consider a record on tape without corresponding transactions, or cards without a corresponding record on tape. Nor did we consider accounting controls and editing. One form of check could have determined if the number of hours worked were within a predetermined limit. The student is strongly urged to study and analyze the flowchart of the problem in Fig. 12-7. Recall that the computer cannot be expected to handle the unexpected unless provisions are included in the program. You should follow the program through closely, investigating all possibilities that could result in incorrect processing.

Problem 3

By working this problem you can test your understanding of flowcharting, reinforce your practical knowledge, and gain experience. The problem is to draw a flowchart to update pay rate, marital status, or withholding exemptions on a master tape file. Facts relative to the problem are:

1.   The original master tape and transaction cards are in employee-number sequence. In addition to updating records involving changes, copy those master records that have no transaction card onto the updated tape.

2.   Each of the three types of changes is punched in separate cards. There is only one transaction card for those records to be updated. If the program identifies an error card (other than a pay rate, marital status, or withholding exemption change), print the entire card and proceed with another record.

3.   When the last card has been processed, write the remaining records onto the updated tape, rewind both tapes, and stop the computer.

We have discussed both types of flowcharting, systems and program. The systems flowchart, generally prepared by systems-analyst personnel, shows the whole of the operation. It is kept as simple as possible, yet must

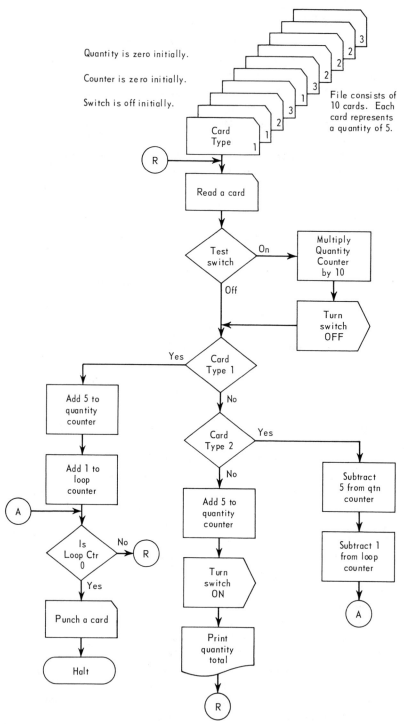

Fig. 12-8 Program flowchart problem.

include sufficient detail to enable others to understand and visualize the sequence in which documents flow from machine to machine. On the other hand, a program flowchart shows every minute detail. For this reason, more creative thinking is necessary to draw this type, especially in light of the many alternate paths possible.

A knowledge of how the computer works is a necessity to effective flowchart preparation. You will find that as we progress, the pieces will begin to fall into place, especially after a few exercises in flowcharting. Do not feel discouraged if at first you have some difficulty, but continue your practice, because without a knowledge of flowcharting it is virtually impossible to progress to computer programming.

QUESTIONS

1. What is the use of narrative instructions? Of flow-charts?

2. What is the difference between a systems flowchart and a program flowchart?

3. Most problems have more than one correct solution. In solving a problem, when should this fact be considered?

4. Proper program flowcharting eliminates much debugging. What is meant by this statement?

5. What is the purpose of the connector symbol?

6. How would you correct the program error in Fig. 12-6?

7. Two errors result from the last-card test in Fig. 12-7. What are they?

8. In Fig. 12-8, how many cards are processed? Punched?

9. In Fig. 12-8, what is the total quantity printed on the first line? The second line?

10. What is the status of the switch in Fig. 12-8 when the computer stops? How many times is the switch turned ON?

13
Introduction to computers

Computers entered the data processing picture in the mid 1950s. Although the government possessed a few in the late 1940s, they were special-purpose computers and were not available commercially. The computer was introduced primarily because of its speed, accuracy, and large memory.

CONCEPTS OF AN ELECTRONIC DATA PROCESSING SYSTEM

A *computer system,* synonymous with electronic data processing system (EDPS), is composed of a number of individual machines that perform some part of the data processing operation. It is completely electronic, except for the input and output units. With the exception of a few models, instructions are stored inside the machine. These instructions, called a *program*, are series of steps followed by the computer in a prescribed sequence to produce the desired processing. The term *processing* applies to handling data by comparing and classifying it in preparation of calculation, and summarizing the results for recording. Since the instructions are stored internally, the machine has access to them at electronic speeds, and we have the term *stored program*.

The heart of a computer system is the central processor (Fig. 13-1). It is from here that the entire system is controlled by the program. The program, stored in a language the computer understands, is interpreted by the central processor, which directs the machine to perform operations such as locating data and moving them to the arithmetic unit, or controlling input-output functions of other units of the system. The electronic storage in the central processor is capable of holding information, in addition to the program, until needed for processing.

The computer requires a number of components that can enter data into the central processor and record the data after processing. The card read–punch (Fig. 13-1) reads the information to be processed from punched

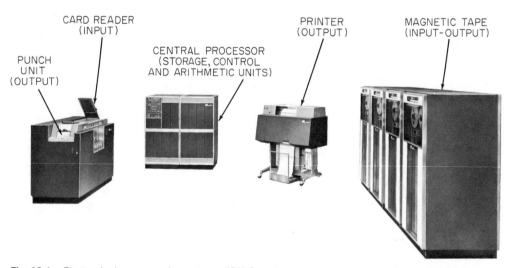

Fig. 13-1 Electronic data processing system. (IBM Corp.)

cards at 800 per minute and makes them available to the central processor. The left section of the unit is able to punch the results of processing at 250 cards per minute. After the input cards are read and the output cards are punched, they are directed into one of five pockets. Processed information may also be recorded on paper forms at 600 lines per minute by the printer (Fig. 13-1). This component is able to print 132 positions in a line, each consisting of one of the 26 letters, 10 digits, or 12 special characters. Magnetic tape units (Fig. 13-1) can be used as input and output. The principal use of tape is to increase the speed of input and to provide compact storage for large quantities of data. Sixteen million characters can be stored on a single tape, and reading speed is about 60 times faster than that of card input.

Although the computer is capable of sorting and merging data recorded on magnetic tape, certain punched-card machines, such as the sorter, interpreter, and collator, have a rightful place with the computer system. So, in general, we may say that a computer replaces the reproducer, calculator, and accounting machine.

NEED FOR COMPUTERS

The philosophy of Charles Babbage, the recognized father of computers, was that mental as well as physical labor should be economized by the aid of machines. The following examples of the fruits of automation readily prove his philosophy and, perhaps, suggest that the computer's full capabilities will never be known.

The computer is used for prediction. A Univac computer came to the attention of millions of people when it was used on television for projecting the results of the campaign between Stevenson and Eisenhower in 1952. The first prediction made by the machine indicated an overwhelming landslide for Eisenhower. The people operating the machine, afraid of the results and consequent public reaction, modified the weighting applied to the various statistical variables, and the subsequent predictions made by the machine indicated a win for Eisenhower, but by a greatly reduced margin. The final results showed

that the initial prediction of 438 electoral votes made by the Univac computer was very close to the final result of 442 votes.*

A savings of time and money can be expected by computer processing, but only when properly applied. Compiling the census of the United States and releasing the findings on a timely basis is a continuing problem. The 1890 census paved the way for processing data by machines. However, every 10 years bring new problems and an ever-expanding population for the Census Bureau to cope with. Consequently, new techniques are devised in search of more efficient and economical approaches. For the 1960 census a method was developed to record collected facts on microfilm. The information on the microfilm was transferred to magnetic tape by specially designed machines and the tapes were used by computers for the processing required. This method of bypassing the manual preparation of punched cards resulted in a savings of $8 million and took half the time required to process the previous census.

Computers process on a timely basis data that would be manually unfeasible. The 10 billion checks processed in 1958 and the 13 billion in 1961 provided the groundwork for developing machines that would read magnetic ink printed on the check. Recorded in a form readable by the human eye, the check contains the transit routing symbol which identifies the bank and its location. This permits the check to be processed electronically through various banks and federal clearinghouses. Upon arrival at the bank of the writer, it is further processed for redemption by the machine since the value of the check and the account number of the depositor are also recorded with magnetic ink. Today's successful processing of 18 billion checks annually has opened the door for other means of direct input, such as typewritten and handwritten documents.

The shortage of white-collar workers has been solved to a great extent by the computer. White-collar workers are those persons in clerical, professional, and similar occupations. This is in contrast with blue-collar workers, usually involved in manual labor necessary for production

---

* By permission of Univac Division of Sperry Rand Corporation.

and servicing. During the past twenty years, white-collar workers have increased in number from 35 percent to almost 50 percent of the labor force. If this rate of growth had continued, eventually there would not be enough people to process clerical and accounting work. In addition to economic and efficient handling of paperwork, computers are used in the design of construction projects, for drawing weather maps used in forecasting, as in medical reseach, and other developments.

Today's scientific need is unparalleled. In 1950, an atomic energy problem at Los Alamos required 9 million calculations. The IBM SSEC computer solved the problem in 150 hours. It would have taken a mathematician 1500 years. You will also recall that John Von Neumann's Maniac computer made possible the building and testing of the hydrogen bomb. Now, a new generation of computers operates thousands of times faster than earlier models to solve many problems in such fields as space exploration.

Computers make possible achievements in space, which might otherwise prove unconquerable. A tremendous amount of calculations, that would require many years by manual means, is necessary; time, therefore, is vital in solving scientific problems. In many instances, the actual success of scientific attempts may be directly attributed to the computer. Let us consider an important happening in the science of space exploration.

The first docking of two space vehicles was performed on March 16, 1966. This preliminary step to the use of orbiting space stations in launching other spacecraft consisted of joining an Agena vehicle with the manned Gemini 8 capsule. With data provided by a small but highly sophisticated computer aboard Agena 8, the astronauts were able to maneuver their space capsule for docking. This incredible docking at 17,500 miles per hour was accomplished in 30 minutes with the aid of a special-purpose computer the size of a bread box. The computations for vital data needed to control Agena 8 during docking would have taken a mathematician about 35,000 hours, or 4 years.

Computers also contribute to public safety; for instance, they can monitor aircraft takeoffs and provide automatic engine shutdown in case of trouble. In addition, they are instrumental in making automatic landings during inclement weather.

As a result of technological advances such as these, the need for the computer will continue to increase rapidly. The undiscovered ways in which data processing machines are used seem almost boundless. With each new application, computers demonstrate new ways in which they can be used to help man advance and enlarge his capabilities.

HISTORY OF COMPUTERS

Howard Aiken, mathematics professor at Harvard University, began work on the first large-scale automatic computer in 1939. He was well along with his work when he read of Charles Babbage, builder of a machine with a remarkable likeness to his. If developed, it would have operated similarly to today's computers with stored programs and punched card input and output. Babbage's work was discussed earlier in the section on the history of data processing.

The advent of mechanization began as a result of the 1880 census. The eight years required to complete it demonstrated that future censuses would take longer to compile than the ten-year span between them. Dr. Herman Hollerith, statistician for the Census Bureau, and engineer James Powers invented a machine that would tabulate. Used in the 1890 census, it caused the census to be completed in 2½ years even though the population had increased nearly 25 percent.

In subsequent years other machines would be built to perform other clerical routines, such as filing and sorting. Development was slow until World War II. Since that time, data processing has grown in leaps and bounds. Although machines available commercially prior to the 1950s were not classified as computers, they have a very important place in the history of computers, for computers are merely an extension of punched-card systems. In fact, earlier computers used the same parts as the punched-card machines.

BEGINNING OF ELECTRONIC DATA PROCESSING

Howard Aiken visualized his electromechanical calculator in 1937. After six years of development work, with the assistance of International Business Machines, the first large-scale computer was completed and put into operation in 1944. Dr. Aiken called his machine the Automatic Sequence Controlled Calculator or Mark I. It was followed by the improved Mark II and Mark III, designed for the government to compute ballistics data.

In the early 1940s, Dr. John W. Mauchly, a physicist, and J. Presper Eckert, Jr., an electronic engineer, conceived of a general-purpose, high-speed digital computer which was entirely electronic except for the input and output units. The machine, built mainly to calculate trajectories, was completed at the University of Pennsylvania in 1946. Named Eniac (Electronic Numerical Integrator and Automatic Computer), it occupied a room over 100 feet in length. The effectiveness of Eniac was somewhat restricted because it had only 200 digits of memory. It also took a long time to change from one problem to another. However, once the machine was properly set up, it could perform 5000 additions per second. Eniac operated in Maryland with high efficiency and dependability for several years.

Eniac was the forerunner of Univac I (Universal Automatic Computer), the first commercial stored-program electronic computer. Univac I was completed in 1951 by Remington Rand and introduced to business in 1953.

Before completion of Eniac, Mauchly and Eckert were designing the first computer to employ the binary system, explained in the next chapter. The machine also had duplicate circuitry for checking, known as parity checking. In general, *parity checking* means that any data moved within the machine arrives at its destination correct. Mauchly and Eckert called their machine Edvac (Electronic Discrete Variable Automatic Computer). It became operational in 1952.

International Business Machines introduced the Selective Sequence Electronic Calculator in 1948. This giant was the first computer to employ *selective sequence programming,* meaning that the instructions need not be performed in sequence. Instead, certain instructions could be bypassed. Thus, the series of steps to be taken by the computer could be altered by returning to subdivisions in the program.

The first computer to operate from instructions stored within it (referred to as a stored program) was Edsac (Electronic Delayed Storage Automatic Computer). Edsac was completed in 1949 at Cambridge University, England. Input to the computer was a standard five-hole teletype tape. Output was in the form of teletype tape or teletype printer. Its memory was capable of storing 17,406 binary digits. Edsac also possessed a characteristic of modern computers, a means by which complex problems could be solved by assembling together methods of solutions (instructions) previously used on simpler calculations.

Although other computers were built about this time, these are mentioned for their significant contributions to electronic data processing. The terminology used to describe their contribution will become clear as we proceed with our study of computers.

CLASSIFICATION OF COMPUTERS

There are two major classifications of electronic data processing machines, analog and digital. Our study will be about the digital computer; the analog computer, after definition, will not be considered further.

The *analog computer* was developed by Dr. Vannevar Bush and others at the Massachusetts Institute of Technology from 1925 to 1930. The most common form of an analog computer is the speedometer. Tire revolutions are converted to miles per hour and translated to digits on a dial. We can say that the analog computer takes a measured amount of information, performs a set routine of processing, and presents the answer in a measurable form. This computer calculates numbers represented by measurable physical quantities such as rotations of wheels, stresses of airplane wings, etc. For example, the slide rule performs numerical calculations with a sliding central piece that moves between two parallel parts, each with a logarithmic scale.

Whereas the analog computer determines the desired answer based upon physical measurement, the digital computer produces the desired result based upon computations of numbers. For this reason digital computers are more accurate than analog computers and the latter are not adaptable to processing of data. We should point out at this time that digital computers rarely use the digits 0 to 9. Instead, they use two-state components that are capable of storing and working with representations such as 0 or 1, yes or no, and off or on. There are two types of digital computers, scientific and business machines.

A *scientific computer,* although it may deal with some business applications, is devoted mainly to solving complex problems, such as those of engineering and research. Generally speaking, the scientific installation requires more sophisticated and faster machines. The problems fed the computer are more closely related to mathematics; thus they are readily stated as formulas. This in turn demands different qualifications, if not higher education, for the programmers who must compile sets of instructions for the machines to operate by. In fact, the person writing the program in a scientific installation is normally more oriented toward the application than the computer.

Advanced computer languages, such as Fortran (*For*mula *tran*slation), have greatly simplified the problem of qualifications for computer personnel in scientific installations. This is so because an engineer with a minimum of computer knowledge may write a program in Fortran. The Fortran programming language is built around the mathematical language; thus the engineer can state the problem in terms he understands and the computer can handle it.

Perhaps the biggest difference between the scientific and business installation is that most scientific jobs are programmed and run only once. On the other hand, a business installation writes a program to be used repeatedly, thus the need for more programming efficiency. Of course, if the scientific installation finds a solution that may be used over and over, it becomes more closely paralleled to its counterpart. The scientific computer can be expected to receive small quantities of input data, perform vast amounts of computations, and provide very

little output. Some scientific computers use only a typewriter for both input and output. Because it is intended primarily for computing, the scientific computer will most likely employ pure binary as opposed to other forms of coded binary discussed in the next chapter.

A *business computer* processes alphabetic and numeric data by accepting vast quantities of input media, performing relatively little processing, and creating the desired output in large quantities. For this reason all business computers consist of many and various input-output devices, such as card readers, card punches, printers, magnetic tape units, etc.

A business application is concerned with accounting controls consisting of editing of the input data, taking batch, money, or hash totals, and performing record counts to ensure that all transactions are processed. For example, a hash total of some descriptive field, such as document, stock or account number, affords a control to see that all of the information has been correctly recorded or that a record has not been omitted. A business computer processes recurring jobs, as opposed to one-time jobs. This necessitates explicit documentation and procedures in the form of console operator instructions, flowcharts, input-output formats, location and disposition of input-output media, and instructions for operating punched card equipment. Since the job is run more than once, program efficiency is important. A long program consisting of many instructions requires more time, therefore more money for computer processing, than a shorter program giving the same results. This means that ingenuity is needed to prepare a successful program with a minimum of machine instructions. All of the former characteristics of a business installation are normally unimportant to a scientific installation because their programs are generally used only once.

The business computer in itself does not save time or money, improve management, deal in increased volumes of data, solve complex problems, or improve customer service. In fact, it does not provide anything beneficial by itself. But with human guidance a computer can read input data, process it, and provide desired results in the desired format. It can compute and print the result where and when you want it but cannot give management miracles. In sum, a computer is only one of many ingredients that make a successful business.

The human guide we allude to is called a programmer. A *programmer* is a person who, essentially, analyzes the problem and source data, determines the solution, and writes a program for the computer. The programmer must know precisely how the computer works and, of equal importance, all about the application or problem in order to meet the requirements expected. Although the programmer knows all about the computer and problem, the computer cannot produce the desired results unless the programmer knows how to solve the problem. Therefore, creative thinking is a must for effective programming.

CONVERSION TO EDP

Although there are a few cases of direct conversion from a manual data processing system to an electronic data processing system, most businesses graduate to a computer system from a system using punched-card machines. The reasons, of course, vary from company to company. There may be problems that cannot be solved with punched-card machines or other reasons such as an expansion of the company's business, mechanization of previously unmechanized areas, or increased volumes of data from increased sales. With the advent of the computer age, many conventional machines are being replaced with computers for speed or economic reasons.

The computer is usually combined with all or some of the punched-card machines to form a new system. We can generalize by saying that a computer augments the old system by replacing the reproducers, calculators, and accounting machines. As we shall see in our discussion of electronic data processing, computers combine all three functions. The remaining machines, such as keypunches, sorters, interpreters, and collators are utilized as support equipment.

Changing from the old data processing system to the new involves planning in order to effect an orderly conversion. Intelligent personnel with the best knowledge of the punched-card system currently installed must be selected and schooled as programmers. Others must be trained to operate the new machines, and personnel from other departments, as well as management, must be educated.

After the programmers are versed in writing programs by which the computer produces the desired processing, the programmers begin the task of writing programs for all jobs. A program represents more than a detailed set of instructions or machine steps. It is the outcome of creative thinking and applied knowledge of the problem and the operation of the computer. The programmer must define the problem, analyze it, find a solution, flowchart it, write the program, then debug (correct) it. Of course, his proficiency is improved as he writes more and more programs, but, nevertheless, a program seldom works the first time.

After the conversion, the programmer's job by no means is through. Program maintenance is a continuing problem. Programs are changed for new business practices, such as new products or discounts. Others are changed to improve program efficiency, for example, to speed up run time. And, of course, new programs must be written for new jobs or special requests.

A dual operation usually accompanies the first month or so of conversion. In one manner the data for each job are run under the new procedure and, if the results are unsatisfactory, the data are processed by the old procedure until the problem is solved. By another conversion method, the data are run under both systems and the results of the old processing are compared with the new. Basically, both are a testing of the new system to assure an orderly conversion with a minimum of problems and delays. Additional personnel may be temporarily needed during the conversion period.

The manufacturer of the new equipment may relieve the pressure of a conversion to some extent by providing system analysts and assistance in program development and testing. The *systems study* is a comprehensive examination, before conversion, of an organization's information-handling procedures. To make the organization run more efficiently, the report requirements are defined and analyzed to ensure that only the necessary information is processed. In the study some reports may be eliminated, others combined, and perhaps some new reports added.

In this chapter you were given a brief introduction to computer equipment, backgrounds, and need, and other facts peculiar to an electronic data processing system. As we progress in our study of computers, you will gain the knowledge needed for programming. You must understand, however, that you cannot learn to program a computer overnight.

QUESTIONS

1. Why must a program be modified after it is initially written and successfully tested?
2. Name the first computer to employ the use of a stored program. The first commercial computer.
3. Name the components of a computer by function and briefly describe them.
4. At which type of computer installation is the programmer more apt to be computer oriented?
5. From a program standpoint, name two ways in which a scientific and business installation differ.
6. What type of computer would likely process a payroll operation?
7. Who is the "father of computers"?
8. Describe a program and the steps a programmer will take before preparing the program.
9. Give the name of the first large-scale automatic computer. The first electronic computer.
10. What stimulated the growth of mechanization?
11. Name several aspects of planning that must go into conversion to a computer system.
12. What is the greatest advantage computers have over punched-card systems?

14
Computer mathematics

The binary system, universal language of the computer, was invented by Gottfried von Leibnitz in Germany during the seventeenth century. The first computer to use the binary numbering system was the Electronic Discrete Variable Automatic Computer, which became operational in 1952.

Previous computers had used the decimal system, thereby requiring 10 bi-stable devices to represent one arabic numeral. This method presented numerous problems, such as excessive heat produced by the extra vacuum tubes and the nearly 2000 square feet required to store the mammoth computer, not to mention the cost factor.

We shall soon see that more numeric and alphabetic characters can be represented with fewer components by using the binary system than by using the decimal system.

DECIMAL NUMBERING SYSTEM

The comprehension of the true value of a number is rare. We shall begin our study of numbering systems by considering the significance of the decimal system.

An important concept in the numbering system is that of positional notation. This means that the numerical value given to a digit is determined by its relative position in a number. Therefore, decimal symbols have varying values depending on the columnar position. A single symbol has a fixed value, but the same symbol in a group of numbers has a different value.

The common decimal system uses 10 marks, the arabic numerals 0, 1, 2, 3, 4, 5, 6, 7, 8, and 9. The radix, or base, is 10.

The value of any number, regardless of its base, is determined by its base being raised to successive higher powers starting with the point (decimal, binary, etc.) and working to the left. Starting with the point and working to the right, the base is raised to successive negative powers. The point shows where positive powers end and negative powers begin. Or expressed another way, a number is made up of coefficients of particular powers of the base of the numbering system. Using this system, a quantity expressed with the symbols 309.75 would mean:

$$(3 \times 10^2) + (0 \times 10^1) + (9 \times 10^0) + (7 \times 10^{-1}) + (5 \times 10^{-2})$$

exponent

base

coefficient

And in expanded form:

$$(3 \times 100) + (0 \times 10) + (9 \times 1) + (7 \times \tfrac{1}{10}) + (5 \times \tfrac{1}{100})$$
$$300 \quad + \quad 0 \quad + \quad 9 \quad + \quad \tfrac{7}{10} \quad + \quad \tfrac{5}{100}$$

When a number is multiplied by itself a given number of times, it is raised to a power. In order to show the power that the base will be raised to, a smaller number, called the exponent, is written above and to the right of the base. For example, 10×10 would be expressed as 10^2, $10 \times 10 \times 10$ as 10^3, and so forth.

Whenever a base (except 0) is raised to the zero power,

it is always 1. This can be proved by the division exponent law, which is

$$\frac{a^m}{a^n} = a^{m-n}$$

Therefore, $\frac{10^5}{10^5}$, which is 1, equals $10^{(5-5)}$ or 10^0. Any number raised to the first power is equal to the number itself, such as $10^1 = 10$.

BINARY NUMBERING SYSTEM

The binary system uses two marks, 0 and 1. Therefore, the base is 2.

To convert decimal to binary, successively divide by 2 and retain the remainder. The remainder becomes the binary equivalent. For example, to find the binary equivalent of 46:

```
        0  1
     2) 1  0
     2) 2  1
     2) 5  1     Remainders
     2)11  1
     2)23  0
     2)46
```

The last remainder is the most significant digit; the binary equivalent of decimal 46 is read as 101110.

In order to convert binary to decimal, the binary-column value is determined by each column base of 2 raised to a successively higher power from the point. For example, decimal 46 equals

$$(1 \times 2^5) + (0 \times 2^4) + (1 \times 2^3) + (1 \times 2^2) + (1 \times 2^1) + (0 \times 2^0)$$

And in expanded form:

$$(1 \times 32) + (0 \times 16) + (1 \times 8) + (1 \times 4) + (1 \times 2) + (0 \times 1)$$
$$32 + 0 + 8 + 4 + 2 + 0$$

We have converted decimal 46 to binary 101110 and converted the binary symbol back to decimal. We see that the value of a binary number, like decimal, is determined by positional notation. That is, the value of any number, regardless of its base, is determined by its base being

raised to successive higher powers beginning at the point.

As in decimal, the zero digits in a binary number have no value. So a shorter method of determining a binary value is to add only the column values having a 1. For example, the decimal value of the binary number 100010 is determined by:

$$2^5 = 32 \times 1 \text{ or } 32$$
$$2^1 = 2 \times 1 \text{ or } \frac{2}{34}$$

The list below shows the relationship between decimal and binary.

0 = 0000	6 = 0110	11 = 1011
1 = 0001	7 = 0111	12 = 1100
2 = 0010	8 = 1000	13 = 1101
3 = 0011	9 = 1001	14 = 1110
4 = 0100	10 = 1010	15 = 1111
5 = 0101		

OCTAL NUMBERING SYSTEM

Although the octal system may be used in some computers as a machine language, we shall be concerned in using it as an intermediate step in determining the binary value.

Consider converting a large decimal number to binary using the previous method. As you have visualized, it takes a long time successively dividing by 2. So let us discover the octal relationship.

The octal system uses eight marks, the arabic numerals 0, 1, 2, 3, 4, 5, 6, and 7. Therefore, the base is 8.

To convert decimal to octal, successively divide by 8 retaining the remainder. The remainder becomes the octal equivalent. As we shall see, each octal number converted to the first three places for pure binary produces a pure binary representation. As an example, consider decimal 239:

```
         0   3     3    5    7₈
      8)  3   5    011  101  111₂
      8) 29   7
      8)239₁₀
         ↑──── Subscript denotes base.
```

We converted decimal 239 to octal 357, thence to binary 11101111. Now let us examine the conversion closer. If we use the first three places of binary, that is 2^2, 2^1, and 2^0, we can represent any one of the eight octal symbols. The list below shows each octal number and its binary equivalent.

0 = 000	4 = 100
1 = 001	5 = 101
2 = 010	6 = 110
3 = 011	7 = 111

So, once we derive the octal number, it is just a simple task of substituting a binary equivalent for each octal number.

Now we will convert the octal number back to decimal. Each octal digit within the number is multiplied individually by its column value, and the sum of the products is the decimal equivalent. For example:

3	5	7_8
8^2	8^1	8^0
64	8	1

3×8^2 or $3 \times 64 = 192$
5×8^1 or $5 \times 8 = 40$
7×8^0 or $7 \times 1 = \underline{\quad 7}$
239

BINARY-CODED DECIMAL

Some computers use binary-coded decimal (BCD), a form of binary which consists of the first four places of binary. This method is the most common means for the computer to communicate with the operator, because it is easy to understand and easy to convert.

BCD uses the first four positions in the binary system and the first 10 decimal numbers. Each position in the decimal number is represented in binary-coded decimal. Thus, each of the 10 decimal symbols has a BCD value as follows:

0 = 0000	5 = 0101
1 = 0001	6 = 0110
2 = 0010	7 = 0111
3 = 0011	8 = 1000
4 = 0100	9 = 1001

Let us assume that we are interested in a dollar amount accumulated in the computer. If the computer displayed

the pure binary configuration

1011100000000000000001000000000100

to us, it would take us quite some time to figure that its decimal equivalent was $61,740,195.88.

However,

01100001011101000000000110010101 10001000

appears at first glance to be even more complicated. But let us take a closer look at the number if it is displayed in units of four binary symbols.

0110 0001 0111 0100 0000 0001 1001 0101 1000|1000
  6   1   7   4   0   1   9   5   8   8

Now we can see that with a little practice, the largest number can be visually translated to decimal with little effort. BCD is an ideal means of communicating with the computer or vice versa.

Although numerous other numbering systems are used in computers, we have covered the ones most widely used. At this point you may feel a little vague as to the necessity for understanding binary. When we discover how the computer memory is constructed in the next chapter, the need for understanding it will be clear.

BINARY ARITHMETIC

The simplicity of the computer's bi-stable components allows binary computations at microsecond (one millionth of a second) speeds. The newest generation of computers performs operations one thousand times faster, at speeds rated in nanoseconds, one billionth of a second.

Binary arithmetic is quite simple to understand, with addition being the easiest. The rules for adding binary digits are:

$0 + 0 = 0$	
$1 + 0 = 1$	
$1 + 1 = 10$	(0 with a 1-carry)
$1 + 1 + 1 = 11$	(1 with a 1-carry)

Of course, the first two rules are no different from decimal addition but the last two rules may seem strange. Let us examine them closer and we shall see that only the base makes them appear different from the decimal system. When we go beyond the base of the decimal system, such as $9 + 1$, the result is 10 or 0 with a 1-carry. Since the binary system has only the 0 and 1 symbols, we have the same situation when we add 1 to 1; that is, 0 with a 1-carry or 10.

An explanation of the last rule makes evident the ordinary arithmetic behind all of the four rules.

$$
\begin{array}{ll}
1 & 1 \\
1 & 1 \\
\underline{1} & \underline{10_2} \quad \text{(partial answer)} \\
3_{10} & 1 \\
& \underline{} \\
& 11_2
\end{array}
$$

Now, recall from our former discussion of binary that decimal 3 is equal to binary 11. The illustrations below use the four rules of addition.

$$
\begin{array}{lll}
2 = 010 & 9 = 1001 & 7 = 111 \\
4 = 100 & 12 = 1100 & 6 = 110 \\
\overline{6 = 110} & \overline{21 = 10101} & \overline{13 = 1101}
\end{array}
$$

Binary subtraction is accomplished by the computer through binary addition. In order to understand binary subtraction, we must add four more rules to the addition rules:

Rule 1. Complement the subtrahend, which is accomplished by changing all 1s to 0 and all 0s to 1.

Rule 2. Add the complemented subtrahend to the minuend, using the rules of addition.

Rule 3. If there is no carry, recomplement the result. The absence of a carry indicates a negative result.

Rule 4. If there is a 1-carry, add the 1-carry to the units position of the result. The presence of a 1-carry indicates a positive result.

Examples

$$
\begin{array}{ll}
\textbf{1.} & \\
19 = 10011 \\
\underline{-10 = 01010} \\
 10101 \\
 01000 \\
 1 \\
9 = 01001
\end{array}
$$

$$
\begin{array}{ll}
\textbf{2.} & \\
6 = 00110 \\
\underline{-21 = 10101} \\
01010 \\
10000 \\
-15 = 01111
\end{array}
$$

Binary multiplication is accomplished in the same manner as decimal multiplication, except using the rules of binary addition. The multiplication rules are:

$$
\begin{array}{l}
0 \times 0 = 0 \\
1 \times 0 = 0 \\
1 \times 1 = 1
\end{array}
$$

Examples

$$
\begin{array}{ll}
\textbf{1.} & \\
14 = 1110 \\
\underline{\times 5 = 0101} \\
 1110 \\
 0000 \\
 1110 \\
\underline{ 0000} \\
70 = 1000110
\end{array}
$$

$$
\begin{array}{ll}
\textbf{2.} & \\
15 = 1111 \\
\underline{\times 15 = 1111} \\
 1111 \\
 1111 \\
 1111 \\
\underline{ 1111} \\
225 = 11100001
\end{array}
$$

A short-cut method for adding long columns of 1s is to count the 1s and divide by 2 to determine the number of carries; the remainder of 0 or 1 is the total of the column.

Binary division is also accomplished in the same way as decimal division, except that the rules of binary multiplication and binary subtraction apply.

Examples

$$
\textbf{1.} \quad 45 \div 5 = 9
$$

$$
\begin{array}{r}
1001 \\
101)\overline{101101} \\
\underline{101} \\
010 \\
\underline{111} \\
000101 \\
\underline{101} \\
010 \\
\underline{111} \\
000
\end{array}
$$

$$
\textbf{2.} \quad 18 \div 4 = 4.5
$$

$$
\begin{array}{r}
100.1 \\
100)\overline{10010.0} \\
\underline{100} \\
011 \\
\underline{111} \\
00010\;0 \\
\underline{10\;0} \\
01\;1 \\
\underline{11\;1} \\
00\;0
\end{array}
$$

We can readily determine that Example 1 is correct because the decimal quotient 9 is equal to the binary quotient 1001.

Before verifying the second example, we must cover another rule for converting decimal numbers to binary.

The integers, or whole numbers, are converted in the manner previously studied. To convert decimal fractions to binary notation, multiply the fractional part of the decimal number by 2. The binary fraction is developed from 0, and 1 carries to the left of the decimal point.

Examples

1.	0.25	2.	0.50	3.	0.75
	$\times\ 2$		$\times\ 2$		$\times\ 2$
	0.50		1.00		1.50
	$\times\ 2$				$\times\ 2$
	1.00				1.00

Therefore, decimal 0.25, 0.50, and 0.75 converted to binary fractions are 0.01, 0.1, and 0.11, respectively. Now we can see that our second division problem is correct since the decimal quotient 4.5 is equal to the binary quotient 100.1.

OCTAL ARITHMETIC

Addition in the octal system follows the same rules as decimal addition except for the absence of the 8s and 9s. Therefore, we must skip two numbers any time addition goes beyond 7. This means that 1 added to 7 results in 0 and a 1 carry or 10, because the 7 is the highest number in the octal system.

Examples

1.	1357_8	2.	351_8	3.	2743_8
	7410_8		564_8		537_8
	10767_8		1135_8		3502_8

Octal subtraction follows the rules of decimal subtraction with two exceptions. Since the octal system has no 8s or 9s, the difference is 2 less than decimal subtraction when the minuend is larger than 7. If the problem requires borrowing from the adjacent column, we borrow the octal base of 8, and not 10 as in decimal.

Examples

1.	375_8	2.	316_8
	-167_8		-227_8
	206_8		67_8

Recall from binary subtraction that we found the difference through a process of complementing the subtrahend and adding. Let us see if the same rules hold true for octal subtraction.

Rule 1. Complement the subtrahend by subtracting the subtrahend from 7s.

Rule 2. Add the complemented subtrahend to the minuend as in octal addition.

Rule 3. If there is no carry (indicates a negative result), recomplement the difference.

Rule 4. If there is a carry (indicates a positive result), add the carry to the unit's position of the difference.

Examples

1.	371_8	2.	1234_8	3.	345_8
	-507		-1521		-127
	270_8		6256_8		650_8
	661		7512	①	215
	-116_8		-0265_8		$\rightarrow 1$
					216_8

BINARY-CODED DECIMAL (BCD) ARITHMETIC

This form of arithmetic is not so simple for the computer as the binary system, but has proved to be the most popular number system, because it is easy to understand.

The rules of binary arithmetic apply, except that a carry must have the value of 10. The relationship of decimal, binary, and BCD addition is shown in the following example:

Decimal	Binary	BCD	
6	0110	0000 0110	
7	0111	0000 0111	
13_{10}	1101_2	0000 1101	
		0110	(correction factor)
		$0001\ 0011_{BCD}$	

The correction factor is based upon the difference between decimal 16 (binary 10000) and the binary-coded decimal equivalent of decimal 10 (BCD 0001 0000). The following example illustrates the correction factor added wherever a BCD number exceeds binary nine.

```
6451        0110  0100  0101  0001
2592        0010  0101  1001  0010
9043₁₀      1000  1001  1110  0011
                              0110          (correction factor)
            1000  1010  0100  0011
                  0110                      (correction factor)
            1001  0000  0100  0011
```

You now have a basic understanding of number systems, especially the binary system. We have covered the decimal, binary, octal, and binary-coded decimal systems. Your comprehension of number systems will provide insight for the internal operation of the computer.

QUESTIONS

1. What are the radices of the decimal, binary, and octal number systems?
2. How do you convert a decimal number to binary? To octal?
3. Why is BCD helpful to the computer operator?

PROBLEMS

1. Convert decimal 46 to binary.
2. Convert 10011100 to decimal.
3. Convert decimal 117 to octal.
4. Convert octal 526 to binary.
5. Convert 10011001 to octal.
6. Convert decimal 957 to binary-coded decimal.
7. Add 1100110 to 1011011.
8. Subtract 11010 from 10110.
9. Subtract 110 from 1010.

15

Components of a computer

A new concept in mass processing of data was introduced to business with the advent of punched-card data processing. Each machine comprising the system performed a limited operation or series of operations. Further, the entire system came into being over a period of years as a result of the components being invented to perform specific operations previously done manually. Consequently, the work flow had to progress from one machine to another during the various phases of processing. This meant also that a machine operator had to accompany the cards to each machine used and, in general, had to perform varying manual operations.

An electronic data processing system, synonymous with computer, is also composed of several components. However, the components are interconnected. During design, emphasis is placed on controlling a variety of functions, such as reading, printing, punching, computing, and even sorting, without human intervention. A computer system consists broadly of machines that provide data input, data processing, and data output. These three types of machines, their characteristics and construction, and the movement of data through them, are the subjects of this chapter.

FUNCTIONAL UNITS OF A COMPUTER SYSTEM

All electronic data processing systems (EDPS) can be divided into five distinct components (Fig. 15-1). They are the input unit; arithmetic-logic, internal storage, control components comprising the central processing unit; and

113

the output unit. All units are connected by electrical cables so as to function as a system. You may begin to get a more complete picture of a computer by considering each component separately.

The heart of a computer system is the *central processing unit* (CPU) (Fig. 15-2). The CPU houses the control, arithmetic-logic, and internal memory components. For many computers it also contains the operator's console which provides neon lights for displaying computer halts, access to memory for the purpose of reading or altering the information, and switches, keys, and buttons for manual control of the system. The nerve center of the whole system is the *control* component. Its prime function is to obtain instructions stored in memory in the proper order and to interpret (decode or translate) and execute (telling the other parts of the system what to do) the instructions. All operations performed by the many possible input-output units, manipulation of data within the central processor, and movement of data between components, are supervised by the control component. In fact, all internal and external operations are coordinated and directed by the control component.

The *arithmetic-logic* component contains the circuitry to perform the operations that its name implies. It is here that the actual work of problem solution involving addition, subtraction, multiplication, and division is accomplished. The logic portion can compare two factors and, based upon the decision made after the comparison, the computer carries out specific operations. It can also distinguish positive, negative, or zero values resulting from arithmetic operations. Based upon the result, the program may be altered by branching to a subroutine to handle exceptional conditions.

Internal memory (also referred to as main or primary memory) has the ability almost instantaneously to accept, remember, and transfer information that has been stored in it. Each position of memory is numbered, permitting the machine to store a character in a specific position, then locate and use that information as needed. All data must be placed in internal storage from an input unit before being processed by the computer. When reading in or storing a character in a memory location, the contents in that position are destroyed. However, a character

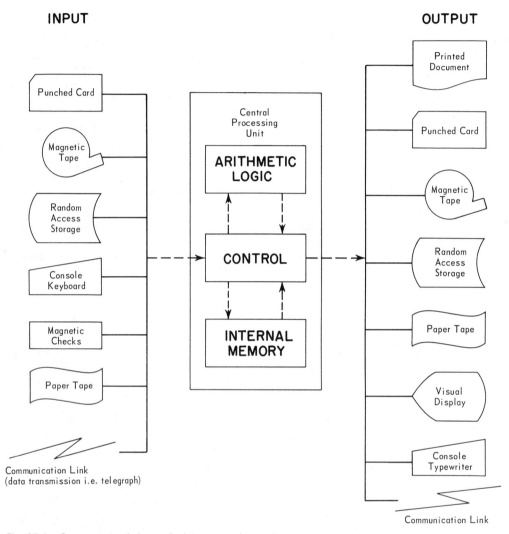

INPUT

OUTPUT

Fig. 15-1   Components of electronic data processing systems.

may be read out for processing without being destroyed. Therefore, readout is nondestructive and read-in is destructive. Storage exists in different forms, and although physically different, their function and operation are basically the same. All processing and data manipulation are performed by a program stored in internal memory.

The *program* consists of a set of instructions to direct processing in sequence to produce the desired results. The amount of internal memory not used to store the program is known as *working storage*. It is here that the data being processed or waiting processing and intermediate results requiring further processing are stored. Working storage also holds tables, constant factors, and input-output areas. The input area contains data transferred from the input components that are waiting proc-

Fig. 15-2   IBM 1401 Central Processing Unit. (IBM Corp.)

essing. The output area stores the results of processing until the output device, such as a printer or card punch, needs the information.

The computer requires an *input* component, such as card reader (Fig. 15-3), that can enter data into the central processor. Input may be in the form of *external* storage, such as punched cards, checks written in magnetic ink, paper tape, and magnetic tape (Fig. 15-11), or in the form of *auxiliary* storage, such as a magnetic drum or magnetic disk (Fig. 15-9). Auxiliary or secondary storage is additional storage to augment the capacity of internal memory. This type of storage holds entire files of information measured in millions of characters and is used in random-access applications such as inventory accounting. Data may be entered in the computer also with a console typewriter or by data transmission machines. The function of the input components is essentially to load the program into internal memory, translate the external form of data into the computer language (usually binary), and transfer the data to be processed into the input area of memory located in the central processor. As the program and input data are transferred to memory, a parity check is performed to ensure that all data are read and stored correctly. Each of the forms of external storage will be explained later in the chapter.

The function of the *output* component, such as a printer (Fig. 15-4) is to translate the machine language in the form of output and to record the results of processed data into the desired format. Output can be a printed report or any medium listed as input, with the exception of checks written in magnetic ink. In addition, a visual display, similar to a television picture, can be

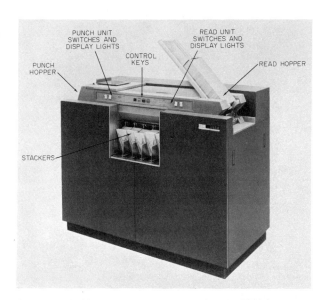

Fig. 15-3   IBM 1402 Card Reader and Punch. (IBM Corp.)

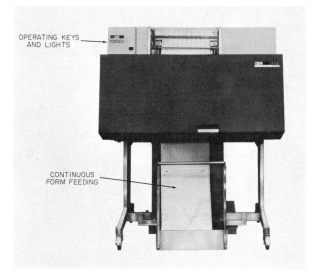

Fig. 15-4   IBM 1403 Printer. (IBM Corp.)

connected to some computers as an output medium. The most common means of input and output are punched cards and printed documents, respectively. In the illustration in Fig. 15-3, the left side of the unit serves as output for punching results after processing.

Although there are many other components, such as the power supply, we are concerned only with the functional components having to do with the flow of data.

PROCESSING OF DATA

You will recall from Chap. 4 that the bottleneck of data processing is input and output. The same applies to computers. Information may be entered directly into a computer system by a console typewriter, but this is rarely done except during debugging or correction stages. A faster means is to read in data from punched cards. This medium is suitable for entering data into most computers at around 800 cards per minute. However, depending upon the amount of processing to be done, this can slow down the operation of the computer considerably. The answer to the problem is to use an input or output medium, such as magnetic tape (Fig. 15-10), which is more compatible with the processing speed of the CPU. Data can be transcribed directly from source documents onto magnetic tape with NCR 735 Tape Encoders. But this may be impractical or uneconomical, and data are usually copied onto magnetic tape from punched cards.

There are several types of machines for conversion purposes. Some are card-to-magnetic-tape converters, magnetic-tape-to-card converters, and paper-tape-to-magnetic tape converters. *Conversion* is a term applying to the changing of one input or output medium to another by machines called converters. When conversion is made a part of an operation, it is called off-line processing. *Off-line* operations are those performed independently of the computer. For instance, magnetic tape produced as output during a computer run may be converted to punched cards for producing printed documents on the accounting machine. In this manner the input-output bottleneck is solved by less expensive equipment, releasing the computer for other jobs. There are no set rules

for this method of processing. The method selected must meet the processing requirement, and, of course, what is economical must be kept in mind.

A computer uses two methods of processing data, sequential and in-line processing. The method used depends upon the application and the type of organization. *In-line processing* requires a large storage capacity because all information concerning the status of a file must be available to the CPU. The information is permanently held in storage as opposed to sequential processing, whereby information is temporarily stored. The benefits gained should outweigh the extra cost resulting from the additional mass memory. Transactions are fed to the computer at random as they occur.

In *random-access processing,* one record is available just about as quickly as any other. This can be contrasted to a deck of cards or reel of tape where the first record in the file is available without delay, but getting the last record involves reading the entire file. A perfect example to illustrate random-access processing is an inventory application. This situation demands that records be kept on a current basis. The stock on hand must be enough to meet demands, yet overstocking cuts down on the profits of the company. To maintain a current inventory, transactions must be processed as they occur.

To accomplish this, all data concerning the application must be stored in a large-capacity storage unit. Data of this nature are usually retained in a magnetic-disk file (Fig. 15-8). This type of storage costs much less than storage inside the central processor. The difference in cost between the two storage devices results because internal storage is extremely fast while external memory is somewhat slower.

As the transactions affecting the contents of the inventory file occur, they are fed into the computer at random. The computer locates the corresponding record in storage and adjusts the data accordingly. Balances of each stock number are constantly maintained; the status of any item is available merely by inquiring into memory. How this is accomplished will be discussed later in the chapter.

In *sequential processing,* data are stored outside the computer on punched cards or magnetic tape. A payroll application is a typical example. There is no real need for maintaining current payroll information on a daily basis. Transactions, such as time attendance cards, pay rate changes, additions, and deletions, can be accumulated until it is convenient to process them. At the beginning of processing, the file is sorted to group together all records concerning a single item. This method is referred to as *batch processing,* a term denoting the saving of transactions for a specified time and processing them in one machine run.

The computer processes the first record or group of like records and the result is written as output. The next record or group of records is brought into storage for processing, and so on. Consequently, the data are transitory, requiring only enough storage for the program and working storage. This is the basis of sequential processing. Each record is processed in the order in which it appears in the file; therefore, the file must be in a particular sequence, such as employee number sequence.

MOVEMENT OF DATA

Referring to Fig. 15-1, we see that information can travel between each of the five components. In manipulation of the data in memory, we must work with groups of characters called *words.* A computer word, in many respects, is similar to a field. You will recall that earlier we set aside certain columns in a card that we defined as fields. These fields are necessary in wiring control panels because this is a means of telling the machine which data to process. A word can be such a thing as customer name, employee number, money amounts, and so on.

There are two types of words, fixed length and variable. In a *fixed word length* computer, information is handled in words containing a predetermined number of characters. The size of a word is designed into the circuitry of the computer. Let us consider a 10-position fixed word length machine. If the computer memory is 4K (a term referring to the size of storage—in our case, 4000 positions), it contains 400 computer words. A 10-position *amount* field can be stored in one word. However, a 15-position field containing customer name would occupy two words. This means that five positions of storage will

be wasted unless we have another word of five positions or less to store.

Although we use a technique known as *packing,* whereby another five-position field is stored in the leftover positions of the word containing customer name, many memory positions invariably are wasted. The smallest unit of information that may be addressed is the word. The five-position field in the example of packing could be identified only by locating the word containing customer name. The precise location within the word can then be located by shifting columnwise left or right.

In a fixed word length computer, operations are performed on complete words. For example, all positions of two factors in an addition operation are combined simultaneously, including carries. In another example, all characters of a complete word are transferred instantaneously between components. Both cases are opposite from variable-length operations. The advantage of a fixed-length machine, because of its parallel feature, is that operations are performed faster. However, this is accomplished at the expense of wasted memory.

In a *variable word length* computer, any number of storage positions may be grouped together to accommodate fields of any size. As a result, information is available by character instead of by word. This method eliminates wasted memory, but the operations are slower than fixed word length machines because data are processed serially, or character by character.

Let us store two words in an example. Assuming that the last word ended in storage location 499, the next word begins in position 500. A 15-position customer name is stored in locations 500 to 514, and the second field, four-position account number, is stored in locations 515 to 518. Stated another way, each word (thus the data which are of variable length by nature) is stored in the next available position which immediately follows the preceding word. Since the size of a word is set by the programmer, the computer hardware must provide a means of identifying the beginning and end of a word. This feature is explained in the following chapter. The term *hardware* applies to the physical construction of the machine, such as mechanical, electrical, and electronic parts.

We have talked about storing data within memory and moving data between components. To do this we must know where the data are located. For this purpose, an address is assigned to each individual *location* in variable word length machines and to every *word* in a fixed word length machine. An *address* is a number identifying a location in memory where information is stored. A storage address can be compared to a post office box number. Storage addresses are actually numbered consecutively beginning with zero. For example, addresses in an 8K variable-length computer are numbered from 0000 through 7999. We can say that storage is divided into locations, each holding specific data and each with an assigned address. We should emphasize at this point that the address identifies a word location, and not the contents of the computer word. For example, location 500 may contain a Z at one time and an 8 a moment later.

This brings us to the explanation of storage devices. There are many types of storage, each designed for a specific purpose. Storage units are available where access time is measured in billionths of a second. *Access time* is the elapsed time between the instant at which information is called for and the instant at which the information is available at the desired location. The speed of access has a direct bearing on the cost of the computer because the faster the memory device the more expensive it is.

MAGNETIC CORE STORAGE

In the previous chapter, we explored the way the binary numbering system can represent numbers. Further, we saw that computations can be made using numbers expressed by 1s and 0s. The following discus-

sion of storage devices clearly points out why and how binary notation is used in computers.

Magnetic core storage is the most widely used memory in computers because it is extremely fast. Its access time is measured in microseconds, that is, in millionths of a second. The first large-scale computer to use core storage was Whirlwind I, built at the Massachusetts Institute of Technology in 1950. This dynamic memory, developed by Jay W. Forrester of MIT, was first offered commercially in the IBM 704 computer in 1955. Soon afterward computers using the slower vacuum tubes were retired and replaced by a new generation of computers using magnetic core storage and transistors.

A magnetic core is a tiny (a few hundredths of an inch in diameter) doughnut-shaped device, made of ferromagnetic material. If we pass a wire through the center of the core and send electrical current through it, the core becomes magnetized. This two-state device may be magnetized in either a positive or negative direction; thus it has the capability to represent a binary 1 or 0 value. When a core is magnetized in a counterclockwise direction (Fig. 15-5a), the core is negative and is said to be OFF. When a core is magnetized in a clockwise direction (Fig. 15-5b), the core is positive and is said to be ON. The core remains magnetized after the current is removed (Fig. 15-5c) and represents a value of 0 if OFF or a value of 1 if ON.

Magnetism of the cores is controlled in two ways. First, by controlling the direction of the current flowing through the wires, we determine whether it is to be magnetized in the positive or negative state. Once the polarity of the core is set up, the core remains magnetized in that direction until current is passed through the wire in the opposite direction. Then the core reverses its magnetic state. Second, the core to be magnetized can

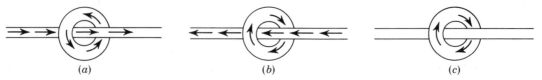

(a)	*(b)*	*(c)*

Fig. 15-5 **(a)** Core magnetized in a counterclockwise direction to represent a 0. **(b)** Core magnetized in a clockwise direction to represent a 1. **(c)** Core remains magnetized after current is removed; 1-value stored in core remains.

be selected when many cores are strung on the same wire.

Selection is accomplished by passing two wires through each core. By sending only half the amount of current necessary to magnetize a core through each wire, only the core at the intersection of the wires with electrical current is affected (Fig. 15-6). In this manner, a screen of wires called a *magnetic core plane* can contain any number of cores. The 1 or 0 representation stored in a core is called a *bit*.

You will recall from Chap. 14 that decimal information may be represented with the binary-coded decimal number system. Using a combination of the first four places of binary, we can express any digit. Therefore, if we stack four planes and give each a value of 1, 2, 4, or 8, each *column* of cores can represent a number. In other words, the cores for any storage position are located one above the other on each of the planes. For example, the value of decimal 6 is represented by the binary notation 0110. This means the cores in planes 1 and 8 of the same storage position are OFF or consist of 0 bits, and the cores in planes 2 and 4 of the same storage position are

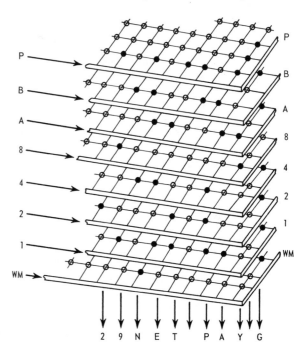

Fig. 15-7   Array of magnetic core planes.

ON representing 1 bits. Figure 15-7 illustrates the storage of numeric characters as well as alphabetic characters to be explained next.

By adding two more planes to the array, we have the capability of storing alphabetic and special characters. In a punched card, zone punches are combined with numeric punches to represent letters. These two additional planes, identified as A and B, serve the same purpose. The 12 zone is represented by a 1 bit in the A and B plane, the 11 zone by a 1 bit in the B plane, and the 0 zone by a 1 bit in the A plane. Although the 0 bits are necessary to represent conditions either written or illustrated, the 1 bits are usually referred to and the other bits are assumed 0. For example, BCD notation 110001, representing the letter A, would be described as having a 1 bit in the A, B, and 1 planes of the storage location. Figure 15-7 illustrates how alphabetic characters appear in memory. The coding structure for all characters of the IBM 1401 EDPS is shown in Table 15-1.

Once information is stored in memory, we must be able

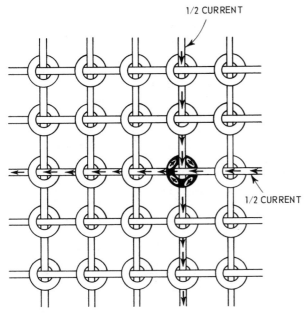

Fig. 15-6   Magnetizing a selected core in a magnetic core plane.

Table 15-1 Standard Binary-coded Decimal Computer Codes

Character	Print	Card code	BCD Code C BA 8421	Operation	Character	Print	Card code	BCD Code C BA 8421	Operation
Blank			1 00 0000		!	—	11-0	0 10 1010	Zero and subtract
.	.	12-3-8	0 11 1011	Halt	J	J	11-1	1 10 0001	
⊐	⊐	12-4-8	1 11 1100	Clear word mark	K	K	11-2	1 10 0010	Select stacker (card)
[		12-5-8	0 11 1101		L	L	11-3	0 10 0011	Load characters to word mark
<		12-6-8	0 11 1110	Less than					
≢		12-7-8	1 11 1111	Tape group mark	M	M	11-4	1 10 0100	Move characters to word mark
&	&	12	1 11 0000		N	N	11-5	0 10 0101	No operation
$	$	11-3-8	1 10 1011		O	O	11-6	0 10 0110	
*	*	11-4-8	0 10 1100		P	P	11-7	1 10 0111	Move characters to record or group mark
]		11-5-8	1 10 1101						
;		11-6-8	1 10 1110		Q	Q	11-8	1 10 1000	Store A-address register
△		11-7-8	0 10 1111						
—		11	0 10 0000		R	R	11-9	0 10 1001	
/	/	0-1	1 01 0001	Clear storage	‡	‡	0-2-8	0 01 1010	Tape record mark
,	,	0-3-8	1 01 1011	Set word mark	S	S	0-2	1 01 0010	Subtract
%	%	0-4-8	0 01 1100	Divide	T	T	0-3	0 01 0011	
γ		0-5-8	1 01 1101		U	U	0-4	1 01 0100	Control tape unit
\		0-6-8	1 01 1110		V	V	0-5	0 01 0101	Branch if word mark and/or zone
⧣		0-7-8	0 01 1111						
#	#	3-8	0 00 1011	Modify address	W	W	0-6	0 01 0110	Branch if bit equal
@	@	4-8	1 00 1100	Multiply	X	X	0-7	1 01 0111	Move and insert zeros
:		5-8	0 00 1101						
>		6-8	0 00 1110	Greater than	Y	Y	0-8	1 01 1000	Move zone bits
√		7-8	1 00 1111	Tape mark	Z	Z	0-9	0 01 1001	Move characters and suppress zeros
?	&	12-0	1 11 1010	Zero and add					
A	A	12-1	0 11 0001	Add	0	0	0	1 00 1010	
B	B	12-2	0 11 0010	Branch	1	1	1	0 00 0001	Read a card
C	C	12-3	1 11 0011	Compare	2	2	2	0 00 0010	Write a line
D	D	12-4	0 11 0100	Move numerical bits	3	3	3	1 00 0011	Write and read
E	E	12-5	1 11 0101	Move characters and edit	4	4	4	0 00 0100	Punch a card
					5	5	5	1 00 0101	Read and punch
F	F	12-6	1 11 0110	Control carriage (printer)	6	6	6	1 00 0110	Write and punch
					7	7	7	0 00 0111	Write, read, and punch
G	G	12-7	0 11 0111						
H	H	12-8	0 11 1000	Store B-address register	8	8	8	0 00 1000	Start read feed
I	I	12-9	1 11 1001		9	9	9	1 00 1001	Start punch feed

to recall it when needed. This is accomplished by a third wire, called a *sense wire,* running through the center of all cores. When information is readout of storage, only the image is transferred. The magnetism of the cores remains unaltered. This is the opposite of reading in data, where previous information in the same core position is automatically destroyed.

During operations involving movement of the bits to and from each storage location, the computer automatically checks the validity of the information. This built-in method of self-checking is called *parity checking.* Some computers, including the IBM 1401 EDPS, employ odd parity while others use even parity. The plane labeled P in Fig. 15-7 contains the parity bit. In *odd parity* the bits that are turned ON in each character position are counted. If the count is an even number, the bit in the parity plane for that position is turned ON. If the count is an odd number, the parity bit is left OFF. For the digits 0 to 9, the check bit is on for digits 0, 3, 5, 6, and 9 while the check bit is OFF for digits 1, 2, 4, 7, and 8. In other words, processing is stopped and the halt is identified on the operator console whenever the total number of 1 bits encountered in a storage position is even. In *even parity* machines, a 1 bit is added to the parity plane for each location in memory containing an uneven number of on bits.

The plane at the bottom of the array (Fig. 15-7) is known as a *word mark* plane and is necessary in variable-length computers to identify the end, or last character, of a word. Since it is of no concern at this point, its purpose will be explained in the next chapter.

BUFFER STORAGE

Whether the most efficient usage is made of a computer is determined by the utilization of the central processor. As previously mentioned, processing information by a computer involves input, processing, and output, each requiring a specified period of time.

In a fully buffered machine, *buffer storage,* which is merely additional core storage, is located between all input units and the CPU, and between the CPU and all output units. The buffer may be a separate unit or it may be located in the individual input, output, and central processing units. Present development of the buffering concept is towards internal buffers instead of external buffers. Buffer storage permits overlapping of the input, output, and internal processing operations, or allows them to occur simultaneously. Let us examine this concept closer, thereby explaining why the CPU is kept from doing useful work if the system is unbuffered.

The CPU is electronic and, therefore, offers no delay from moving parts. On the other hand, the input-output units have many moving parts, such as the printing mechanism on the printer, the punching device on the punch unit, and rollers to transport cards past the reading brushes in the reader. Obviously, operations involving these input-output devices are relatively slow in comparison with the speed of the central processor.

With no overlap in operation, a record is transferred to the CPU where computing takes place. Then processing is suspended while the results are written by the output unit and another input record is placed into the CPU. In this type of data flow, much of the available time of the CPU is wasted while the input and output devices perform their functions. With electronic buffer storage, data are collected in the buffer at the same time the CPU is busy doing other work. When called for by the program, the contents of the buffer are transferred to main storage with almost no delay. While these data are being processed by the CPU, another record is being placed in the buffer. After processing is completed, the results are moved from main storage to the output buffer instantaneously, and the input buffer contents are again summoned by the computer. In this manner computation by the CPU continues while transfers between buffer storage and the input-output devices take place.

Some computers have no buffering while some are partially buffered. The IBM 1401 EDPS may be equipped with a buffered printer. A print cycle normally requires 100 ms (1 ms is $\frac{1}{1000}$ of a second). The print buffer permits the contents of the print area to be moved to the buffer in 2 ms. Therefore, the CPU gains an additional 98 ms of processing that otherwise would not be available.

In effect the buffer provides temporary storage between

input-output units and the CPU. This enables the program to process one record at the same time other records are readied for reading, printing, or punching. In fact, some large computers are buffered to the extent that more than one program can be processed during the same run, resulting in maximum efficiency of the central processor.

MAGNETIC DISK STORAGE

The IBM 1405 disk storage unit (Fig. 15-8) is used for storing entire files. This storage medium is less expensive than core storage, but it is also slower. The primary advantage of disk storage is that it provides random-access processing for large quantities of data at a reasonable cost.

Let us illustrate this technique with an example. Suppose we have the contents of the dictionary stored in a huge deck of cards. To find a certain word we merely thumb through to the approximate location, then search each card until we find the one containing the word we are looking for. This is retrieving stored-data randomly. We had immediate access to specific areas of the file

without examining each individual card. In sequential processing the computer does not have this ability. It must begin searching at the beginning of the card or tape file and check sequentially through each record until the desired word is located.

A magnetic disk file is constructed in such a manner as to permit bypassing unwanted records and proceeding directly to the area concerned. This is similar to locating the word "magnetic" in the dictionary by thumbing to the tab labeled M. Random-access storage is made possible by a stack of magnetized disks, stacked one above the other and slightly separated from each other. This space provides for the movement between disks of a read-write arm that also moves up and down the disks to the one desired, in much the same manner as we located tab M in the dictionary.

Each disk unit contains either 25 or 50 disks, storing either 10 or 20 million characters. The metal disks are 1/8 inch in thickness and 2 feet in diameter. They are coated on both sides with magnetic recording material and are mounted on a vertical shaft. The disks rotate at 1200 revolutions per minute, permitting the reading and writing of data at 22,500 characters per second. An access arm, having two read-write heads, records or reads binary-coded decimal characters stored as magnetized spots called bits. One read-write head is for the top of the disk face and the other is for the bottom disk face; therefore, information can be recorded on each side of the disk.

Each disk (Fig. 15-9) has concentric tracks for storing characters in the form of seven BCD bits, including a parity bit. Each surface of the disk contains 200 tracks or grooves, each divided into sectors. There are five sectors on the top surface of the disk, numbered 0 to 4, and five sectors on the bottom surface of the disk, numbered 5 to 9. A track sector, which contains 200 characters, is the smallest unit of disk information that can be addressed. In this sense a track sector can be compared to a computer fixed-length word.

As with magnetic core storage, information is checked for parity during movement between the central processor and the disk unit. Data to be changed on the disk is brought to the CPU for computation and, based upon

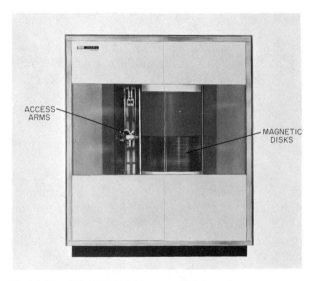

Fig. 15-8   IBM 1405 Disk Storage. (IBM Corp.)

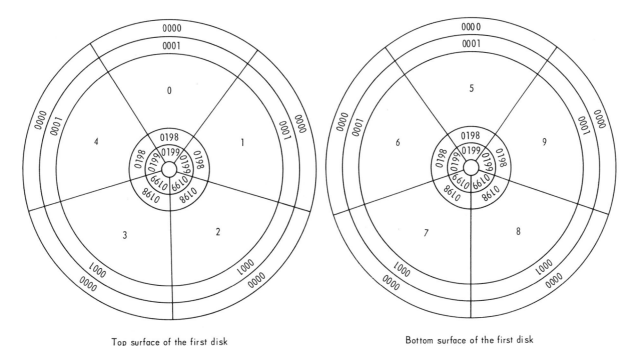

Top surface of the first disk   Bottom surface of the first disk

Fig. 15-9   Schematic of the IBM 1405 Magnetic Disk.

input transactions recorded on cards or tape, the updated information is placed back on the disk. Recording the updated data erases the previous information. Since the information on the disk must be moved to the CPU for processing, disk storage must be classified as auxiliary storage.

An access arm moves to the position specified by program instructions by moving vertically to the correct disk, and horizontally to the specified track and sector on that disk. Access time varies from 100 to 800 ms, depending on how far the access arm must move. Each sector has a seven-digit address. The first digit specifies the disk storage unit in case the file being stored requires more than 50 disks. The second to fifth digits specify the tracks which are numbered from 0000 to 4999 for 25 disks or 0000 to 9999 for 50 disks. The outermost track of the bottom disk has the address 0000 and the innermost track of the bottom disk has the address 0199. The tracks on the twenty-fifth disk have addresses running

from 4800 at the outside to 4999 at the inside. The tracks on the fiftieth disk have addresses running from 9800 at the outside to 9999 at the inside. The sixth digit specifies the track sector or computer word. The seventh digit must always be zero.

There are many other considerations involved in programming Ramac (Random Access Method of Accounting and Control) computers. However, it is not the intent of this book to fully explain disk storage, but to give a basic knowledge helpful in understanding the concept of data processing.

MAGNETIC TAPE STORAGE

A typical 2400-foot reel of tape can store 16 million characters or the equivalent of 200,000 fully punched cards. Unlike cards, magnetic tape can be used over and over again. This is possible because information that is no longer useful can be erased by recording new data on the tape. In addition to the advantages of providing compact storage for large amounts of data, magnetic tape is more compatible to computer speeds than other forms of input or output. As previously mentioned, large computers may use magnetic tape exclusively as input-output, while slower operations involving reading, punching, and printing are accomplished off line.

Magnetic tape is made of a mylar base coated with magnetic oxide. Although tape comes in varying widths, it is usually ½ inch wide and wound on individual reels 10½ inches in diameter. The tape is read and written in a tape unit (Fig. 15-10). The number of tape units attached to computers varies, depending upon the need of the user and the computer characteristics. The tape is in motion during read-write operations and moves at 75 or 112.5 inches per second, depending on the tape unit. Density

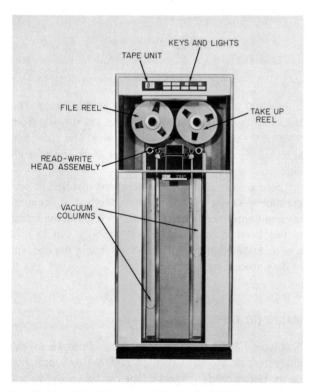

Fig. 15-10 IBM 729 Magnetic Tape Unit. (IBM Corp.)

of recording, a term denoting characters per inch, is 200 or 556, and data is read at rates varying from approximately 15,000 to 62,500 characters per second. Faster tape units have a density of 800 characters per inch and reading speeds up to 340,000 numeric characters per second.

To prepare the tape unit for operation, a full reel of tape is loaded on the left spindle of the tape unit and an empty reel on the right spindle. The tape is manually wound approximately 12 feet onto the takeup reel and the appropriate button pushed to position the tape at the load point. The machine finds the load point by sensing an aluminum *reflective strip* located 10 feet from the beginning of the tape. Another reflective strip, called an *end-of-reel marker*, is located about 14 feet from the physical end of the tape. The read-write head assembly for reading and writing is automatically closed and loads the tape into the vacuum columns (Fig. 15-10) to prevent tape breakage during high-speed starts and stops. Tape may be rewound or backspaced at speeds of 500 inches per second.

The tape unit, under direction of the central processor, moves the magnetic tape across the read-write heads and accomplishes the actual reading and writing of information. Characters are recorded in BCD on the tape in the form of magnetized spots called bits. The bits are recorded in seven parallel channels or rows along the length of the tape. As you have recognized in Fig. 15-11, the bit pattern is the familiar numeric-and-zone bits with a parity check bit. In some tape units data are recorded in binary or binary-coded decimal. Like other magnetic storage devices, the information can be retained indefinitely or erased by recording new data on the tape.

A spot of dust on the tape can cause a bad reading or writing. To detect this condition, as well as errors in tape or equipment, reading and writing are subject to several built-in checks. There is the usual parity check of each character. As each character is written, the bits are added and a parity bit recorded whenever necessary to make even parity. Tapes are always even parity, as contrasted with central processors, some of which have odd parity and some have even. This is strictly a hardware characteristic and is of no vital concern. Another parity check,

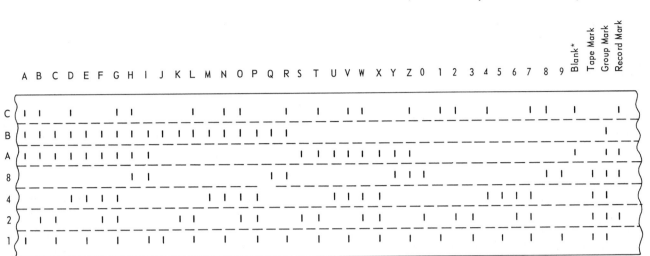

Fig. 15-11   Magnetic tape character codes.

* A no-bit blank character cannot be written on tape. The substitute blank character is composed of a CA bit combination on tape.

called the *horizontal check character,* is provided by counting the number of bits in each channel or row. The horizontal check character is recorded at the end of each block. A *block* can be one record or a group of records.

The parity checks are made only when the tape is read. A two-gap head is used to ensure that information is correctly written. There is one head for writing and one for reading. The writing head is located immediately before the reading head. When a character is written, it is immediately read by the read head to determine if the data written are readable and if parity counts are correct. If a read or write error is detected, a tape error routine illustrated in the program flowchart (Fig. 12-7) attempts to correct the difficulty.

Characters are written on the tape in blocks (Fig. 15-12). A block may contain 80 characters from a card or any number of characters. Blocks are separated from each other by a blank ¾-inch gap, called an *interrecord gap.* This is created by the distance the tape moves in coasting to a stop (⅜ inch), plus the distance to accelerate to reading speed again (⅜ inch).

It is necessary that the beginning and end of the tape

be recognized. The load point, where reading or writing is begun, is automatically positioned under the read-write head when the reflective spot is sensed. Detection of the end-of-reel reflective spot turns on an indicator in the computer during writing only. This is a signal that

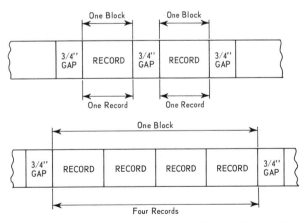

Fig. 15-12   Recording records on magnetic tape. End-of-block is indicated by an inter-record gap.

the programmer checks for in his program in order to write a final block. The end-of-reel indicator is not turned on during reading operations. The reason is that sometimes we have only a partial reel of information. In this case we would want the computer to stop at the end of the data since it would be useless to read the remainder of the blank tape. Therefore, when the end-of-reel or the last record is written, we write a *tape mark* on the tape. Then we can write the program to test for a tape mark during reading operations and, when detected, cause the computer to halt.

To prevent writing accidentally on tape containing permanent data, thus destroying valid information, *a file protection ring* is provided. This removable plastic ring must be inserted on the back of the reel to write on tape. The usual procedure is to remove the ring immediately after writing a tape, thus lessening the possibility of inadvertently destroying master files.

Paper tape is similar to magnetic tape. Instead of magnetic spots, data are recorded in the form of punched holes. Reading is accomplished by a photoelectric sensing device, which senses the presence or absence of holes in the tape. The tape is read at speeds up to 1000 characters per second. Although not so fast as magnetic tape, paper tape does have the advantage of being inexpensive. It is an excellent medium for storing permanent data, such as tax information for history purposes. Paper tape can also be especially valuable where data are received over wire circuits, such as teletype, or created by typewriters coupled with paper tape punches as a by-product of other operations. Paper tape has basically the same characteristics described for magnetic tape, so we shall not describe it in detail.

OTHER STORAGE DEVICES

Magnetic-drum storage was originally designed for use as primary memory, but is mainly used now to serve as random-access storage. Binary-coded decimal information is written on the outer surface of the rotating cylinder by read-write heads that are suspended slightly from the drum. The drum revolves under 30 read-write heads, one for each of the 30 channels or bands. Each channel is divided into 10 sections, each section storing 200 characters. As the drum rotates, the words pass serially character-by-character under the heads and the bits comprising a character pass in a parallel manner under the heads. Average access time is 8.6 ms for newer models with 400 channels that rotate under 400 read-write heads at 3500 revolutions per minute.

Disk storage is also available in interchangeable disk packs. Six 14-inch-diameter disks, with recording surfaces on both sides except for top and bottom disks, are mounted as a disk pack. They are readily removed from a specially constructed disk storage unit and are stored in a library of disk packs in much the same manner as reels of magnetic tape are stored. A special feature of the disk pack is that it has an access arm for each disk, thus providing faster access time. Each disk pack can store around 3 million characters.

Other storage devices in the developmental stages promise to increase computer speeds and provide increased storage capacity in compact forms. Kodak mini-cards, 16 mm x 32 mm in size, can be mechanically searched at 1000 a minute. The equivalent of 500 file cabinets of documents can be stored in a mini-card file system consisting of 900,000 mini-cards. National Cash Register Company has developed a storage device, called Photochromic Micro Image, that is capable of storing a 300-page book on 1 square inch of film. Technological advance in the IBM 360 EDPS resulted in processing speeds rated in nanoseconds (1 nanosecond is one billionth of a second). Its mammoth memory can be built up to 8.5 million characters of addressable internal storage. In addition, auxiliary memory in the form of magnetic drum or disk storage provides random-access storage for several hundred million digits. We can surmize that computers in the near future will operate in picoseconds, one thousandth of one nanosecond, with virtually unlimited storage.

QUESTIONS

1. Name two ways the magnetism of cores is controlled.
2. Assuming the buffer storage to be a separate device,

at what place should a block(s) be inserted in Fig. 15-1 to represent the buffer?

3. Which component is said to coordinate and direct all operations in the entire electronic data processing system?

4. By what means is a computer word located in memory?

5. How may a special character be stored in core storage as opposed to a numeric character?

6. What is the difference between a fixed word length computer and a variable word length computer?

7. Name three functions of the input component.

8. How many planes are there in a fixed word length computer?

9. How many tape records can be included in a block?

10. What is the purpose of machines called *converters*?

11. Magnetic disk storage makes possible which type of processing?

12. What popular type of memory has the fastest access time? Name the input medium with speed most compatible with the CPU.

13. Prove arithmetically that a magnetic disk unit containing 50 disks will store 20 million characters.

14. What is the highest-numbered address of the second disk in a magnetic-disk unit?

15. Define the difference between auxiliary and internal storage. What is working storage?

16. What do we mean when we say a computer performs validity checking by odd parity?

17. Define the terms in-line and off-line processing.

18. What is the purpose of buffer storage?

19. Is the statement "the parity bit along with other bits making up a character are transferred from core storage and written on tape" true? Why?

20. How is an end-of-reel detected during tape reading? During writing?

16
Principles of basic programming

The computer is a tool which assists management in solving business problems. These problems, for the most part, deal with the processing of business data. *Business data* can be thought of as elements of information needed in processing to produce the desired results. This collection of information consists of the names and addresses of employees, the number of hours worked and the rates of pay; facts relative to inventory accounting such as quantities of items received and shipped, their nomenclature, price, terms used to describe an object such as size and color; and areas of accounts receivable or accounts payable involving names and addresses of vendors or customers, the quantity and amount owed, and so forth. In processing of business data, checks are prepared in payment of money owed, invoices and inventory reports are produced, and ledgers are maintained in order to inform management of company assets and liabilities—the formula of profitable business.

The computer cannot think, but, when properly instructed, can solve problems at phenomenal speeds. To solve problems, the computer performs operations by processing data. This entails arithmetic operations, logic operations, and moving data from one place to another. For example, input data must be transferred to the processing unit where the data are shifted to align decimal points, the results of arithmetic computations are moved to temporary storage areas as intermediate answers, and processed data in final form are transferred to the output unit for printing or punching. In a sense, the computer is capable of decision making. It can examine data to de-

termine whether it is positive or negative. Two items can be compared to determine which is larger and to determine if they are equal or unequal. The computer can be given alternate courses of action to take, based upon the answers, and, depending on the circumstances, can be left to decide which course to take.

COMMUNICATING WITH THE COMPUTER

There is quite a contrast between communicating with people and communicating with machines. We can say to an accountant, "Give me a list of customers who have not made a purchase within the previous 90 days." The computer must be given explicit instructions as to what data are to be used, how to process them, and when to record the solution. These requirements are translated into machine instructions, punched onto cards, and stored in the machine. The step-by-step instructions in the stored program are followed sequentially and performed automatically by the computer to accomplish reading and storing of data, calculation and decision-making operations necessary to give the desired result, and selection of the output device required to record the finished product.

Where do we start in the process of communicating with the computer? First, we must analyze and describe the data. The description of the data includes the names of each field comprising the record, the length of each, whether the data are numeric or alphabetic, location of decimal points, and so on. Then we must determine the steps the computer must take in solving the problem. This is accomplished by drawing a program flowchart as described in Chap. 12. As you recall, a program flowchart is accomplished through a combination of logic, common sense, the programmer's knowledge of the machine, the known facts about the data being processed, and the aims of the project.

Let us consider some operations that figure in the picture. We must know the type of source data. Initially, we will be concerned only with punched cards. We must also obtain the specific record to be processed. This is done, as an example, by comparing the master name-address card with each detail card to ensure that the transaction matches the corresponding account number. We must examine the data to determine which of several possible operations is to be performed, the calculations that are necessary, and how the final format is to be printed or punched. After the first record is processed, the program must be repeated in whole or in part until all desired transactions have been processed.

When the solution is flowcharted, each symbol in the flowchart is translated or coded into machine language. This is essentially the task of programming, but we cannot minimize the importance of planning and flowchart development. Since a computer cannot exercise judgment, we cannot say, "If anything out of the ordinary comes up, do what you think is best." Consequently, it is certain that during coding, improvements and even flowchart errors will necessitate changes in the program logic. Coding is facilitated by writing the instructions on a program coding sheet with special columns for each item of the instruction.

Before proceeding, let us define the term *machine language*. The instructions to be acted upon by the computer must be located in internal memory. The stored program consists of actual machine instructions made up of numbers, letters, and special characters which the computer understands. Of course, these characters are represented internally in binary, but this is relatively unimportant because the input device converts them automatically.

In any case, these characters are written in a language directly executable by the computer. For example, the machine code 4 means punch a card, the machine code D means move numeric bits, the machine code @ means multiply. In other words, a program written in machine language is one which is written in absolute codes which the engineers have designed as its vocabulary. We should point out at this time that in order for a machine-language program to be run directly on a particular computer, it must be written in a language which that machine will accept. Since computers differ, a machine-language program written for one model cannot necessarily be run on a different model.

IBM 1401 ELECTRONIC DATA PROCESSING SYSTEM

Our discussion of computers up to this point has been in general terms and could apply to any EDPS. To go deeper into the art of programming, we must concentrate on a specific computer. We have chosen the 1401 EDPS because it is the most widely used computer in the industry and it has simple programming logic, making it a very suitable instrument for learning.

Let us begin by expanding our knowledge of selected components covered in the previous chapters. These consist of 1402 card read (input), 1401 central processor (processing), 1402 card punch (output), and 1403 printer (output). Such a system is known as a punched-card-oriented EDPS.

The 1402 card reader (Fig. 15-3) is located in the right half of the unit. This component reads the punches, translates the holes into the BCD computer language, and transfers the data to the central processor. The card is read by two sets of 80 reading brushes (Fig. 16-1). No data are transferred into storage at the first reading station. Instead, a count is made of the number of holes in each column of the card. At the second reading station, the information is transferred to the CPU internal storage and a second hole count is made and compared with the first. If the two readings are not the same, the entire system stops and a light on the card reader and CPU console signals the error. After the information is stored correctly in memory, the card falls into the NR (normal-read) pocket unless selection is desired. The card may be selected to pockets labeled 1 or 8/2 by the program.

The 1402 card punch (Fig. 15-3) is located in the left half of the unit. During punching operations, a blank card moves past the punching station and processed information from the CPU is punched as directed by the program. A hole count is made as punching takes place and is verified with the hole count taken as the punched card passes the 80 punch-check reading brushes. If the count is invalid for any column, a light on the card punch and CPU console signals the error. As with reading, the cards may be selected into one of three stackers. If undirected,

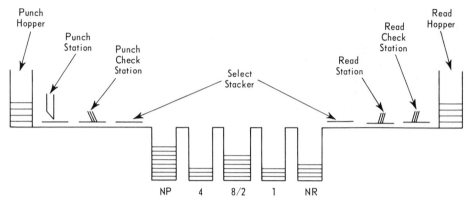

Fig. 16-1   IBM 1402 Card Reader and Punch schematic.

the cards fall into the NP (normal-punch) pocket. Otherwise, the card can be selected to the 4 or ⅝ pocket by programmed instructions. Note that cards from both feeds may be combined in the middle pocket.

Printed output is accomplished by the 1403 printer (Fig. 15-4). One of the 26 letters, 10 digits, or 12 special characters can be printed in each of the 132 printing locations. These characters are printed from a single print chain traveling in a horizontal direction as each reaches the appropriate print location. The characters are automatically translated from the BCD machine language before printing. In addition, each character set up for printing is checked against the corresponding position in the print area of the CPU to ensure that the document is correctly printed.

The central processing unit (Fig. 15-2) houses the circuitry for the control, arithmetic-logic, and internal memory components. The control component interprets or decodes each instruction in the program, carries out the execution of them, and directs the operation of the input and output components. Internal memory stores the program and data being processed. In the arithmetic-logic component, the four operations of addition, subtraction, division, and multiplication are performed. Logical decisions and shifting of data are also performed here.

We should point out that the 1401 has an add-to-memory feature, and so does not have an arithmetic unit

as such. This simply means that arithmetic and logic operations are executed wherever the data are located in memory as opposed to some other computers where data must be physically moved to counters for computing or comparing.

Internal memory is divided into reserved areas (Fig. 16-2) for input data and output data, and storage for the program and work areas. Assuming that our 1401 is a 4K machine, memory positions are numbered from 0000 to 3999. Positions 0001 to 0080, called card read-in area, are reserved for 80 columns of information from the card. A *card-read* instruction transfers the data read by 1402 card reader into this area, destroying any previous information. The second reserved area, called card-punch area, is located at positions 101 to 180. Information to be punched must be stored here. When a *punch* instruction is executed, the contents in positions 101 to 180 are transferred to the 1402 card punch for punching. The print area, positions 201 to 332, is the third reserved area. Data is stored here for printing. When a *print* instruction is executed, the contents of the print area are transferred to the 1403 printer, where an entire line is printed. The rule, read-in is destructive and read-out is non-destructive, applies to all three reserved input-output areas.

The areas are reserved as given for the programmer's convenience. If the three areas were reserved in consecutive locations beginning in position 0000, the input-output formats would be difficult to work with. For instance, column 1 of the card would be stored in position 0000, column 80 would be stored in position 0079, and so on. Therefore, the input-output areas have been designed to correspond to card columns and print positions.

The 1401 is a variable word length machine, meaning that each word can vary in length and occupies the positions adjacent to the preceding word. So unless we prevent it, the program will be stored beginning at core location 333. Immediately following the last character in the final instruction, working storage begins for the data being processed. Assuming that the program is stored in positions 333 to 1500, working storage consists of locations 1501 to 3999. In this manner no position in memory is unintentionally wasted. In fact, the unused positions in the reserved areas can be used, with the exception of locations 0000 and 0100.

Since instructions and data words are not limited in size, a method of determining their length is required.

This identification is provided by a *word mark* and is illustrated by underlining the leftmost character of an instruction or field of data. This word mark is a bit stored in memory (Fig. 15-7) and is assigned by the programmer for data words when he writes the program. Word marks for instructions are automatically set into core storage when the program is loaded. The function of the word mark is described in each type of instruction covered. It is not moved with data during processing except when a *load* instruction is used.

We have introduced additional facts about the computer and reinforced earlier learning about the components. A little later, core storage will be explained in more detail. But in the meantime, let us explore the instruction format and discuss a simple program.

PROGRAM INSTRUCTION FORMAT

A computer *instruction* is an element of a program. It is an order to carry out some simple operation such as

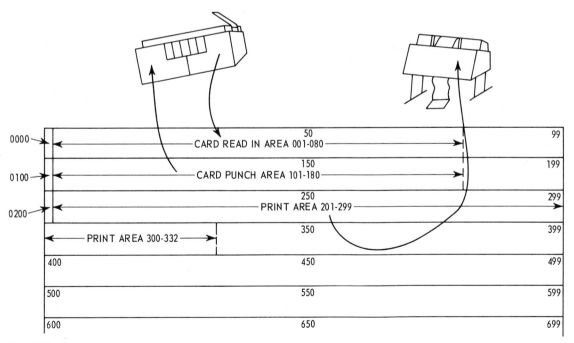

Fig. 16-2 Core storage layout.

card reading or movement of data to the output area. An instruction consists basically of two parts, an operation code (referred to as OP code) and one or two operands. The OP code designates the operation to be performed and the operand(s) designates the address of data or tape unit needed for that specific instruction. In the case of *branch* instructions, the operand specifies the address of the next instruction to be executed.

A 1401 instruction can be from one to eight characters in length. Every instruction must have an OP code and any parts that are not used in a particular instruction are simply omitted. The format of the instruction is:

OP code	A-address	B-address	d-modifier
X	XXX	XXX	X

The OP code is a single character that defines the operation to be performed. It always has a word mark, a bit in core to signal the beginning of the instruction (Fig. 15-7), which we shall consider carefully later in the chapter. As discussed above, we shall identify a word mark by underlining it. *Note:* A repertory of OP codes and their functions is included in Table 15-1 for reference. The A-address is a three-character address used to identify the units position of the A-data field. In addition, an input-output device (tape or disk unit) or the location of an instruction may be included in the A-address. We should emphasize that an address identifies a word location, not the contents of the word. As an example, address 875 refers to the location of the word NET PAY and not the word itself. The B-address specifies the address of the B-data field. The d-modifier is used to modify an OP code and will be explained later.

Before we see how these parts fit together, we must consider how data in storage are addressed. Each position of memory is given an address beginning with 0000 and each location is capable of holding a BCD character. The storage positions are filled one character at a time in reverse order beginning with the low-order (rightmost) position. This means the low-order position of the word has the largest address. For instance, in the example of NET PAY, the Y is located at address 875 and the N at address 869.

A word mark is set in the high-order position or under the N to identify the beginning of the word. Now we can say that when a character position is addressed the computer moves the character in that position and all characters to its left until a character with a word mark (WM bit on) is reached.

All storage locations are identified and written as three-character addresses. The first thousand addresses are written as numbers between 000 to 999. Addresses of 1000 and over are stored in a special manner to fit into three characters. The units and tens positions are identified numerically, while the hundreds position is identified by a character consisting of combined numeric and zone bit(s). Looking at Table 16-1, we see that address 3802 would be written as H02. The complete pattern of three-character addresses for a 4K computer is shown in this table.

Now let us proceed with an example. Suppose we have to move the constant NET PAY from location 875 to location 1240. We write the following instruction:

OP code	A-oddress	B-address	d-modifier
M	875	S40	

The OP code M means move the word in the A-field to the B-field and stop at the first word mark encountered. Assume the storage contents as follows:

A-field	B-field
NET PAY	936515043
↑	↑
875	1240

The result of the instruction after execution would be as follows:

A-field	B-field
NETbPAY	93NETbPAY
↑	↑
875	1240

Since we need a space between the two names, a blank space is left in memory. Henceforth, a small letter "b" will indicate a blank where appropriate. The important things about this move are that the first word mark encountered stopped the operation, that the contents from which the word was moved were not affected, and

**Table 16-1   Machine-language Codes for
Core Storage Addresses**

Actual addresses		3-character addresses
000–999	No zone bits	000–999
1000–1099		‡00–‡99
1100–1199		/00–/99
1200–1299		S00–S99
1300–1399	A bit (0-zone)	T00–T99
1400–1499	over-hundreds	U00–U99
1500–1599	position	V00–V99
1600–1699		W00–W99
1700–1799		X00–X99
1800–1899		Y00–Y99
1900–1999		Z00–Z99
2000–2099		!00–!99
2100–2199		J00–J99
2200–2299		K00–K99
2300–2399	B-bit (11-zone)	L00–L99
2400–2499	over-hundreds	M00–M99
2500–2599	position	N00–N99
2600–2699		Ø00–Ø99
2700–2799		P00–P99
2800–2899		Q00–Q99
2900–2999		R00–R99
3000–3099		?00–?99
3100–3199		A00–A99
3200–3299		B00–B99
3300–3399	AB-bits (12-zone)	C00–C99
3400–3499	over-hundreds	D00–D99
3500–3599	position	E00–E99
3600–3699		F00–F99
3700–3799		G00–G99
3800–3899		H00–H99
3900–3999		I00–I99

that the contents to which the word is moved are destroyed. Thus, it is the programmer's responsibility to be sure that the previous contents are no longer needed before a *move* instruction is executed.

MACHINE-LANGUAGE CODING SHEET

The program we are about to discuss is written in actual machine language. To illustrate the use of a few basic instructions, we shall write the program flowcharted in Fig. 12-2. The program essentially provides an 80-80 list of the cards with spacing between fields. The card and print format are:

Columns	Print positions	Description
1–16	1–16	Customer name
17–20	20–23	Account number
36–40	27–31	Invoice number
41–47	35–41	Amount due

First we must write the program and punch it onto a format the machine will accept. Then the program is loaded into memory and the instructions control the computer without further action by the programmer or operator. Instructions are stored in the same internal memory used for the data to be processed. However, program storage must not overlap the locations used to store data. In other words, a location can store either one instruction character or one character of data, but not both.

In general, instructions are stored together in ascending sequential locations in the order in which they are to be executed. Each instruction in turn, beginning with the first one, is brought from internal storage to the control unit for execution. The first instruction is carried out, then the second instruction is located and moved into the control component for execution. This process continues until the program is completed or until the computer is instructed to stop. Let us view the program (Fig. 16-3) as it appears in storage.

/ 080 / 332 / 299 ˌ 001 017 ˌ 036 041 1 M 016 216 M
↑
333
020 223 M 040 231 M 047 241 2 B 398 A B 359 ˌ
↑
398

Confusing as it may seem, each character and its meaning will be understood by the student before he

IBM 1401 PROGRAM CHART

FORM X24-6437-0
PRINTED IN U.S.A.

Program:

Programmer: Date:

Step No.	Inst. Address	OP	Instruction A/I	Instruction B	Instruction d	Remarks	Effective No. of Characters Inst.	Effective No. of Characters Data	Effective No. of Characters Total
1	333	/	080			Clear Read-in Area 001-080	4		4
2	337	/	332			Clear Print Area 300-332	4		8
3	341	/	299			Clear Print Area 201-299	4		12
4	345	,	001	017		Set Word Mark for Name and Account Number	7		19
5	352	,	036	041		Set Word Mark for Invoice No and Amt Due	7		26
6	359	1				Read a Card	1		27
7	360	M	016	216		Move Name to Print Area	7		34
8	367	M	020	223		Move Account Number to Print Area	7		41
9	374	M	040	231		Move Invoice Number to Print Area	7		48
10	381	M	047	241		Move Amount Due to Print Area	7		55
11	388	2				Print a Line	1		56
12	389	B	398		A	If Last Card, Branch to Halt	5		61
13	394	B	359			Branch to Repeat Program	4		65
14	398	.				Halt	1		66
							66		66
	332								
	66								
	398								

Fig. 16-3 Machine-language program to clear storage, set word marks, read cards, and print the data.

finishes this chapter. This does not imply that it is necessary to memorize them. It would be inconvenient to write instructions in a continuous line as shown above. In order to simplify program writing, a program-coding sheet (Fig. 16-3) is provided. The step number assists the programmer in sequencing the instructions. The instruction address is used to keep track of the core locations for each instruction. Addressing instruction words is opposite to that of data words. This means we must refer to the high-order position of an instruction location, as opposed to referring to the low-order position of data words (see the move NET PAY example above). We might add at this point that instruction words are moved from left to right within memory, whereas data words are moved from right to left. This will be explained later. Let us continue describing the coding sheet and concentrate on the program.

The eight-position instruction is the only portion entering storage. The remarks column is used to explain what the instruction accomplishes. This descriptive information is a very important part of documentation, which greatly assists the programmer at a later time by refreshing his memory as to the purpose of the instruction. Comments by the programmers are not stored. The effective-number-of-characters column is used to determine how much computer memory will be used by the program. The total number of characters used can be added to the beginning-instruction address minus 1 to ensure the programmer of the address he has determined for all instructions.

DEVELOPING A MACHINE-LANGUAGE PROGRAM

As we begin the task of writing the program, we do not know what is in the input-output areas. For this reason, we must clear the card-input area to eliminate unwanted word marks and the print area to eliminate unwanted data. The latter is necessary because the words or fields moved into the print (or punch) area will not ordinarily occupy every position. In our program this would apply to the spaces between fields and positions 242 to 332.

The clear-storage instruction clears up to 100 positions of memory. The operation stops at the nearest hundreds

position. That is, the instruction / 299 clears 100 positions or 200 to 299, whereas the instruction / 332 clears 33 positions or 300 to 332. Therefore, the first three instructions in Fig. 16-3 clear the card read-in and print areas. Each instruction we cover will usually list some things that are unrelated to the example and are given in their entirety for two reasons. First, the serious student will carefully study them in order to learn a good deal more about programming, and, second, some items will be explained now but used later. The timing formulas and their use are explained in Chap. 19 and can be ignored until needed. Also, the additional information is worthwhile reference material.

Clear-Storage **Instruction**

Instruction format

Mnemonic	OP code	A-address	B-address	d-modifier
CS	/	XXX		

Function   As many as 100 positions of core storage can be cleared of data and word marks when this instruction is executed. Clearing starts at the A-address and continues leftward to the nearest hundreds position. The cleared area is set to blanks.

Word marks   Word marks are not required to stop the operation.

Timing $T = N (L_I + 1 + L_X)$ ms

Note   During the execution of this instruction, only the B-address register is used. Therefore, when chaining is being considered, the contents of the A-address register can be ignored.

As soon as the contents of a card are transferred to the read-in area, it is necessary to move the data to the print area. In order to provide spacing between all fields printed, we must transfer each of the four fields individually, making it necessary to define the length of each. This is accomplished with word marks by steps 4 and 5. As far as this particular example goes, it would not matter whether the word marks were set in the read-in area or print area. We shall mention three points in set-ting word marks. First, it is useless to set word marks for each program loop; therefore, it is desirable to set them before reading a card in order to save instruction-execution time. In this manner the program branches to *read-a-card*, thus by-passing the *set-word-mark* instruction for all but the first card. Second, a word mark must be set in the high-order position of each data field. Third, word marks are not affected by most instructions. This means that when word marks are set, they become permanent unless cleared by special instructions.

Set-Word-Mark **Instruction**

Instruction format

Mnemonic	OP code	A-address	B-address	d-modifier
SW	,	XXX	XXX	

Function A word mark is set at each address specified in the instruction. If only one word mark is needed, only the A-address is coded. The data at either address is undisturbed.

Word marks Word marks are set at both the A- and B-address specified. It is not necessary to follow this in-struction by a character with a word mark.

Timing $T = N(L_I + 3)$ ms

Address registers after operation

I-add Reg	A-add Reg	B-add Reg
NSI	A-1	B-1

We now have memory that is pertinent to the problem cleared and word marks have been set to identify the be-ginning and end of each field or word. Next, we read a card. The single-character instruction does not need an address since the only place to read information into storage is card read-in area. Reading a card destroys any previous contents of positions 001 to 080 except for word marks. Column 1 of the card is placed in core loca-tion 001, column 2 is placed in core location 002, and so on. There are two basic input-output instructions involv-ing cards.

Read-a-Card **Instruction**

Instruction format

Mnemonic	OP code	A-address	B-address	d-modifier
R	1			

Function This code causes a card to feed and causes all 80 columns of information to be read into core-storage locations 001 through 080.

Word marks Word marks are undisturbed.

Timing $T = N(L_I + 1)$ ms $+ I/O$. A card-read cycle requires a total of 75 ms. The cycle is divided into three separate parts.
1. Read-start time is 21 ms. The *read* instruction must be given before card-reading time in order to activate the card feed for that particular cycle. If the *read* instruction is given too late in the cycle, processing is delayed until the next card-reading time occurs in the following read cycle. The processing unit is interlocked during read-start time.
2. Card-read time is 44 ms. The actual reading of the card takes place during this part of the cycle and the data is read into core storage. The processing unit is inter-locked during card reading time.
3. Processing time is 10 ms. This part of the cycle is for processing. If processing time requires more than 10 ms, the reader speed drops from 800 to 400 cards per minute.

Address registers after operation

I-add Reg	A-add Reg	B-add Reg
NSI	Ap	081

Punch-a-Card **Instruction**

Instruction format

Mnemonic	OP code	A-address	B-address	d-modifier
P	4			

Function The data in storage locations 101 to 180 is punched into a card.

Word marks   Word marks are not affected.

Timing $T = N (L_I + 1)$ ms $+ I/O$. There are four points in the cycle (occurring at 60-ms intervals) when the punch-feeding mechanism can receive an impulse to start the punch cycle. The punch cycle is divided into three separate parts.

1. Punch-start time is 37 ms. After the feed mechanism has been impulsed, the time required for the card to feed and be positioned for punching is called punch-start time. The 1401 processor is interlocked during punch-start time.

2. Card-punching time is 181 ms. The actual punching of the card takes place during this part of the cycle. The 1401 processor is always interlocked during card-punching time.

3. Processing time is 22 ms. This is the remainder of the punch cycle that is allotted for processing by the system.

Address registers after operation

I-add Reg	A-add Reg	B-add Reg
NSI	AP	181

Now that the card is located in memory, we move the data to the print area by steps 7 to 10. We could move the entire 80 positions simultaneously, but we specified earlier that spacing between fields is necessary so that they can be more easily read. In order to do this we must *format* the print area, that is, move each field one-by-one and leave spacing as needed. The instruction is stopped by a word mark in either the A- or B-field and we have set them in the A-field or read-in area. It is, therefore, unnecessary to have them in the print area.

Move Characters to A or B Word Mark **Instruction**

Instruction format

Mnemonic	OP code	A-address	B-address	d-modifier
MCW	M	XXX	XXX	

Function   The data in the A-field is moved to the B-field.

Word marks   If both fields are the same length, only one

of the fields must have a defining word mark. The first word mark encountered stops the operation. If the word mark is sensed in the A-field, the machine takes one more B-cycle to move the high-order character from A to B. At the end of the operation, the A-address register and the B-address register contain the addresses of the storage locations immediately to the left of the A- and B-fields processed by the instruction. The data at the A-address is unaffected by the move operation. Word marks in both fields are undisturbed.

Timing $T = N (L_I + 1 + 2L_W)$ ms
Note: If the fields are unequal in length, chaining can produce unwanted results, because one of the fields has not been completely processed. Thus, one of the registers will not contain the address of the units position of the left-adjacent field.

Address registers after operation

I-add Reg	A-add Reg	B-add Reg
NSI	A-L_W	B-L_W

Next, we print the data. Like the *read-a-card* instruction, it is necessary to give only the print OP code since all 132 positions from the print area are transferred to the printer. Often the print image will occupy less than every position, so care must be taken to clear all positions. Otherwise, unwanted information from a previous job may be left in the print area. Recall that two *clear* instructions are necessary to erase the 132 print positions because a *clear* instruction stops at the first hundreds position, in this case 200 and 300.

Write-a-Line **Instruction**

Instruction format

Mnemonic	OP code	A-address	B-address	d-modifier
W	2			

Function   This instruction causes the data in the print area to be transferred to the printer. The program continues after printing is complete. The printer takes one automatic space after printing a line.

Word marks   Word marks are not affected.

Timing $T = N(L_I + 1)$ ms $+ I/O$
Note: The normal 84-ms interlock (1403, models 1 and 2) during printing can be greatly reduced, if the print buffer storage is installed.

Address registers after operation

I-add Reg	A-add Reg	B-add Reg
NSI	Ap	335
		333 (print storage)

At this point in the program, steps 12 and 13, the computer must make a decision, either to repeat the program if there are additional cards to be processed or to halt if processing is completed. Let us briefly review this subject of branching, covered also in Chap. 10. *Branching* is the selection of one of several paths based upon control punches in a card, switches set by the programmer, or indicators set by the machine. *Indicators* are set internally to record conditions such as high, low, or equal resulting from a comparison of two fields, or detection of the last card. If sense switch A (located on the operator's console) is ON and the last card in the hopper has been read, the last-card indicator is turned ON. Therefore, we can say that a decision to continue or not to continue processing can be made by testing the last-card indicator.

When the last instruction of the main program is executed, we shall cause the program to branch and repeat itself (called a loop) if there are additional records to be processed. This is accomplished with a conditional branch. With this instruction, the machine branches to the specified address only if some condition is met. Otherwise, the machine *falls-through,* a term referring to execution of the next sequential instruction. An unconditional branch causes the program to branch to the address specified regardless of any condition in the machine. Therefore, the A-address for *branch* instructions is the location of an instruction word instead of a data word. For this reason it is referred to as I-address (instruction address) although it is written in the A-address column.

Unconditional-Branch **Instruction**

Instruction format

Mnemonic	OP code	I-address	B-address	d-modifier
B	B	XXX		

Function   This instruction always causes the program to branch to the address specified by the I-address portion of the instruction. This address contains the OP code of some instruction. This unconditional branch operation is used to interrupt normal program sequence and continue the program at some other point, without testing for specified conditions.

Word marks   A word mark must be associated with the core-storage position of the I-address.

Timing

Branch without indexing. $T = N(L_I + 1)$ ms
Branch with indexing. $T = N(L_I + 2)$ ms

Address registers after operation

Branch without indexing.

I-add Reg	A-add Reg	B-add Reg
NSI	BI	Blank

Branch with indexing.

I-add Reg	A-add Reg	B-add Reg
NSI	BI	NSI

Branch-if-Indicator ON **Instruction**

Instruction format

Mnemonic	OP code	I-address	B-address	d-modifier
B	B	XXX		X

Function   The d-modifying character (Table 16-2) specifies the indicator tested. If the indicator is ON, the next instruction is taken from the I-address. If the indicator is OFF, the next sequential instruction is taken. Table 16-2 shows characters that are valid for the d-modifier and for the indicators they test. This table also shows testing for

Table 16-2   d-characters for Branch Instructions

d-character	Branch conditions
b	Unconditional
9	Carriage channel 9
@	Carriage channel 12
A	Last-card switch (sense switch A)
B	Sense switch B*
C	Sense switch C*
D	Sense switch D*
E	Sense switch E*
F	Sense switch F*
G	Sense switch G*
K**	End of reel*
L	Tape transmission error*
N	Access inoperable*
?**	Reader error if I/O check stop switch is OFF
!**	Punch error if I/O check stop switch is OFF
P	Printer busy (print buffer storage)*
≠**	Printer error if I/O check stop switch is OFF
/	Unequal compare (B ≠ A)
*	Inquiry clear*
Q	Inquiry request*
R	Printer carriage busy (print buffer storage)*
S	Equal compare (B = A)*
T	Low compare (B < A)*
U	High compare (B > A)*
V	Read-write parity check or read-back check error*
W	Wrong-length record*
X	Unequal address compare*
Y	Any disk unit error condition*
Z**	Overflow
%**	Processing check with process check switch OFF

* Special feature

** Conditions tested are reset by a *branch-if-indicator* ON instruction

high, low, or equal, which is used when the high-low-equal compare feature is installed. The indicators tested are not turned OFF by this instruction except as noted by **. When carriage tape channels 9 or 12 are sensed, the corresponding indicators are turned ON. These carriage-channel indicators are turned OFF when any other carriage tape channel is sensed. The next *compare* instruction turns OFF the compare indicators.

Word marks   Word marks are not affected.

Timing

No branch. $T = N(L_I + 1)$ ms
Branch without indexing. $T = N(L_I + 1)$ ms
Branch with indexing. $T = N(L_I + 2)$ ms

Address Registers After Operation

No branch.

I-add Reg	A-add Reg	B-add Reg
NSI	BI	dbb

Branch without indexing.

I-add Reg	A-add Reg	B-add Reg
NSI	BI	Blank

Branch with indexing.

I-add Reg	A-add Reg	B-add Reg
NSI	BI	NSI

Now we can say that the d-modifier conditions the OP code if the condition being tested is present. If the condition specified in the d-modifier column is OFF or absent, the program falls through. Step 12 is a *branch conditional* instruction. If the last card in the hopper has been read (sensed by A-character in d-modifier column), the program branches to the *halt* instruction located at 398, thus bypassing the next sequential instruction. If there are more cards in the hopper to be processed, the conditional branch is nullified and the program falls through. The next sequential instruction is an unconditional branch to instruction location 359.

A review of the instructions indicates that it is unnecessary to repeat the *clear-storage* and *set-work-mark* instructions in the looping process. Therefore, we might say that these instructions are used only for initialization. Such a routine is called housekeeping. *Housekeeping* is a set of instructions that do not contribute directly, but are necessary to the program solution. The *halt* instruction at step 14 stops the computer. There are two types of *halt* instructions.

Halt **Instruction**

Instruction format

Mnemonic	OP code	A-address	B-address	d-modifier
H	⌐			

Function   This instruction causes the machine to stop and the *stop-key* light to turn on. Pressing the *start* key causes the program to start at the next instruction in sequence.

Word marks   Word marks are not affected.

Timing $T = N(L_I + 1)$ ms

Address registers after operation

I-add Reg	A-add Reg	B-add Reg
NSI	Ap	Bp

Halt-and-Branch **Instruction**

Instruction format

Mnemonic	OP code	I-address	B-address	d-modifier
H	⌐	XXX		

Function   This is the same as the *halt* instruction, except that the next instruction is at the I-address.

Word marks   Word marks are not affected.

Timing

Without indexing. $T = N(L_I + 1)$ ms
With indexing. $T = N(L_I + 2)$ ms

Address registers after operation

Without indexing.

I-add Reg	A-add Reg	B-add Reg
NSI	BI	Blank

With indexing.

I-add Reg	A-add Reg	B-add Reg
NSI	BI	NSI

MACHINE CYCLES

We write a program, punch it onto cards, and load it into storage. By the time the instructions are executed, we are no longer in the picture. If something comes up that we failed to consider, the computer does what the program says to do, even though the results may be meaningless. Hence the data processing axiom GIGO—garbage in, garbage out. By understanding how instructions and data are handled as they pass through various registers, we can expect to gain knowledge to help us write a better program and assist us in debugging.

All computer processing takes place within a fixed interval of time, called a *machine cycle*. These cycles are measured in thousandths (milliseconds), millionths (microseconds), and billionths (nanoseconds) of a second. To comprehend such a minute interval of time, consider that a spaceship traveling at 100,000 miles per hour would travel less than two inches in one millionth of a second. Within a machine cycle, the computer can perform a specific machine operation. The number of operations required to execute a single instruction depends on the instruction. Thus, various machine operations are combined to execute each instruction.

The 1401 instruction is carried out in two phases, an I-phase (instruction phase) and an E-phase (execution phase). Basically, the instruction is brought to the control unit and placed in registers during the I-phase in order to interpret the instruction. Next, the data is acted upon character-by-character during the E-phase as directed by the instruction. In the next section we shall describe the various registers and the movement of instructions and data through them.

REGISTERS

A *register* is an electronic device capable of temporarily storing a character(s) of information while or until it is used. It is capable of receiving the information, decoding that information, and processing the data as directed by the control unit. There are six registers that interpret instructions and operate on data stored in memory (Fig. 16-4). Other registers are involved in

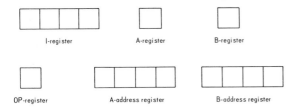

Fig. 16-4 Control unit registers.

arithmetic operations and transferring data between internal memory and input-output units. Registers have various functions. Some registers are involved in movement of data, some are used to hold parts of an instruction while it is being executed, and others are used to hold data being computed or results of arithmetic operations.

The A-address and B-address registers are actually three-character registers, designed to hold a three-position address as shown in Table 16-1. For convenience, they are shown on the operator's console and in the diagram of Fig. 16-4 as four characters. Therefore, we can say that the A- and B-address registers are used to keep track of the addresses of data. Likewise, the I-address register keeps track of the location of the next instruction to be executed.

The most heavily used register is the B-register. Every character leaving memory, whether it be an instruction or data, enters the B-register and is then directed elsewhere. As a character passes through the B-register, it is checked for parity and a word mark. As we shall see, a word mark sensed here terminates the I-phase and signals the beginning of the E-phase or vice versa.

When the I-phase begins, the OP code of the instruction is brought from the storage location specified in the I-register and placed in the B-register. The word mark with the OP code tells the computer that this character is the first of an instruction and transfers it to the OP-register. The OP-register deciphers the OP code and determines what function the instruction will be. The I-register is increased by 1, giving the address of the next character of the instruction (first character of A-address). This is then obtained, passing through the B-register to the A-address register. The I-register is again increased by 1 and the second character of the A-address is brought through the B-register to the A-address register. This process continues until all characters of the A- and B-address are placed in the A- and B-address registers. The d-modifier is not stored in a separate register; it simply conditions the OP code.

As soon as all characters of an instruction are placed in the OP-register and A- and B-address registers, the I-register contains the address of the next instruction. The first character, which is an OP code, is brought to the B-register and a word mark is detected. The word mark signals that the entire instruction is in the control registers, thus the end of the I-phase and beginning of the E-phase. *Note:* In the case of *branch* instructions, the I-register is completely replaced with the contents of the A-address register.

Before we explain the operation of the E-phase, let us demonstrate the I-phase in terms of an example. The instruction and storage contents are:

OP code	A-add	B-add
M̲	875	S40
↑		
500		

A-field	B-field
NETbPAY̲	936515043̲
↑	↑
875	1240

The last character of the previous instruction was located at position 499. We said that the I-register contains the address of the next instruction, which would be 500. The M̲ goes through the B-register to the OP-register and the contents of the I-register are incremented by 1, giving the address (501) of the next character. Then the 8 is placed in the A-address register and the I-register increments to 502. The process continues until the word mark of the next instruction is detected. Figure 16-5*a* shows the contents of the registers after the operation.

At this point no data have been moved. The I-phase has simply prepared the instruction for execution. That is, the OP code has been decoded as meaning "move the word at A-address to B-address" and the starting addresses of

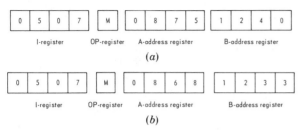

Fig. 16-5   (a) End of I-phase. (b) End of E-phase.

the A- and B-field are in the address registers. The first step of the E-phase is to obtain the first character of the A-field as given by the address in the A-address register. Thus the character Y is placed in the B-register, checked for a word mark, moved to the A-register, and placed back in memory at the location specified by the contents in the B-address register. When the Y character is stored, a check is made to determine if the position at which it is being stored has a word mark. The A- and B-address register are both decreased by one, giving the address of the next character to be moved. The character A is moved, the address decremented, and the process continues until a word mark is detected by the B-register. When this happens, we go back to the I-cycle and obtain the next instruction. Figure 16-5*b* shows the contents of the registers at the end of the E-phase.

CHAINING

It is important to know the contents of the three address registers when the instruction has been fully executed. We know that instructions are picked up from left to right; therefore, the I-address register always contains the first character of the next instruction. We also are aware that data are moved from right to left, so the A- and B-address registers always contain the address of the next data character after the last one transferred. This fact can be most useful in conserving memory and processing time. Frequently, we can take advantage of the contents of the registers after an instruction is executed. If both address registers contain the desired address, both addresses may be omitted from the instruction. This technique is known as *chaining*.

For example, assume that the five characters at locations 868 (now standing in A-address register) are added to the contents at location 1233 (now standing in B-address register). Then the instruction following the previous example appears as:

M̲ 875 S40
A̲

Now the A-address register contains 863 and the B-address register contains S28. If we desire to M̲ 400 S28, we simply omit the B-address (M̲ 400 bbb) since it is already located in the B-address register. This technique is known as *partial chaining*. However, great care must be taken or incorrect processing may result. For example, had the example been M̲ 863 400, partial chaining would not have been possible. If we omit the B-address (M̲ bbb 400), then the B-address 400 would have been placed in the A-address register during the I-phase, destroying the needed A-address 863. This happens because characters are placed in the registers from left to right in a consecutive manner. In other words, we may omit the B-address, but not the A-address during partial chaining.

The description of each instruction includes the contents of the address registers after the operation has been performed. Table 16-3 gives the meaning of each abbreviation.

PROBLEMS IN ABSOLUTE PROGRAMMING

Programming is communication between man and computer. Without this communication and without a skillful programmer, the computer cannot live up to its reputation. The computer accepts only instructions that the engineers have designed as its vocabulary, which is an absolute (machine language) program. Earlier computers could only accept machine-language programs. For this reason, only the best of experts could program them. The difficulties encountered when writing in absolute machine language are:

1. Instructions and addresses must be coded in machine language.

Table 16-3 Codes for Address-register Contents after Operation

Abbreviation	Meaning
A	A-address of the instruction
B	B-address of the instruction
NSI	Address of the next sequential instruction
BI	Address of the next instruction if a branch occurs
L_A	Number of characters in the A-field
L_B	Number of characters in the B-field
L_D	Number of characters in a disk record
L_W	Number of characters in the A- or B-field, whichever is smaller
Ap	Previous setting of the A-address register
Bp	Previous setting of the B-address register
dpp	d-character and the tens and units positions of the previous register setting
dbi	d-character and the tens and units positions of the *branch* instruction
dbb	d-character and blank in the units and tens position

2. Allocation of storage locations for instructions and data must be kept track of.

3. Instructions must be written in the sequence by which they are executed, so if an instruction is added or deleted, all succeeding instructions must be relocated.

For example, every instruction except an unconditional branch must be followed by a character with a word mark. By examining Fig. 16-3 we see that this rule has been broken at the end of the program. This means that another instruction is needed in housekeeping to set a word mark in location 399. But, is it really that simple? When we add the *set-word-mark* instruction, it makes the location of every succeeding instruction incorrect. Consequently, the I-address of both *branch* instructions must be changed. As you can see, inserting additional instructions or mislabeling the location of only one instruction can be disastrous, especially with complicated programs.

To relieve the programmer of the difficulties of writing absolute programs, a number of programming languages have been developed which are easier to use and under-

stand than machine language. The next chapter is about one such language, symbolic programming.

QUESTIONS

1. What storage positions from 0000 to 0332 may be used as working storage?
2. In relation to the registers and machine phases, why must the last instruction in a program be followed by a character with a word mark?
3. Chaining is possible in the program shown in Fig. 16-3. Which instruction(s) can be chained? Write the new instruction(s).
4. In Fig. 16-3, name two instructions that could be reversed without harming the program, but would prevent chaining.
5. What signals the end of the I-phase? The E-phase?
6. Name four things that happen during the I-phase. During the E-phase.
7. Define the program terms *coding* and *machine language*.
8. What happens to the data and word marks in positions 001 to 080, 101 to 180 and 201 to 332 when an *input-output* instruction is executed?
9. Name at least five requirements for a programmer in order to communicate with the computer.
10. Which part of an instruction must always be present?
11. Define fall through.
12. A validity light located on an input-output unit turns on. What does this indicate?
13. What is the purpose of a word mark? How is it represented in memory?
14. On the coding sheet, which columns of data actually enter core storage?
15. In the *clear-storage* instruction, when is the operation terminated?
16. Identify the reserved areas of memory.
17. What purpose does the effective number of characters serve on the coding sheet?
18. What stops the operation when a *move-characters* instruction is executed?

19. In the 1402 card read-punch, identify the stackers that accept cards selected by program instruction.
20. Of the instructions discussed, which one would not be necessary in a fixed word length machine?
21. In what manner are instructions picked up from storage? Data?

PROBLEMS

1. Write a program to produce a new deck of cards in the format as follows:

Input columns	Output columns	Description
1–15	1–15	Employee name
38–46	16–24	Social security number
47–49	25–27	Occupation code
50–51	28–29	Pay grade
55–56	35–36	Number of dependents
70–75	37–42	Salary
76–79	43–46	FICA

2. Write the storage location to be addressed in each of the examples. Write the storage location in which the word mark should be set.

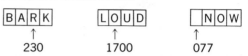

3. In the examples above, write the instruction to move NOW to replace BARK, setting word marks as appropriate.
4. Write the instruction(s) necessary to clear the word LOUD in the above example.
5. Assuming the last instruction is to be written at location 450, write the *halt* instruction in such a manner as to stop the computer in case the *start* key is depressed.

17
Symbolic programming (I)

We have seen so far that the computer must work with actual machine-operation codes and addresses. However, programming in machine language burdens the programmer with looking up or memorizing practically every address and OP code. Not only does this increase the chance of program error, but debugging and correction are intensified. The first language developed to permit the programmer to concentrate more on the problem and less on machine characteristics was called the symbolic programming system (SPS).

Each instruction in the preceding chapter, as you recall, contained an operation code called mnemonic. In symbolic programming, we use mnemonic OP codes because they are much easier to remember than actual OP codes. For example, P is the mnemonic OP code for punch-a-card, which is easier to remember than the machine-language equivalent of 4. Soon after development of mnemonic OP codes, it became evident that the computer was capable of assigning storage addresses to data that could be referred to mnemonically. Instead of specifying an absolute address, we could then use symbolic names called labels. As an example, the address of an area containing invoice number could be referred to as INVNO. The computer, acting under control of a special conversion program provided by the manufacturer, would then translate INVNO into an equivalent machine-language address. Thus, when the programmer uses the symbolic programming system, he is relieved of the task of remembering absolute operation codes and actual locations of data or instructions in memory.

The computer cannot execute a program written in symbolic language. It is necessary to translate the symbolic program, called a *source program,* into machine-language instructions. These instructions, resulting from the translation, are called an *object program.* This process of translation from the source program into an object program is done by another program called a *processor.* The operation carried out by the processor, which results in punching of an object program from the source program, is called *assembling.* Thus, the processor is often called an assembler or assembly program. Figure 17-1a shows a simplified assembly process from a programmer standpoint and Fig. 17-1b shows the operation of processing a job with the object program from a machine operator's standpoint. Next, we shall discuss the coding sheet on which the programmer writes his program and from which the source program is keypunched.

SYMBOLIC CODING SHEET

We see from Fig. 17-4 that addresses are written as descriptive symbols and that the operation codes are written mnemonically. We have used absolute addresses where convenient. The machine distinguishes between symbolic and absolute addresses by the first character in the address. If it is a letter, the address is *symbolic.* If it is a digit, the address is *absolute.* In general, symbolic-address labels of the programmer's choice are assigned that are descriptive of the information referenced by them.

The 1401 symbolic coding sheet contains special columns for each item of information required in the translation process. Each statement is written on a separate line and keypunched as indicated by the column numbers. The function of each column is explained in the following paragraphs.

Page number (columns 1 and 2) is a two-character numeric field used for sequencing the coded sheets. Line number (columns 3 to 5) is a prenumbered three-character code for sequencing instructions on each page. The line entries are numbered in increments of 10 to facilitate inserting additional instructions between lines. The six unnumbered lines at the bottom of the sheet are reserved for these insertions, or can be used to continue line numbering. For example, if an insert is necessary between lines 170 and 180, it can be numbered 171. All instructions must be in the proper sequence before assembly; the keypunched instructions may be sequenced by sorting or collating columns 3 to 5 minor and columns 1 and 2 major. Identification (columns 76 to 80) is coded to identify the program.

Certain pseudo-instructions require the number of characters in the word be specified. A *pseudo-instruction* provides information to the assembler program as opposed to an instruction which provides information to the computer. For example, if the programmer needs a working storage area in order to save the employee number for comparison with the following card, then he must give the size of the field. This number is written *right-justified* (a term referring to the placing of significant digits to the right) in the *count* field (columns 6 and 7). If the count columns contain 04, four storage locations are allocated for the information.

As we have seen, every instruction word and data word has an address. In symbolic programming, addresses may be referred to by the absolute address or by a label. *Labels* (columns 8 to 13) are descriptive terms that the

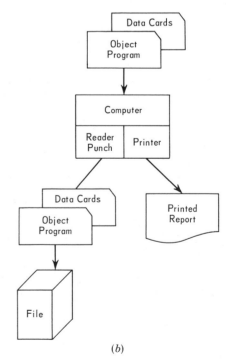

(a)

(b)

Fig. 17-1 **(a)** Assembling an object program. **(b)** Processing data with object program.

programmer selects to identify specific addresses. In other words, the label is an equivalent address that is used in lieu of actual machine addresses. During assembly, the computer sets up a table of labels and their actual addresses. Addresses of labels are punched in the object deck as absolute storage locations. The equivalent address of the label of an instruction is the high-order core position whereas the address of the label of data is the low-order core position. A label can be from one to six alphanumeric characters in length, except for the first position, which must be alphabetic. The label is coded *left-justified* (a term referring to the placing of significant digits to the left) and punched beginning in column 8. Blanks must not appear within the label. For instance, employee number may be coded EMPNO, but not EMPbNO.

The operation code (OP code) can be either mnemonic or absolute. Actual OP codes are punched in column 16 and mnemonic OP codes are coded beginning in column 14. For example, the clear-storage OP code is coded CS in columns 14 and 15 as mnemonic or / in column 16 as absolute.

The A- and B-Operand (columns 17 to 27 and 28 to 38) may be from 1 to 11 characters in length. In the operand the programmer designates the addresses of instructions and data, constant data, information pertinent during assembly, or a specific tape unit. The operand may include a symbolic label representing an address, actual address, asterisk, or blank.

A symbolic address in the A- or B-address (columns 17 to 22 and 28 to 33) can be from one to six alphanumeric characters in length, except for the first, which must be alphabetic. Each symbolic address must have a corresponding label elsewhere in the program. Actual addresses are sometimes preferred over symbolic addresses, especially when the address is referred to

only once. They are easy to work with since they are written as four-digit numbers. For example, core location 80 is coded as 0080 and core location J99 is coded as 2199. Both symbolic and absolute addresses are left-justified. Figure 17-2 illustrates the use of a symbolic and an actual address. Blank addresses are used where no operand is needed; for example, the instruction R (read-a-card) needs no address since core location 0001-0080 is permanently set up to accept input data. The use of the asterisk will be explained as needed.

Character adjustment (columns 23 to 26 and 34 to 37) makes it possible to reduce the number of labels needed and permits addressing characters within a word. For example, in Fig. 17-4, line 140, the I-address of the unconditional branch is coded as SELECT+002. We see that the address of the next instruction is labeled SELECT. If the instruction SS (select stacker) is located at position 1548 and its d-modifier at location 1549, then we must add two to the label SELECT in order to bypass the select-stacker instruction. Figure 17-5 illustrates that this technique produces the same result in the object program if we give the instruction at line 160 a separate label. Figure 17-3 illustrates the technique of addressing characters within a word.

Indexing (IND—columns 27 and 38) permits modification of addresses. The operation is accomplished by *registers,* which are similar to counters. Indexing, in general, allows the address of an instruction to be modified without actually changing the address itself. This is accomplished by adding the contents of the index register to the address without changing the instruction as it appears in storage. This is particularly useful when working with tables stored in memory. Assume that we have a stored table consisting of 50 two-position codes, each representing a state. Each card in the file has a two-position state code that must be matched to the corre-

LINE	COUNT	LABEL	OPERATION	(A) OPERAND				(B) OPERAND				d	COMMENTS
				ADDRESS	±	CHAR. ADJ.	IND	ADDRESS	±	CHAR. ADJ.	IND		
3	5 6	7 8	13 14 16 17		23		27 28		34		38 39	40	55
0 1 0			B	T A X R T N				0 0 7 5				A	

Fig. 17-2   SPS instruction showing symbolic and actual addresses.

LINE	COUNT	LABEL	OPERATION	(A) OPERAND				(B) OPERAND				d	COMMENTS
				ADDRESS	±	CHAR. ADJ.	IND.	ADDRESS	±	CHAR. ADJ.	IND.		
3	5 6 7 8		13 14 16 17		23		27 28		34		38 39 40			55
0 1 0			S	D I S C N T	–	0 0 2		T O T D U E	–	0 0 2			D R O P C E N T S

Fig. 17-3   Character adjustment.

sponding code in the table. Without indexing, this would require 50 compare instructions. With indexing, one compare instruction suffices. Specific items in the table are referred to by comparing the two-position code in the card to the first state code. If an unequal occurs, the table address is modified so as to shift two positions, giving the address of the second state code, and so on. For example, a card is compared with the first state (Alabama) in the table and, if found unequal, the program adds 2 to the index register, loops to the original *compare* instruction, whose address has been increased by the two core positions, giving the address of Alabama plus 2 (as modified by the index register) or Alaska. This process of looping and address modification continues until the card is matched with the correct state in the table. The index register is reset to zero for each card; therefore, the compare always begins at the address of the code that represents Alabama.

The d-character (column 39) is written in machine language and performs the same function as described in the previous chapter. You will recall that the d-character modifies the OP code. Comments (columns 40 to 55) are used by the programmer to describe each entry so that the instruction can be more easily understood. Comments have no effect on the program; however, incorrect processing occurs if they overlap beyond column 55. Columns 56 to 75 must be left blank because they are used during the assembly process. The foregoing discussion about the coding sheet probably left you with many unanswered questions. To see how all of the columns fit together, let us discuss the coding of a symbolic program.

Symbolic Payroll Program Problem

Given the following information, you are encouraged to draw a program flowchart to produce a payroll register.

The purpose of this program is to compute net pay and print the report in the format given in Table 17-1. In addition, the job calls for separating the overtime-pay cards (stacker 1) from the other cards (NR stacker), double spacing between lines, and printing a card count at the end of the report. Net pay is determined by the formula: regular pay plus overtime pay, minus insurance and withholding tax and FICA deductions. The program used for illustration (Fig. 17-4) is written from the flow-chart solution located with the answers to the end-of-chapter questions.

Specific information must be provided the processor during assembly. These instructions are included at both the beginning and end of the source program. Called pseudo-instructions, they are instructions to the processor and are not actually executed by the program, as opposed to instructions that are executed by the computer. The first pseudo-instruction (CTL) in Fig. 17-4 tells the processor the amount of storage in the computer that assembles the object program and the storage size of the computer that will use the object program. This is

Table 17-1   Input-output Format

Input columns	Print position	Description
1–15	1–15	Name
16–20	21–25	Employee number
30–38	29–37	Social security number
40–45	41–46	Regular pay
46–49	50–53	Overtime pay
50–53	57–60	Insurance
70–73	64–67	Withholding tax
74–77	71–74	FICA
	100–107	Net pay
80		Overtime cards are punched 9
	130–132	Card count

necessary since the machine performing the assembly may be different from the machine that actually processes the data.

CTL (Control) Statement

Description   The control card is placed at the beginning of the source deck so that the SPS processor is able to distinguish the storage sizes of the processing machine (that *assembles* the object program), and the object machine (that *executes* the assembled object program).

The programmer writes the mnemonic code (CTL) in the operation field and indicates in column 17 the size of the processor machine. This determines the maximum number of labels that can be processed per iteration, a term indicating execution of passes 1 and 2 of the processor. The programmer indicates in column 18 the size of the object machine. This indicates to the processor how much storage space has to be cleared at load time for the assembled program.

Col 17 and 18 codes	Storage positions
1	1400
2	2000
3	4000
4	8000
5	12000
6	16000

The next pseudo-instruction (*ORG*) causes the processor to load the program at a specific area in memory. For no other reason than illustration, we shall cause the program to begin loading at core position 1500. In the absence of an *ORG* statement, the first instruction is automatically placed beginning at location 333. This is the first position beyond the reserved input-output areas.

ORG (Origin) Statement

Description   An *ORG* statement causes the processor's storage-assignment counter to assign addresses beginning at a particular location specified by the programmer.

If it is entered as the first card (excluding *CTL* statement) of the source program, an ORG card can cause the initial assignment of addresses to be at a location other than 333. An *ORG* statement may be included at any desired point in the source program. This causes the counter to be reset and causes all future entries to be assigned addresses beginning at the particular location designated by the programmer. Character adjustment and indexing are *not* valid in an *ORG* statement.

The programmer writes ORG in the operation field and the actual machine address at which assignment is to begin (left-justified) in the A-address; he inserts the card in the desired place in the program.

The processor assigns addresses to instructions, constants, and work areas beginning at the address specified in the A-address; he causes the storage-assignment counter to assign subsequent addresses beginning at the address written in the A-address if an *ORG* statement is encountered at any point in the source program.

Another pseudo-instruction is written as the last instruction in Fig. 17-4. The END card signals the processor that assembling is completed. If the programmer wishes to begin processing immediately after loading the object program, he writes the actual storage location or label of the first instruction in the A-address. We should emphasize that only an object program deck is punched during assembly. After assembling the source program, the object deck may be loaded into memory with the data to be processed. Then the computer begins executing the instructions, beginning with the one specified in the A-address of the END card.

END Statement

Description   An *END* statement is a signal to the processor that the last card in the source program has been processed. If the programmer specifies in the A-operand the actual or symbolic address at which the object program is to begin execution, an *END* statement produces an instruction that starts program execution immediately after loading. If the A-operand is blank, the 1401 halts when the last instruction has been loaded.

IBM

INTERNATIONAL BUSINESS MACHINES CORPORATION
IBM 1401 SYMBOLIC PROGRAMMING SYSTEM
CODING SHEET

FORM X24-1152-3
PRINTED IN U.S.A.

Program ___Symbolic Programming Problem___

Programmed by ___I. Q. STUDENT___

Date ___SEPT 3___

Page No. |0 1| of ___2___

Identification _P R O B_

LINE	COUNT	LABEL	OPERATION	(A) OPERAND ADDRESS	±	CHAR. ADJ.	IND.	(B) OPERAND ADDRESS	±	CHAR. ADJ.	IND.	d	COMMENTS
0 1 0			C T L	3 3									4 K M A C H I N E
0 2 0			O R G	1 5 0 0									S T O R E P G M 1 5 0 0
0 3 0		* P A Y R O L L	R E G I S T E R ,	P R O B L E M									
0 4 0		H K E E P	C S	0 3 3 2									C L E A R P R I N T 2 0 1 -
0 5 0			C S										3 3 2 , , P U N C H 1 0 1 -
0 6 0			C S										1 8 0 A N D R E A D 0 0 1
0 7 0			C S										- 0 8 0 B Y C H A I N I N G
0 8 0			S W	0 0 0 1				0 0 1 6					
0 9 0			S W	S S N O	- 0 0 8			R E G P A Y	- 0 0 5				S E T W O R D M A R K S
1 0 0			S W	O T P A Y	- 0 0 3			I N S	- 0 0 3				I N R E A D I N A R E A
1 1 0			S W	W H T A X	- 0 0 3			F I C A	- 0 0 3				
1 2 0		L O O P	R										R E A D A C A R D
1 3 0			B	S E L E C T				N I N E 8 0				9	G O T O S E L E C T C D
1 4 0			B	S E L E C T	+	0 0 2							B Y P A S S S E L E C T
1 5 0		S E L E C T	S S									1	S E L E C T O V E R T I M E
1 6 0			Z A	R E G P A Y				N E T C T R					C O M P U T E N E T P A Y
1 7 0			A	O T P A Y				N E T C T R					B Y F O R M U L A ; R E G
1 8 0			S	I N S				N E T C T R					P A Y + O V E R T I M E P A Y
1 9 0			S	W H T A X				N E T C T R					- I N S U R A N C E , - W I T H
2 0 0			S	F I C A				N E T C T R					H O L D I N G T A X , - F I C A
2 1 0			M C W	N E T C T R				0 3 0 7					P R T N E T 1 0 0 , - 1 0 7
2 2 0			M C W	N A M E				0 2 1 5					P R T N A M E 1 , - 1 5
2 3 0			M C W	E M P L N O				0 2 2 5					P R T E M P N O 2 1 , - 2 5
2 4 0			M C W	S S N O				0 2 3 7					P R T S S N O 2 9 , - 3 7
2 5 0			M C W	R E G P A Y				0 2 4 6					P R T R E G P A Y 4 1 , - 4 6
2 6 0			M C W	O T P A Y				0 2 5 3					P R T O T P A Y 5 0 , - 5 3

AREA—DEFINITION CHARACTER COUNT ⟶ I   5   10   15   20   25   30   32

o402250MSP

Fig. 17-4 Example of symbolic program.

The programmer writes END in the operation field, and may write a symbolic, blank, or actual machine address (left-justified) in the A-operand. An asterisk address is not permissible.

The processor clears the read area (positions 001 to 080) of core storage and assembles an instruction that branches to the address specified in the A-address after loading is completed.

As many lines as are needed may be listed on the program-assembly listing (Figs. 17-1α and 17-4) to de-scribe the program. Its presence in the program does not affect the program. Comment cards may be inserted throughout the program at the programmer's discretion.

COMMENT Card

Description To provide the programmer with the ability to insert more extensive descriptive information in the program listing than is possible by using the *comments* field on a program-entry card. Comment cards are not

IBM

INTERNATIONAL BUSINESS MACHINES CORPORATION
IBM 1401 SYMBOLIC PROGRAMMING SYSTEM
CODING SHEET

FORM X24-1152-3
PRINTED IN U.S.A.

Program Symbolic Programming Problem   Page No. |0,2| of ___2___

Programmed by I. Q. STUDENT   Date SEPT 3   Identification P,R,O,B, 76 80

LINE	COUNT	LABEL	OPERATION	(A) OPERAND ADDRESS	±	CHAR. ADJ.	IND.	(B) OPERAND ADDRESS	±	CHAR. ADJ.	IND.	d	COMMENTS
0 1 0			MCW	INS				0260					PRT INS 57-60
0 2 0			MCW	WHTAX				0267					PRT WH TAX 64-67
0 3 0			MCW	FICA				0274					PRT FICA 71-74
0 4 0			W										PRINT
0 5 0			CC									K	SPACE 2
0 6 0			A	LOOP				COUNT					ADD 1 TO CD CTR
0 7 0			B	LAST								A	TO LAST CD RTN
0 8 0			B	LOOP									REPEAT PROGRAM
0 9 0		LAST	CS	0332									CLEAR PRT 332-300
1 0 0			CS										CLEAR PRT 201-299
1 1 0			MCW	COUNT				0332					PRT CC 330-332
1 2 0			W										PRT CARD COUNT
1 3 0		HALT	H	HALT									LOCKED HALT
1 4 0			H										
1 5 0		NAME	DS	0015									NAME
1 6 0		EMPLNO	DS	0020									EMPLOYEE NUMBER
1 7 0		SSNO	DS	0038									SOCIAL SEC NO
1 8 0		REGPAY	DS	0045									REGULAR PAY
1 9 0		OTPAY	DS	0049									OVERTIME PAY
2 0 0		INS	DS	0053									INSURANCE
2 1 0		WHTAX	DS	0073									WITHHOLDING TAX
2 2 0		FICA	DS	0077									FICA
2 3 0	0.8	NETCTR	DCW	*				0000 0000					NET PAY COUNTER
2 4 0	0.3	COUNT	DCW	*		b b b							CARD COUNT CTR
2 5 0		NINE8.0	DS	0080									OVERTIME CODE
2 6 0			END	HKEEP									TO PROGRAM START

AREA–DEFINITION CHARACTER COUNT ⟶ 1   5   10   15   20   25   30 32

6402250MSP

Fig. 17-4   Example of symbolic program (continued).

assembled nor do they affect the assembling procedures. When encountered by the processor, they are reproduced unaltered in the SPS output deck, but are bypassed when the object program is being loaded.

The programmer indicates with an asterisk (*) in the first position of the *label* field (column 8) that the card is a comment card; he may write the comment beginning at any position between columns 9 to 55. Comments extending beyond position 55 may cause an error during processing.

The processor reproduces unaltered the comment in proper sequence in the program listing.

The first four instructions in the housekeeping routine are used to clear the input-output areas using the technique of chaining. The next four instructions set word marks that are shown as absolute and symbolic in order to illustrate both techniques. The address of a word containing data is the low-order (units) position. This is usually of no concern when setting word marks in the high-order position of each field. However, we must consider both since our problem sets them by using labels originally set up for data. This represents somewhat of a problem since we must address a position within the word. Character adjustment solves the problem, allowing us to use labels whose address is different from the address needed. Looking at the format (Table 17-1), we see that social security number is punched in columns 30 to 38. Therefore, the word mark should be set in the read-area position 0030. Yet, the equivalent of the label SSNO (located at page 2, line 170) is storage location 0038. By coding character adjustment (SSNO−008), 8 is subtracted from the actual address which is established as the equivalent of the symbol SSNO. In other words, the word mark is set in core location 0030.

After executing the housekeeping instructions, we read the first card in the data deck. The job specification calls for selecting the card to stacker 1 if overtime is involved; otherwise the card should be stacked in NR pocket. Since the overtime cards are punched with a 9 in column 80, we can make the decision by testing column 80. This testing of the type card uses a new variation of the *branch* instruction that combines the functions of comparing and branching. If the single character located at the address specified in the B-address (label NINE80 is defined elsewhere in the program as being column 80) is equal with the character in d-modifier, then a branch is taken to the instruction shown in the I-address. This instruction, whose address is labeled SELECT, stacks the card into pocket 1.

Branch if Character Equal Instruction

Instruction format

Mnemonic	OP code	I-address	B-address	d-modifier
B	$\underline{B}$	XXX	XXX	X

Function　This instruction causes the single character at the B-address to be compared to the d-character. If it has the same bit configuration as the d-character, the program branches to the I-address; otherwise the program continues sequentially. The d-character can be any combination of the six BCD code bits (BA8421).

Word marks　Word marks in the location tested have no effect on the operation.

Timing
No branch. $T = N (L_I + 2)$ ms
Branch without indexing. $T = N (L_I + 2)$ ms
Branch with indexing. $T = N (L_I + 3)$ ms
Care must be taken if the specified d-character is also the same d-character that can test and reset an indicator OFF, when it is used with a $\underline{B}$ XXX d instruction. If the indicator is ON during the execution of the $\underline{B}$ XXX XXX d instruction, it is turned OFF.

Address registers after operation

	I-add Reg	A-add Reg	B-add Reg
No branch.	NSI	BI	B-1
Branch without indexing.	NSI	BI	Blank
Branch with indexing.	NSI	BI	NSI

If the condition is not met, the program falls through to the next instruction, an *unconditional branch*. We have said that the adjustment factor is added to or subtracted from the actual address assigned to the label by the processor during assembly. Thus, one label can serve more than one address. For example, we could simply give a label to the instruction at page 1, line 160. But since we already have a label for the preceding instruction, why create new labels? Instead, the label SELECT +002 will produce an actual address equal to the address that would have been assigned if a new label had been given the instruction at line 160. Figure 17-5 shows how

Line		Instruction
130		B V48 080 9
140		$\underline{B}$ V50
150		K 1
	Loc V48 or 1548 _____↑	
160		? 045 W92
	Loc V50 or 1550 _____↑	

Fig. 17-5　Assembled instructions showing one label being used with character adjustment.

the object program would be assembled regardless of the technique used.

The above two *branch* instructions constitute the decision as to select or not to select the card. The first *branch* instruction results in a YES answer if the branch is taken. This causes the program to take the symbolic I-address as the next executable instruction, which selects the card into stacker 1. If the condition being tested is absent, the answer to the decision is NO, resulting in the next sequential instruction being executed. The program transfers to the symbolic address SELECT+002, thus by-passing the *select-stacker* instruction. We use stacker selection to put all 9 in column 80 cards into pocket 1. This instruction needs only a character (to determine which stacker is to be selected) in the d-modifier and, of course, the OP code.

Select-Stacker Instruction

Instruction format

Mnemonic	OP code	A-address	B-address	d-modifier
SS	K̲			X

Function   This instruction causes the card that was just read or punched to be selected into the stacker pocket specified by the d-modifier.

d-character	Feed	Stacker pocket
1	Read	1
2	Read	8/2
4	Punch	4
8	Punch	8/2

Read select   A *select-stacker* instruction must be given during the first 10 ms after actual card reading is completed. Otherwise the command is ineffective. After a card is read, it continues to the stackers without stopping. Therefore, if no select-stacker signal is received within the next 10 ms, the card stacks in the NR (normal stacker). Read-select instructions cannot be used following RP and WRP instructions because the select signal cannot be given with the prescribed 10 ms.

Punch select   The *select-stacker* instruction is effective if given at any time between two *punch-card* instructions. However, if a punch check occurs, the error card is directed to the NP (normal punch) stacker.

Word marks   Word marks are not affected.

Timing $T = N(L_I + 1)$ ms

Address registers after operation

I-add Reg	A-add Reg	B-add Reg
NSI	dbb	dbb

Select Stacker and Branch Instruction

Instruction format

Mnemonic	OP code	I-address	B-address	d-modifier
SS	K̲	XXX		X

Function   This is the same as select stacker, except that the next instruction is taken from the I-address.

Word marks   Word marks are not affected.

Timing $T = N(L_I + 1)$ ms

Address registers after operation

I-add Reg	A-add Reg	B-add Reg
NSI	BI	dbb

The next five instructions are used to compute net pay. This involves adding regular pay and overtime pay, and subtracting insurance, withholding tax, and FICA deductions. Net pay is computed in a counter that we have given the symbolic label NETCTR. Before using the counter, we must clear it of any contents that may remain from a previous computation. One method is to move a field of blanks into the counter and yet another way is to move, instead of adding, the first field to be added into the counter. However, we shall use another instruction that clears the area to zeros before addition takes place.

Zero and Add Two Fields **Instruction**

Instruction format

Mnemonic	OP code	A-address	B-address	d-modifier
ZA	?	XXX	XXX	

Function   This instruction adds the A-field to a zeroed B-field. Technically, this is accomplished by moving the A-field to the B-field. The high-order positions of the B-field are set to zero if the B-field is larger than the A-field. The data from the A-field move directly from the A-register to storage. Zone bits are stripped from all positions except the units position. Blanks in the A-field are stored as blanks in the B-field.

Word marks   A word mark is required for definition of the B-field. It is required in the A-field, only if it is shorter than the B-field. If the A-field is shorter than the B-field, all extra high-order B-field positions contain zeros. But the transmission of data from the A-field stops when the A-field word mark is detected.

Timing $T = N (L_I + 1 + L_A + L_B)$ ms. The sign of the result always has both A- and B-bits if it is positive. If the sign is negative, it has only a B-bit.

Address registers after operation

I-add Reg	A-add Reg	B-add Reg
NSI	$A-L_W$	$B-L_B$

We now have the contents of the area labeled REGPAY, which consist of the contents from card columns 40 to 45, added into the counter labeled NETCTR. Even though you have recognized how easy it is to associate the A- and B-fields with the problem at hand, you are most likely confused as to how the machine knows where REGPAY and NETCTR are located. They are defined at the end of the program; therefore, we shall delay explaining them until that time. The next instruction adds the overtime field to the contents of NETCTR. The idea of addition is that the field located at the address specified in A-operand is added to the number located at the address in the B-operand. The sum replaces the B-field.

Add-Two-Fields **Instruction**

Instruction format

Mnemonic	OP code	A-address	B-address	d-modifier
A	A	XXX	XXX	

Function   The data in the A-field are added to the data in the B-field. The result is stored in the B-field.

Word marks   The B-field must have a defining word mark, because it is this word mark that actually stops the add operation.

The A-field must have a word mark only if it is shorter than the B-field. In this case, the transmission of data from the A-field stops after the A-field work mark is sensed. Zeros are then inserted in the A-register until the B-field word mark is sensed.

If the A-field is longer than the B-field, the high-order positions of the A-field that exceed the limits imposed by the B-field word mark are not processed. For overflow conditions and considerations, assume that the A-field is the same length as the B-field.

Timing   If the operation does not require a recomplement cycle: $T = 0.0115 (L_I + 3 + L_A + L_B)$ ms. If a recomplement cycle is taken: $T = 0.0115 (L_I + 3 + L_A + 4L_B)$ ms.

Notes
1.   *Sign Control.* If a recomplement cycle is automatically taken, the sign of the B-field (result) is changed and the result is always stored in true form.
2.   *Zone Bits.* If the fields to be added contain zone bits in other than the high-order position of the B-field and the sign position of both fields, only the digits are used in a true-add operation. B-field zone bits are removed except for the units and high-order position in a true-add operation. If a complement add takes place, zone bits are removed from all but the units positions of the B-field.
3.   *Overflow.* If an overflow occurs during a true-add operation, the arithmetic overflow indicator is set and the overflow indications are stored over the high-order digit of the B-field. When the A-field exceeds, or is equal to,

the B-field length, and the A-field position that corresponds to the high-order B-field position contains a zone bit, this zone bit is added to any zone bits present in the high-order B-field position.

Condition	Result
First overflow	A-bit
Second overflow	B-bit
Third overflow	A- and B-bits
Fourth overflow	No A- or B-bits

Conditions 1 to 4 are repeated for five and more overflow conditions. Overflow indication does not occur for a one-position field.

The *branch if arithmetic overflow indicator* ON (B XXX Z) instruction tests and turns OFF the arithmetic overflow indicator and branches to a special instruction or group of instructions if this condition occurs. There is only one overflow indicator in the system. It is turned OFF by a *branch if arithmetic overflow indicator* ON instruction, or by pressing the *start-reset* key.

Address registers after operation

I-add Reg	A-add Reg	B-add Reg
NSI	A-L_W	B-L_B

Add-One-Field **Instruction**

Instruction format

Mnemonic	OP code	A-address	B-address	d-modifier
A	A	XXX		

Function This format of the *add* instruction causes the data in the A-field to be added to itself.

Word marks The A-field must have a defining word mark. It is this word mark that stops the add operation.

Timing $T = 0.0115 (L_I + 3 + 2L_A)$ ms

Address registers after operation

I-add Reg	A-add Reg	B-add Reg
NSI	A-L_A	B-L_A

The next three instructions involve subtracting the deductions one-by-one from the gross pay standing in NETCTR. In subtraction, the word or field in the A-address is subtracted from the word in the B-address. The difference replaces the contents previously standing in the B-address. Upon execution of the five arithmetic instructions, net pay is computed and available at core-storage location called NETCTR.

Subtract-Two-Fields **Instruction**

Instruction format

Mnemonic	OP code	A-address	B-address	d-modifier
S	S	XXX	XXX	

Function The numerical data in the A-field are subtracted from the numerical data in the B-field. The result is stored in the B-field. Refer to Fig. 17-6 for the sign that results from a specific subtract operation.

Word marks A word mark is required to define the B-field. An A-field requires a word mark only if it is shorter

Type of operation	A-field sign	B-field sign	Type of add cycle	Sign of result
A D D +	+	+	True add	+
		−	Complement add	Sign of greater value
	−	+	Complement add	
		−	True add	−
S U B T R A C T −	+	−	True add	−
		+	Complement add	Sign of greater value
	−	−	Complement add	
		+	True add	+

Fig. 17-6 Types of add cycles and sign of result for add and subtract operations.

than the B-field. In this case, the A-field word mark stops transmission of data from the A-field.

Timing   Subtract (no recomplement) $T = 0.0115 (L_I + 3 + L_A + L_B)$ ms. Subtract (recomplement cycle necessary) $T = 0.0115 (L_I + 3 + L_A + 4L_B)$ ms. If a recomplement cycle is automatically taken, the sign of the B-field (result) is changed and the result is always stored in true form.

Address registers after operation

I-add Reg	A-add Reg	B-add Reg
NSI	A-L_W	B-L_B

Zero and Subtract Two Fields **Instruction**

Instruction format

Mnemonic	OP code	A-address	B-address	d-modifier
ZS	!	XXX	XXX	

Function   This instruction subtracts the A-field from a zeroed B-field. Technically, this is accomplished by moving the A-field to the B-field. The high-order positions of the B-field are set to zero if the B-field is larger than the A-field. The data from the A-field are moved directly from the A-register to the B-field. Zone bits are stripped from all but the sign (units) position.

Word marks   A word mark is required to define the B-field. If the A-field is shorter than the B-field, the A-field must have a defining word mark to stop transmission of data to B. The extra high-order B-field positions contain zeros if A is shorter than B.

Timing $T = N (L_I + 1 + L_A + L_B)$ ms. If the A-field is positive, the B-field result is negative. If the A-field is negative, the B-field result is positive.

Address registers after operation

I-add Reg	A-add Reg	B-add Reg
NSI	A-L_W	B-L_B

Subtract-One-Field **Instruction**

Instruction format

Mnemonic	OP code	A-address	B-address	d-modifier
S	S	XXX		

Function   The data at the A-address are subtracted from itself. If the A-field sign is minus, the result is a minus zero. If the A-field sign is plus, the result is a plus zero.

Word marks   The A-field must have a defining word mark.

Timing $T = 0.0115 (L_I + 3 + 2L_A)$ ms

Address registers after operation

I-add Reg	A-add Reg	B-add Reg
NSI	A-L_A	A-L_A

The next symbol in the flowchart calls for the fields to be moved to the print area. In order to provide spacing between printed fields as specified in Table 17-1, they are moved one-by-one to the print area. We shall use both absolute addresses and addresses identified by labels to primarily illustrate the technique. After the nine fields are moved to the print area, we write a line. Neither the *move characters to A or B word mark* nor *write-a-line* instruction presents any new concepts except for the use of symbolic labels.

Normal printing causes only one space after printing. In order to obtain the desired printing with two spaces, we must execute a new instruction. This instruction causes the carriage in the printer to give up to three additional spaces. If further spacing is desired, such as skipping to the next page, certain characters in the d-modifier cause the paper to be advanced in the carriage to a predetermined channel in the carriage tape (located in the printer). The skip or print after printing results in the action becoming effective only after the next line is printed as opposed to the immediate space or skip which takes place immediately after the last line is printed.

There are two types of *control-carriage* instructions. One merely provides additional spacing and the program continues with the next sequential instruction. The other instruction carries out the prescribed spacing or skipping and branches to the instruction specified in the I-address.

This *control-carriage* and *branch* instruction is commonly used in carrying out end-of-page routines, such as page numbering and skipping to a new page. Its use will be demonstrated later.

Control-Carriage Instruction

Instruction format

Mnemonic	OP code	A-address	B-address	d-modifier
CC	$\underline{F}$			X

Function This instruction causes the carriage to move as specified by the d-character. A digit causes an immediate skip to a specified channel in the carriage tape. An alphabetic character with a 12 zone causes a skip to a specified channel after the next line is printed. An alphabetic character with an 11 zone causes an immediate space. A zero-zone character causes a space after the next line is printed. Table 17-2 shows the function of the d-character. If the carriage is in motion when a *control-carriage* instruction is given, the program stops until the carriage comes to rest. At this point the new carriage action is initiated, and then the program advances to the next instruction in storage.

Table 17-2 d-characters for Control Carriage

d-character	Immediate skip to—	d-character	Skip after print to—
1	Channel 1	A	Channel 1
2	Channel 2	B	Channel 2
3	Channel 3	C	Channel 3
4	Channel 4	D	Channel 4
5	Channel 5	E	Channel 5
6	Channel 6	F	Channel 6
7	Channel 7	G	Channel 7
8	Channel 8	H	Channel 8
9	Channel 9	I	Channel 9
0	Channel 10	?	Channel 10
#	Channel 11	.	Channel 11
@	Channel 12	⌑	Channel 12
	Immediate space		**After-print space**
J	1 space	/	1 space
K	2 spaces	S	2 spaces
L	3 spaces	T	3 spaces

Word marks Word marks are not affected.

Timing $T = N\ (L_I + 1)$ ms plus remaining form movement time, if carriage is moving when this instruction is given. The form movement time is determined by the number of spaces the form moves. Allow 20 ms for the first space, plus 5 ms for each additional space.

Address registers after operation

I-add Reg	A-add Reg	B-add Reg
NSI	dbb	dbb

Control Carriage and Branch Instruction

Instruction format

Mnemonic	OP code	I-address	B-address	d-modifier
CC	$\underline{F}$	XXX		X

Function This format of the *control-carriage* instruction causes a program branch to the location specified by the I-address for the next instruction after interpretation of the d-character.

Word marks Word marks are not affected.

Timing $T = N\,(L_I + 1)$ ms plus remaining form movement time, if carriage is moving when this instruction is given. The form movement time is determined by the number of spaces the form moves. Allow 20 ms for the first space, plus 5 ms for each additional space.

Address registers after operation

I-add Reg	A-add Reg	B-add Reg
NSI	BI	dbb

A card count symbol in the flowchart tells us to add a 1 for each card processed. This figure, representing the total cards processed, is printed at the end of the report for control purposes. In lieu of setting up a constant 1, which is used to increment the counter each time the program is repeated, we shall illustrate a programming shortcut. By referring to the *read-a-card* instruction, we see that the OP code R is translated into machine language 1 at the time the source program is assembled. In actuality, the computer adds the contents of the symbolic address LOOP, which is the machine language OP code 1, to a three-position card counter that we have labeled COUNT. Referring to the *add* instruction, we see that the transmission of data from the A-field is stopped as soon as a word mark is sensed. Since the OP code 1 (as well as all operation codes) has a word mark, zeros are assumed in the high-order positions of the A-field until the B-field word mark is sensed.

The following two *branch* instructions are used for the last-card decision. If the first conditional branch condition is met, program control is transferred to the end-of-job routine. If not, the program falls through to an unconditional branch that causes the program to repeat itself beginning at the instruction labeled LOOP.

In the last-card routine, the entire print area is cleared. This is necessary since an image of the last card remains in the print area of core storage. The contents of the counter in which the card count was accumulated are moved to the print area and printed. The last instruction in the program shows a new version of the *halt* instruction. In the *halt-and-branch* instruction, the next instruction is taken from the I-address if the start button on the console is pressed. A common practice when ending a program is to code the location of the *halt* instruction itself in the I-address. Consequently, the machine simply halts again if the start button is inadvertently pressed. This technique is called a locked halt. The second halt merely provides a word mark following the last instruction to be executed, since every instruction except an *unconditional branch* must be followed by a word mark.

We said earlier that labels are selected by the programmer to identify addresses of locations in memory. They can represent data or instruction words and the same label may be used as many times as needed in the program. This relieves the programmer of having to keep up with the addresses as he writes the program. These labels must be defined and are generally placed at the end of the program. There are four instructions that are used to define labels, reserve work areas, or set up constants. We shall cover three of them. These declarative operations are not instructions to the computer but to the processor. They do not result in the creation of any executable instructions in the object program.

Our first instruction to the processor is *DS* for *define symbol*. This establishes absolute addresses as the equivalent for labels we have chosen as descriptive for the problem. For example, 0015 is the absolute equivalent of the label NAME. Our concern here is to move the *name* field (columns 1 to 15) to the print area. Since an instruction to move data must be addressed by the low-order or units position, we define NAME as being at location 0015. We could have defined every field in the print area, thus eliminating all need to use absolute addresses. Instead, we have used both methods for illustration.

Next, we have two *DCW* (*define constant with word mark*) instructions that reserve two work areas. The first *DCW* instruction sets up a counter eight positions (specified in the count field) in length. A word mark is set by this instruction in the high-order position of the counter so there is no need to set a word mark in the housekeeping area. The asterisk (*) in column 17 tells the processor to put the reserved area in any available location. In this area we perform calculations in order to compute net pay. A three-position counter is similarly set up for the card count by a second *DCW* instruction.

Numerous constants can be set up in storage using the *DCW* or *DC* instructions. They can consist of blanks, numeric, alphabetic, or punctuation characters. In fact, it is possible to use a combination of three, such as MARCHb20,b1953. The constant being stored is coded beginning in column 24. In our sample program, we show one counter initialized to all zeros and the other set to blanks. Blank constants appear as blanks in storage and the symbol b is reflected on the coding sheet and post list simply for clarity. Initializing the counter to zeros or blanks has no effect on the computations.

It is not permissable to use a *DCW* in the read-in area because this area is used when loading the object program. Otherwise, we could have made the *DS* instructions

DCW and eliminated the need for setting word marks in the housekeeping section. In any case, the *DS* with a *set-word-mark* instruction accomplishes the same result. We should mention as a last comment that *DS*, *DCW*, and *DC* instructions do not have to be in any particular sequence. The *END* instruction, explained earlier in the chapter, must be the last instruction in the program.

DCW (Define Constant with Word Mark) Statement

Description   A *DCW* statement causes a constant to be loaded into a core storage area and a word mark to be set in the high-order position of this area at program load time.

Programmer's actions

1.   Writes *DCW* in the operation field.
2.   Writes in the *count* field the number of core storage positions needed to store the constant or work area.
3.   Writes a symbol in the *label* field if he wishes to refer later to the address of the field where the constant is stored.
4.   Writes the address of the area in which the constant is to be stored. If the programmer wishes to let the processor assign the address, he simply puts an asterisk (*) in column 17. Otherwise, he writes an actual address beginning in column 17. In any case the address refers to the low-order (units) position of the defined area.
5.   Writes the constant beginning in column 24 of the coding sheet. The constant may extend to the end of the *comments* field (column 55). Thus, the maximum size of a constant is 32 core storage positions.
6.   May write a comment in columns 40 to 55 if these positions are outside the range of the constant itself as specified in the *count* field.

Processor's actions

1.   Allocates a field in core storage to store the constant. The number in the *count* field determines the number of positions allocated.
2.   Adds the number in the *count* field to the number that was standing in the storage assignment counter if there is an asterisk (*) in column 17. The result becomes the address of the constant. This address is made equiva-

lent to the label, and the two are stored in the label table.
3.   Substitutes the equivalent addresses of labels in the operands of symbolic program statements which have corresponding symbolic addresses during assembly of the object program.
4.   Produces a card, as part of the object program, containing the data defined, with a sign if required, and instructions to load the constant into core storage with a word mark in the high-order position. This card is loaded with the object program and the constant is stored exactly as the *DCW* source-program statement defined it. For blank constants, the area is cleared for all existing word marks except the high-order word mark for the *DCW* constant.

DC (Define Constant) Statement

Description   This statement is the same as a *DCW* statement except that the processor does not set a word mark in the high-order position of the constant. Care should be taken to clear all word marks from the storage area to which the constant is to move.

DS (Define Symbol) Statement

Description   *DS* statements cause the processor to assign equivalent addresses to labels or to assign storage for work areas. *DS* statements differ from *DCW* and *DC* statements in that no data are loaded into the defined area at program load time. A *DS* defined area is unaffected during the loading of the object program. Data, word marks, and instructions previously put in the area remain unaltered. Thus, if *DS* statements are used only to define areas, use of a clear-storage routine before loading the program is recommended.

Some *DS* statements affect the storage assignment counter. These can be used to bypass areas needed for independent routines (instructions or data not included in the source program being assembled) or for storing constants for which the programmer has selected the actual storage locations.

Programmer's actions

1.   Writes *DS* in the operation field.

2.   Writes a symbol in the *label* field if he wishes to refer symbolically to the low-order position of the area.

3.   Writes the address of the area. If the processor is to assign the address, he writes an asterisk (*) in column 17 and writes a number in the count *field* to indicate the size of the area.

If the programmer wants to equate the label to an actual address or I/O unit operand, he writes the address or I/O operand beginning in column 17. In this case no storage is allocated by the processor, so the *count* field is left blank.

DS statements cannot be character adjusted or indexed.

Processor's actions

1.   Adds the number in the *count* field to the storage-assignment counter and equates the resulting address to the label if one appears in the *DS* statement if there is an asterisk (*) in column 17. If the asterisk or I/O unit operand appears in the *DS* statement, the processor equates the label to the operand.

2.   Substitutes the equivalent addresses of labels in the operands of symbolic program statements which have corresponding symbolic addresses during the assembly of the object program.

3.   Leaves the defined area unaltered during object program loading.

ASSEMBLING THE PROGRAM

The 1401 assembly process is accomplished by five separate programs:

Preprocess listing program
Processor assembly program (two parts):
Processor, pass 1
Processor, pass 2
Postprocessing listing program
Condensing program

In general, the source program is punched onto cards (one card per line) as indicated by the columns on the SPS coding sheet (Fig. 17-4). The preprocess program is placed in the card reader (Fig. 15-3) followed by the source deck. Pressing the load button on the reader transfers or loads the program into storage and lists each source-program card on the printer (Fig. 15-4). The purpose of this listing is to detect coding, such as undefined labels, and keypunch errors. Each field on the coding sheet is listed with spacing between fields along with error codes. The error legends are:

ERR 1   Page-line sequence: indicates that a page or line number is out of sequence.

ERR 2   Count: indicates the count for a *DC* or *DCW* is greater than 32 or less than 1, or that the programmer has not indicated the count for a *DC*, *DCW*, or *DS* statement.

ERR 3   Label: indicates that the first character in a label is blank, numeric, or a special character. Also recognizes a *DS* card without a label whose A-operand is not an asterisk. This type of card is meaningless to the processor and is noted as a potential error.

ERR 4   Illegal OP code: indicates illegal mnemonic operation code or a blank operation code field. A CTL card in any other position than the first in the source deck is processed as an instruction card and thus gives an illegal OP code error. These cards are created as *DCW*s if there is a count.

ERR 5   Illegal A-operand indicates:

1.   An instruction with a B-operand but not A-operand.

2.   A blank or symbolic A-operand for a *DCW*, *DC*, *DS*, or *DSA* statement.

3.   A nonnumeric address for an *ORG* statement.

4.   An asterisk address for an *END* statement.

5.   In a general operand error:

    a.   The indexing is not 1, 2, or 3.

    b.   Character adjustment is nonnumeric or left-justified.

    c.   Character adjustment sign is not + or −.

    d.   The first character of the operand is blank, but the balance of address is not.

    e.   The operand begins with % but is greater than three characters. It does not appear to be an I/O device.

    f.   The first character is numeric but the remaining are not.

Symbolic programming (I) 161

g. The numeric operand is fewer than four characters.

h. The numeric operand is greater than the object machine size specified.

i. The first character of the address is the asterisk but the balance is not blank.

ERR 6 Illegal B-operand: indicates the sign position (column 23 is not $+$, $-$, or blank) in a *DCW* or *DC* statement or a general operand error.

ERR 7 Columns 56 to 75 not blank: the information in columns 56 to 75 can cause an improper assembly.

The comments (columns 40 to 55) in a source-program card are entered in this field on the printed page. The preceding format is adhered to in the pre-process listing with the following exceptions:

1. Comments cards. The routine lists the comments (columns 8 to 55) centered in the middle of the page.

2. Constants. Constants are right-justified beyond the d-character column. The count determines the length of a constant. In this way, low-order blanks appear more distinctly. The sign (column 23) appears in the high-order position.

In addition, the preprocess listing prints, at the end of the source program listing, the total number of cards and the highest storage address that the processor assigns (exclusive of actual addresses assigned by the programmer).

After correction of all errors in the source program, it is inserted between pass-1 deck and pass-2 deck of the SPS processor and loaded into the computer. After pass-1 processor is loaded into core storage, the program starts immediately to assemble the source program by punching an intermediate (partial) deck. The three decks (pass-1 processor, source program, and intermediate deck) are stacked in separate pockets. The intermediate (partial) deck is a one-for-one translation, meaning that the intermediate deck contains one card for each one in the source program. After the one-for-one intermediate translation, pass-2 processor is automatically loaded into memory and the machine stops. Essentially, pass 1 changes mnemonic OP codes to absolute OP codes, assigns all instructions an equivalent core address, and

puts the label, if any, and its equivalent address into a table.

The intermediate deck (punched output resulting from pass 1) is placed in the read hopper as input for pass 2. Pressing the start button begins execution of pass 2 and punches the actual object program, a one-instruction-per-card program with self-loading cards. Each card of the object program contains the source-program symbolic instruction and the machine-language translation. The intermediate (partial) deck is destroyed. Pass 2, upon encountering a symbolic operand, searches the table for the label and translates it into the machine-language equivalence; then it converts four-character actual addresses to three-character machine addresses. Figure 17-7 shows the procedure of SPS assembly.

The object program is now ready to be combined with data for testing. Even after correction of errors discovered by the preprocess program, there are undoubtably additional errors. These most likely are program-logic errors, such as failing to have a subroutine for the computer to go to, after a *branch* instruction is executed. Most helpful in the debugging process is an assembly listing of the program (Fig. 17-8). Called a *post listing*, it shows both the source program and the final machine-language object program produced from it.

Note that the *count* field contains the number of core positions the instructions occupy. The processor provides this for the programmer's convenience. Also, we see that the assembled program addresses (LOC) are correct for data, constants, and instructions. Of particular importance in the post list, we have proved that chaining saves core storage. Note that nine positions are saved with the *clear-storage* instructions in the housekeeping area. We should emphasize that the processor is not yet through assisting us in isolating errors. Post-processing errors are indicated on the post listing by the *error indicator* ⋈, a lozenge printed between the page and the line number. This indicates that at least one of the following errors appears on the card:

1. An undefined symbol in A- or B-operand.

2. A blank operation code in the assembled instruction.

3. Data to be loaded has been assigned an address in the read area.

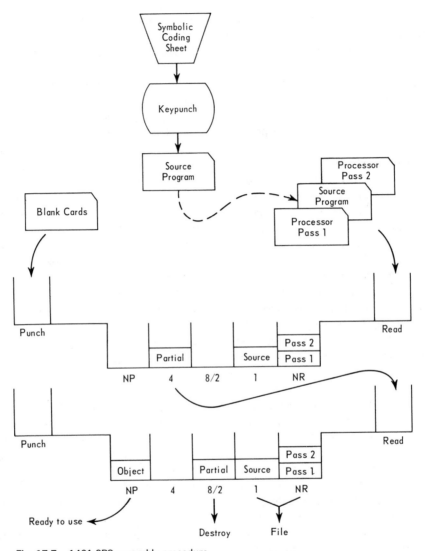

Fig. 17-7   1401 SPS assembly procedure.

4. A constant has been assigned a count greater than 32.

5. The count column in a *DC*, *DCW*, or instruction card is blank or zero. This causes a halt in the condensing routine. A blank instruction count cannot occur as a result of assembling. However, it may have been inadvertently left out of patch (correction) cards.

If a card does not appear to the listing routine as an assembled card, the words unassembled card are printed out with a complete reproduction of the card data. This error is most likely to occur when the operator attempts to list an unassembled (source program) deck, fails to reiterate a partially assembled deck, or lists the output from pass 1.

PG Line	CNT	Label	OP	A-operand	B-operand	d	LOC	Instruction			Comments
1 010			CTL	33							4K MACHINE
1 020			ORG	1500							STORE PGM 1500
1 030				* PAYROLL REGISTER PROBLEM							
1 040	4	HKEEP	CS	0332			1500	/	332		CLEAR PRINT 201–
1 050	1		CS				1504	/			332, PUNCH 101–
1 060	1		CS				1505	/			180 AND READ 001
1 070	1		CS				1506	/			–080 BY CHAINING
1 080	7		SW	0001	0016		1507	,	001	016	
1 090	7		SW	SSNO–008	REGPAY–005		1514	,	030	040	SET WORD MARKS
1 100	7		SW	OTPAY–003	INS–003		1521	,	046	050	IN READ-IN AREA
1 110	7		SW	WHTAX–003	FICA–003		1528	,	070	074	
1 120	1	LOOP	R				1535	1			READ A CARD
1 130	8		B	SELECT	NINE80	9	1536	B	V48 080 9		GO TO SELECT CD
1 140	4		B	SELECT+002			1544	B	V50		BYPASS SELECT
1 150	2	SELECT	SS			1	1548	K	1		SELECT OVERTIME
1 160	7		ZA	REGPAY	NETCTR		1550	?	045 W92		COMPUTE NET PAY
1 170	7		A	OTPAY	NETCTR		1557	A	049 W92		BY FORMULA: REG
1 180	7		S	INS	NETCTR		1564	S	053 W92		PAY+OVERTIME PAY
1 190	7		S	WHTAX	NETCTR		1571	S	073 W92		–INSURANCE–WITH
1 200	7		S	FICA	NETCTR		1578	S	077 W92		HOLDING TAX–FICA
1 210	7		MCW	NETCTR	0307		1585	M	W92 307		PRT NET 100–107
1 220	7		MCW	NAME	0215		1592	M	015 215		PRT NAME 1–15
1 230	7		MCW	EMPLNO	0225		1599	M	020 225		PRT EMP NO 21–25
1 240	7		MCW	SSNO	0237		1606	M	038 237		PRT SS NO 29–37
1 250	7		MCW	REGPAY	0246		1613	M	045 246		PRT REGPAY 41–46
1 260	7		MCW	OTPAY	0253		1620	M	049 253		PRT OT PAY 50–53
2 010	7		MCW	INS	0260		1627	M	053 260		PRT INS 57–60
2 020	7		MCW	WHTAX	0267		1634	M	073 267		PRT WH TAX 64–67
2 030	7		MCW	FICA	0274		1641	M	077 274		PRT FICA 71–74
2 040	1		W				1648	2			PRINT
2 050	2		CC			K	1649	F	K		SPACE 2
2 060	7		A	LOOP	COUNT		1651	A	V35 W95		ADD 1 TO CD CTR
2 070	5		B	LAST		A	1658	B	W67 A		TO LAST CD RTN
2 080	4		B	LOOP			1663	B	V35		REPEAT PROGRAM
2 090	4	LAST	CS	0332			1667	/	332		CLEAR PRT 332–300
2 100	1		CS				1671	/			CLEAR PRT 201–299
2 110	7		MCW	COUNT	0332		1672	M	W95 332		PRT CC 330–332
2 120	1		W				1679	2			PRT CARD COUNT
2 130	4	HALT	H	HALT			1680		W80		LOCKED HALT
2 140	1		H				1684				
2 150		NAME	DS	0015			0015				NAME
2 160		EMPLNO	DS	0020			0020				EMPLOYEE NUMBER
2 170		SSNO	DS	0038			0038				SOCIAL SEC NO
2 180		REGPAY	DS	0045			0045				REGULAR PAY
2 190		OTPAY	DS	0049			0049				OVERTIME PAY
2 200		INS	DS	0053			0053				INSURANCE
2 210		WHTAX	DS	0073			0073				WITHHOLDING TAX
2 220		FICA	DS	0077			0077				FICA
2 230	8	NETCTR	DCW	*		00000000	1692				NET PAY COUNTER
2 240	3	COUNT	DCW	*		bbb	1695				CARD COUNT CTR
2 250		NINE80	DS	0080			0080				OVERTIME CODE
2 260			END	HKEEP				/	V00 080		TO PROGRAM START
		52 CARDS									

Fig. 17-8 Assembly listing of the program in Fig. 17-4.

The final program, a condensing routine, is used to convert the one-instruction-per-card object deck into a condensed deck with several instructions per card. Thus, the condensed deck does not contain the symbolic instruction as does the object program. Condensing a program is advisable when it consists of several hundred or several thousand instructions.

In this chapter we have used numerous symbolic instructions. We also included some instructions that were not used in the sample program, but were similar in function to those used. In addition, most of the instructions contained information that was meaningless to the program, but which will be useful in future problems or as reference material. Our next problem, in Chap. 18, uses the same instructions covered in the previous two chapters and is an expanded program, requiring new instructions. In addition, we shall concentrate on programming techniques, such as program switches and programming shortcuts.

QUESTIONS

1. How many core positions are saved in the sample program in Fig. 17-8 as a result of chaining?
2. Assume that the label SELECT at line 150, page 1 in Fig. 17-4 is omitted. Write the new instruction at line 140 to accomplish the branch to the instruction at line 160 without creating a new label.
3. Name at least three reasons why programmers prefer symbolic programming over absolute programming.
4. What is a source program? An object program?
5. How many positions may be coded for an instruction (OP, A-operand, B-operand, d-modifier) using the SPS coding sheet? How many of these characters are actually stored in memory?
6. Which of the following are considered to be valid labels: PRT332, 332PRT, STUDENT, QUOTbX, QUOTX, 0080, TAX, CTRb1, A? Which of the following are valid absolute addresses: 0180, 180, P180, E75?
7. Since the source-program cards must be loaded in a certain sequence, how would you cope with this requirement if you dropped the program deck?
8. What is a pseudo-instruction?
9. In which program deck(s) would you find absolute addresses of labels?
10. If the address of ADDPAY is 1560, what is the address of ADDPAY+004? Of ADDPAY−004?
11. What does the instruction CTL 43 mean?
12. Concerning the symbolic program in Fig. 17-4, write the instruction that will cause the two working storage counters to be stored beginning at location 3000. Where would this instruction be inserted?
13. How should the program in Fig. 17-4 be changed in order to stop the computer once the object program has been loaded?
14. What condition must be met in order for the *select-stacker* instruction, line 150 in Fig. 17-4, to be executed?
15. What is the difference between the instructions SS 2 and SS PCHRTN 8?
16. Assuming an A-field of 000CB2 whose address is FIELDA and B-field of 00947 whose address is FIELDB, what will the contents of each field be after execution of ZA FIELDA FIELDB?
17. Upon execution of the instruction S 0076 COST, what will the contents of COST be if the A-field contains 31072 and B-field contains 04086?
18. What action occurs as a result of the instruction CC ENDPG 1? The instruction CC L?
19. Define the term *fall through*.
20. Write the instruction to define a label of your choice for the field *hourly pay*. The field is punched in card columns 31 to 36.
21. Write an instruction to reserve a constant whose image appears as $bb,bbb.bb. A word mark is to be set in the high-order position.
22. What is the purpose of the preprocess program? The condensing program?
23. Which assembly program produces the final object program?
24. In Fig. 17-8, the address of all instructions is shown as being the high-order position. Explain

why the address at line 240 is 1695 instead of 1693.

25. Explain why the computer cannot use the source deck to process data.

PROGRAM PROBLEM

Draw a flowchart and write a program to accomplish the following: crossfoot punched net pay to computed net pay (regular pay + overtime pay − withholding tax − FICA − insurance) and print or punch the difference, whichever is applicable. If the card contains an X-80, produce an output card; if not, print and double-space the information. Combine both the source cards and newly punched cards into the same stacker. Assume a 2K processor and object computer. Begin instruction assignment at location 400. You are to use labels in the print area.

Input columns	Output columns	Print	Description
1–15	1–15	1–15	Name
72–80	16–24	20–28	Social security number
60–66	25–31	52–58	Regular pay
35–39	32–36	65–69	Overtime pay
40–44	37–41	75–79	Withholding tax
45–49	42–46	85–89	FICA
50–53	47–50	95–98	Insurance
54–59	51–56	104–109	Net pay
	57–62	115–120	Difference

18
Symbolic programming (II)

The presentation in the last chapter gave us an opportunity to see one of the many programming languages in use. In this chapter we shall expand our knowledge of the symbolic programming system by studying other programming techniques and at the same time introduce new instructions. In addition, we shall study program modification using program switches.

CASE PROBLEM

This problem has relatively little processing, but is representative of larger programs. It gives an idea of a typical program used in business. The problem involves printing identifying information punched in master cards, accumulating regular and overtime hours punched in time-attendance cards, and computation of total hours, regular earnings, overtime earnings, and gross earnings. Earnings are computed by multiplying the accumulated regular and overtime hours by hourly wage, which is punched in each employee's master card. This report, called an employee earnings register, is group printed with columnar headings over each field of information at the top of the page. In addition, provision is made to stop printing a few lines before the end of each page, print the page number, and skip to the first printing line of the next page.

Information for this report is taken from two records, a master card and time-attendance card. All data are contained in the master card with the exception of hours worked, which are included in the time-attendance (detail)

cards. In general, the master card is read first, identifying data for that master are stored, then detail cards are read and hours are accumulated until a different employee number is recognized. Then computations are made and a single line of information is printed for that employee. Since we must ensure that the proper master is used with the corresponding details, employee number must be stored and compared against each detail for that group. Hourly rate must also be saved from each master in order to compute employee earnings. (See Table 18-1.)

After the master information is stored, all corresponding details are processed by separately accumulating the total regular and overtime hours worked. When a new employee master is recognized, regular pay is computed by multiplying the accumulated regular hours by hourly wage. Overtime is computed under the time-and-one-half policy by multiplying the accumulated overtime hours by hourly wage, increasing the amount by 50 percent, and rounding the total to the nearest penny. Salesmen employees are paid an hourly wage for regular and overtime hours, but are not paid time-and-one-half for overtime. Total hours are calculated by adding regular and overtime hours, and total pay by adding regular and overtime pay. All six totals are transferred to final counters in order to print overall totals at the end of the report.

Program switches and decisions are generously used in the program. A *program switch* is a technique whereby the result of a decision, made at one point in the program, is stored for use at one or more places later in the program. In still another case, it is often necessary to make a decision from one record and store the answer for later use with other records. Both uses are employed in this program. We shall talk more about program switches a little later.

Controls are illustrated at two points in the program. We previously said that each group of cards for every employee contains one master and one or more time-attendance cards. For this problem we assume one time-attendance card for each day in the two-week pay period. Consequently, the computer can be controlled to stop whenever the number of details exceeds 14 (one card for each day). Since a master is the first card of a group, this means that a change in employee number is recog-

Table 18-1 Card and Report Format for Employee Earnings Register

Master columns	Detail columns	Print position	Print image	Description
1–4	1–4	1–4		Employee number
5–23		7–25		Employee name
24–32		28–38	XXX XX XXXX	Social security number
33–36		41–45	XX.XX	Hourly wage
	63–64	48–50	XXX	Regular hours
		53–63	$ XX,XXX.XX	Regular pay
	65–66	66–68	XXX	Overtime hours
		71–81	$ XX,XXX.XX	Overtime pay
		84–86	XXX	Total hours
		89–99	$ XX,XXX.XX	Total pay
37–39		102–104	XXX	Department
75				Master card code M
		47–50	XXXX	Regular hours final total
		53–63	$ XXX,XXX.XX	Regular pay final total
		65–68	XXXX	Overtime hours final total
		71–81	$ XXX,XXX.XX	Overtime pay final total
		83–86	XXXX	Total hours final total
		89–99	$ XXX,XXX.XX	Total pay final total

nized by a comparison between the last detail of the previous group and the first card (which is a master) of the new group. Therefore, if the first card of a group is found not to be a master, the computer is instructed to stop. Otherwise, incorrect processing occurs.

EARNINGS REGISTER PROGRAM

Before attempting to understand this symbolic program, the student should become thoroughly familiar with the flowchart solution in Fig. 18-1. Every possible path that the computer can take should be traced and retraced. In fact, you can understand the problem even better by redrawing the flowchart and changing the comments in each block into your own wording. In so doing, keep in mind how you would have solved the problem, because this program is not necessarily the shortest or best solution. It has been designed with primary emphasis on illustrating programming techniques and demonstrating the use of new instructions, as well as old ones. If your total line entries are fewer than in the sample program, we can assume that yours is a more effective program.

In Fig. 18-2, the program begins by setting word marks in the read area and clearing the counters used in accumulating regular and overtime hours. Notice that the counters are cleared by subtracting the information from itself. As we proceed, you will see that other working storage areas are cleared by other techniques, such as *zero* and *add* instructions or simply by moving new information in, thus destroying the old. LOOP counter is set to 14 each time a new master is read so that we can control the number of time-attendance cards being processed.

Immediately after reading each card, we make a test to determine if the last card has been read. If not, the program branches around the instruction that sets the *last-card-program* switch. If the last-card indicator is ON,

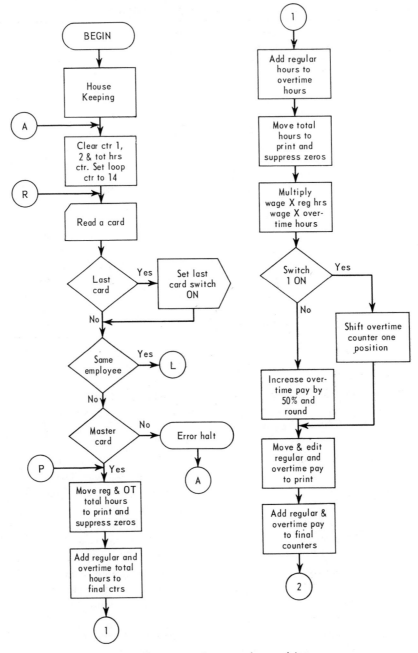

Fig. 18-1 Flowchart to produce an employee earnings register.

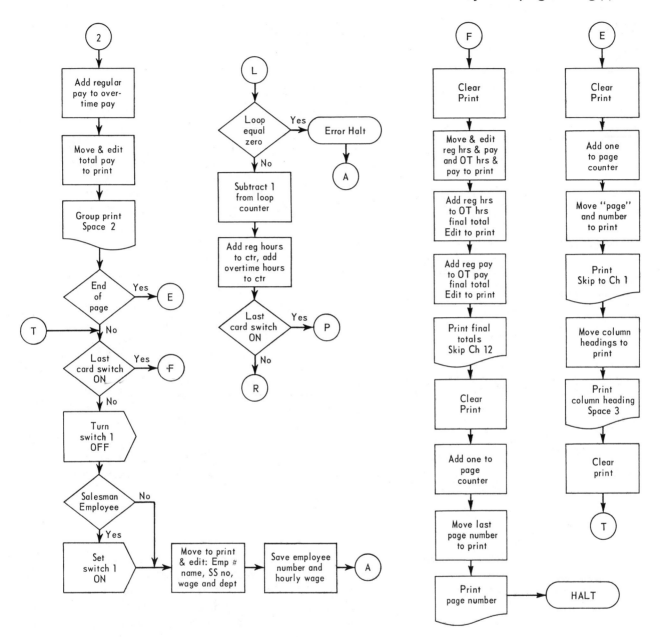

Fig. 18-1   Flowchart to produce an employee earnings register (continued).

IBM.

INTERNATIONAL BUSINESS MACHINES CORPORATION
IBM 1401 SYMBOLIC PROGRAMMING SYSTEM
CODING SHEET

FORM X24-1152-3
PRINTED IN U.S.A.

Program __EARNINGS REGISTER__

Programmed by __I. Q. STUDENT__

Date __JAN 1__

Page No. |0 , 1| of ___6___

Identification |E , A , R , N ,|

LINE	COUNT	LABEL	OPERATION	(A) OPERAND ADDRESS	±	CHAR. ADJ.	IND.	(B) OPERAND ADDRESS	±	CHAR. ADJ.	IND.	d	COMMENTS
0 1 0			C T L	2 2									
0 2 0		* T H I S	P R O G R A M	A C C U M U L A T E S	R E G U L A R H O U R S A N D									
0 3 0		* O V E R T I M E H O U R S ,	M U L T I P L I E S T H E M B Y R A T E , A D									
0 4 0		* J U S T A N D R O U N D O T	H R S , P R O D U C E S A N E A R N I N G S ,									
0 5 0		* R E G I S T E R W I T H C O L U M N A R H E A D I N G S A N D F I N A L									
0 6 0		* T O T A L S . P R O G R A M S W I T C H E S A R E I N T R O D U C E D A S									
0 7 0		* W E L L A S N E W I N S T R U C T I O N S .									
0 8 0		*											
0 9 0		B E G I N	S W	0 0 0 1				0 0 0 5					H O U S E K E E P I N G
1 0 0			S W	0 0 2 4				0 0 3 3					
1 1 0			S W	0 0 6 3				0 0 6 5					
1 2 0			S W	0 0 3 7				0 0 7 5					
1 3 0		R E P E A T	S	T O T H R S									R E S E T
1 4 0			S	C T R 1									C O U N T E R S
1 5 0			S	C T R 2									T O Z E R O
1 6 0			M C W	C 1 4				L O O P					S E T C T R T O 1 4
1 7 0		R E A D	R										R E A D A C A R D
1 8 0			B	S E T S W								A	T E S T L S T C D I N D
1 9 0			B	S E T S W	+ 0 0 7								B Y P A S S L C S W I T C H
2 0 0		S E T S W	M C W	O N E				L A S T S W					S E T L C S W I T C H O N
2 1 0			C	E M P N O				L S T E M P					C O M P A R E E M P L N O
2 2 0			B	M A S T E R								/	U N E Q U A L E M P L N O
2 3 0			C	L O O P				Z E R O					M A X I M U M 1 4 C A R D S
2 4 0			B	S T O P								S	T O O M A N Y C A R D S
2 5 0			B	O K									B Y P A S S H A L T
2 6 0		S T O P	H	R E P E A T									O P R I N T E R V E N E S

AREA—DEFINITION CHARACTER COUNT ⟶ 1   5   10   15   20   25   30   32

6402250MSP

Fig. 18-2   Program to produce employee earnings register in Fig. 18-1.

the program branches to set a *last-card* switch, which then can be tested elsewhere in the program.

A program switch can be set in at least two ways. One possibility is to store a 1 for "yes" decisions or a zero for "no" decisions. For example, we set the last card switch to zero initially. Then we move a 1 to the location of the switch when the last card is detected. Later in the program, the *last-card* switch can be tested and if ON (presence of a 1), the course of the program can be changed, suggesting the term program modification.

Switches are useful for various reasons. Sometimes we are able to repeat the instruction that makes a decision, but in other cases the condition or data on which the decision was originally made is no longer available. Or it may happen that the decision, which is used at two or more points in the program, involves several instructions. Therefore, computer time and memory are saved through the use of program switches if the decision is needed more than once. The second way of setting a switch will be discussed later in the program.

IBM

INTERNATIONAL BUSINESS MACHINES CORPORATION
IBM 1401 SYMBOLIC PROGRAMMING SYSTEM
CODING SHEET

FORM X24-1152-3
PRINTED IN U.S.A.

Program Earnings Register

Programmed by I. Q. STUDENT

Date JAN 1

Page No. |0,2| of ___6___

Identification E,A,R,N
                76   80

LINE	COUNT	LABEL	OPERATION	(A) ADDRESS	±	CHAR. ADJ.	IND	(B) ADDRESS	±	CHAR. ADJ.	IND	d	COMMENTS
0,1,0		O,K	S	O,N,E				L,O,O,P					DECREASE COUNTER
0,2,0			A	R,E,G,H,R				C,T,R,1					REG HOURS CTR
0,3,0			A	O,T,H,R				C,T,R,2					OVERTIME HR CTR
0,4,0			B	P,R,T,R,T,N				L,A,S,T,S,W				1	TEST LAST CARD
0,5,0			B	R,E,A,D									REPEAT LOOP
0,6,0		M,A,S,T,E,R	B	P,R,T,R,T,N				0,0,7,5				M	TEST FOR MASTER
0,7,0			H	R,E,P,E,A,T									OPR INTERVENES
0,8,0		P,R,T,R,T,N	M,C,S	C,T,R,1				0,2,5,0					PRT REG HR 48-50
0,9,0			M,C,S	C,T,R,2				0,2,6,8					PRT OT HRS 66-68
1,0,0			A	C,T,R,1				C,T,R,3					ROLL REG & OT HR
1,1,0			A	C,T,R,2				C,T,R,4					-INTO FINAL CTRS
1,2,0			A	C,T,R,1				T,O,T,H,R,S					ADD REG HRS & OT
1,3,0			A	C,T,R,2				T,O,T,H,R,S					-INTO TOT HR CTR
1,4,0			M,C,S	T,O,T,H,R,S				0,2,8,6					PRT TOT HR 84-86
1,5,0			Z,A	C,T,R,1				R,E,G,P,A,Y	-	0,0,5			REGHR MULTIPLIER
1,6,0			M	S,A,V,E,H,W				R,E,G,P,A,Y					MULT WAGE X HRS
1,7,0			Z,A	C,T,R,2				M,U,L,T,O,T	-	0,0,5			OT MULTIPLIER
1,8,0			M	S,A,V,E,H,W				M,U,L,T,O,T					MULT WAGE X OTHR
1,9,0		S,W,I,T,C,H	N,O,P	A,R,O,U,N,D									BRANCH BY OT RTN
2,0,0			Z,A	X,1,5				O,T,P,A,Y	-	0,0,9			1.5 MULTIPLIER
2,1,0			M	M,U,L,T,O,T				O,T,P,A,Y					MULT OTPAY X 1.5
2,2,0			S,W	X,1,5									ADJUST TO .5
2,3,0			A	X,1,5				O,T,P,A,Y					ROUND TO CENTS
2,4,0			C,W	X,1,5									RESTORE TO 1.5
2,5,0			B	A,R,O,U,N,D	+	0,1,4							BYPASS SHIFT
2,6,0		A,R,O,U,N,D	Z,A	X,1,0				O,T,P,A,Y	-	0,0,9			1.0 MULTIPLIER

AREA—DEFINITION CHARACTER COUNT ──▶ 1   5   10   15   20   25   30 32

6402250MSP

Fig. 18-2 Program to produce employee earnings register in Fig. 18-1 (continued).

Our next instruction is a decision to see if the employee number of the card just read is equal to the employee number in the last master card. We shall see later in the program that employee number is stored from the master. Since the program has just started, no employee number has been previously stored, and consequently, employee number in the first card (which should be a master) compares against a blank area of memory, resulting in an unequal-compare result. *Note:* At the time of assembly two clear-storage cards are created in the object program deck that clear the amount of memory specified in the CTL card.

In the last chapter we used a form of comparing with the *branch if character equal* instruction. However, this instruction compares only one position. Since the employee number is four positions in length, we need a new instruction that will handle more than one character. The following instruction compares the data in the A-field against the data in the B-field and sets an indicator that reflects if the comparison is unequal (B ≠ A), equal

IBM

INTERNATIONAL BUSINESS MACHINES CORPORATION
IBM 1401 SYMBOLIC PROGRAMMING SYSTEM
CODING SHEET

FORM X24-1152-3
PRINTED IN U.S.A.

Program Earnings Register

Programmed by I. Q. STUDENT

Date JAN 1

Page No. |0, 3| of 6

Identification E, A, R, N,

LINE	COUNT	LABEL	OPERATION	(A) OPERAND ADDRESS	±	CHAR. ADJ.	IND.	(B) OPERAND ADDRESS	±	CHAR. ADJ.	IND.	d	COMMENTS
0,1,0			M	MULTOT				OTPAY					SHIFT 1 POSITION
0,2,0			LC	AMASK				0,2,6,3					EDIT WORD TO PRT
0,3,0			MC	EREGPAY				0,2,6,3					PRT REGPAY 5,3-6,3
0,4,0			LC	AMASK				0,2,8,1					EDIT WORD TO PRT
0,5,0			MC	EOTPAY	-,0,0,1			0,2,8,1					PRT OT PAY 7,1-8,1
0,6,0			A	REGPAY				CTR,5					ROLL REG&OT PAY -
0,7,0			A	OTPAY	-,0,0,1			CTR,6					-INTO FINAL CTRS
0,8,0			A	OTPAY	-,0,0,1			REGAY					ADD REG & OT PAY
0,9,0			LC	AMASK				0,2,9,9					EDIT WORD TO PRT
1,0,0			MC	EREGPAY				0,2,9,9					PRT TOTPAY 89-9,9
1,1,0			W										GROUP PRINT
1,2,0			CC									K	SPACE 2
1,3,0			B	OVERF								@	TEST END OF PG
1,4,0	LC,TEST		B	FINAL				LASTSW				1	TEST LAST CD SW
1,5,0			MCW	NOPSW				SWITCH					TURN SW 1 OFF
1,6,0			C	DEPT				S,9,4					TEST IF SLSM CD
1,7,0			B	MOVE								/	JUMP IF UNEQUAL
1,8,0			MCW	MASTER				SWITCH					TURN SWITCH 1 ON
1,9,0	MOVE		MCS	EMPNO				0,2,0,4					PRT EMP NO 1-4
2,0,0			MCW	NAME				0,2,2,5					PRT NAME 7-2,5
2,1,0			LC	AEDITSS				0,2,3,8					MASK TO PRT
2,2,0			MC	ESSNO				0,2,3,8					PRT SS NO 2,8-3,8
2,3,0			LC	AEDITHW				0,2,4,5					MASK TO PRT
2,4,0			MC	EHRWAGE				0,2,4,5					PRT HRWAGE 4,1-4,5
2,5,0			MCS	DEPT				0,3,0,4					PRT DEPT 102-104
2,6,0			MCW	EMPNO				LSTEMP					STORE MSTR EMPNO

AREA-DEFINITION CHARACTER COUNT ⟶ 1   5   10   15   20   25   30 32

6402250MSP

Fig. 18-2 Program to produce employee earnings register in Fig. 18-1 (continued).

(B = A), high (B > A), or low (B < A). These indicators can be tested by the *branch if indicator* ON instruction.

Compare Instruction

Instruction format

Mnemonic	OP code	A-address	B-address	d-modifier
C	C	XXX	XXX	

Function The data in the A-field are compared to an equal number of characters in the B-field. The bit con-

figuration (BA8421) of each character in the two fields is compared. The comparison turns on an indicator that can be tested by a subsequent *branch if indicator* ON instruction. The indicator is reset by the next 7-character *compare* instruction. Note: The ascending sequence of characters is as follows: blanks, special characters, letters A to Z, and digits 0 to 9.

Word marks The first word mark encountered stops the operation. If the A-field is longer than the B-field, the extra A-field positions at the left of the B-field word mark are not compared. If the B-field is longer than the A-field, an unequal compare results.

IBM

INTERNATIONAL BUSINESS MACHINES CORPORATION
IBM 1401 SYMBOLIC PROGRAMMING SYSTEM
CODING SHEET
FORM X24-1152-3
PRINTED IN U.S.A.

Program _____ EARNINGS REGISTER _____   Page No. |0_4| of __6__

Programmed by ____ I. Q. STUDENT ____   Date __JAN 1__   Identification _E_,A_,R_,N_,_
                                                                                76   80

LINE	COUNT	LABEL	OPERATION	(A) OPERAND ADDRESS	±	CHAR. ADJ.	IND.	(B) OPERAND ADDRESS	±	CHAR. ADJ.	IND.	d	COMMENTS
0 1 0			M C W	H R W A G E				S A V E H W					S T O R E M S T R W A G E
0 2 0			B	R E P E A T									P R O C E S S N E W E M P L
0 3 0		O V E R F	C S	0 3 3 2									C L E A R -
0 4 0			C S										P R I N T A R E A
0 5 0			A	O N E				P G C T R					I N C R E A S E P G C N T
0 6 0			M C W	P A G E				0 2 7 0					M O V E P A G E T O P R T
0 7 0			M C S	P G C T R				0 2 7 4					P A G E N O T O P R T
0 8 0			W										P R I N T P A G E N O
0 9 0			C C									1	S K I P T O N E W P G
1 0 0			M C W	C O L H D G				0 3 0 5					C O L U M N H D G F O R M T
1 1 0			W										P R I N T C O L M H D G
1 2 0			C C									L	S P A C E 3
1 3 0			C S	0 3 0 5									C L E A R -
1 4 0			C S										P R I N T A R E A
1 5 0			B	L C T E S T									G O T O T E S T L C S W
1 6 0		F I N A L	C S	0 3 3 2									C L E A R
1 7 0			C S										P R I N T A R E A
1 8 0			M C S	C T R 3				0 2 5 0					R E G H R F I N A L T O T
1 9 0			L C A	M A S K				0 2 6 3					P R T & E D I T R E G
2 0 0			M C E	C T R 5				0 2 6 3					P A Y F I N A L T O T
2 1 0			M C S	C T R 4				0 2 6 8					O T H R S F I N A L T O T
2 2 0			L C A	M A S K				0 2 8 1					P R T & E D I T O V E R -
2 3 0			M C E	C T R 6				0 2 8 1					T I M E F I N A L T O T
2 4 0			A	C T R 3				C T R 4					A D D R E G & O T H R S
2 5 0			M C S	C T R 4				0 2 8 6					T O T A L H R S T O P R T
2 6 0			A	C T R 5				C T R 6					A D D R E G & O T P A Y

AREA-DEFINITION CHARACTER COUNT ⟶ 1   5   10   15   20   25   30 32

6402250MSP

Fig. 18-2   Program to produce employee earnings register in Fig. 18-1 (continued).

Timing $T = N(L_I + 1 + 2L_W)$ ms

Address registers after operation

I-add Reg	A-add Reg	B-add Reg
NSI	A-L_W	B-L_W

Since we are following the first card through the program, let us follow the unequal path and return to the equal routine later. On an unequal condition, the program branches to a routine labeled MASTER (line 60, page 2) that tests the card to see if it is a master. If the card does not have an M in column 75, the computer stops and the machine operator takes corrective action, either by locating the correct master card or by having the cards sequenced by the collator. If the card is a master, the computer branches to a routine called PRTRTN. Following the flowchart, we shall jump directly to the last-card—decision symbol (line 140, page 3 in Fig. 18-2). We have chosen this course because the areas skipped involve counters which are zero initially, and thus the computations are meaningless during the processing of the first card.

The *last-card* switch is OFF (contains a zero) for the first card, so the next sequential instruction is executed.

174 Data processing concepts

IBM

INTERNATIONAL BUSINESS MACHINES CORPORATION
IBM 1401 SYMBOLIC PROGRAMMING SYSTEM
CODING SHEET

FORM X24-1152-3
PRINTED IN U.S.A.

Program ___Earnings Register___

Programmed by ___I. Q. STUDENT___

Date ___JAN 1___

Page No. |0,5| of ___6___

Identification ___E,A,R,N___

LINE	COUNT	LABEL	OPERATION	(A) OPERAND ADDRESS	±	CHAR. ADJ.	IND.	(B) OPERAND ADDRESS	±	CHAR. ADJ.	IND.	d	COMMENTS
0,1,0			L,C	M,A,S,K				0,2,9,9					P,R,T, &, E,D,I,T, F,I,N,A,L
0,2,0			M,C	C,T,R,6				0,2,9,9					T,O,T,A,L, P,A,Y
0,3,0			W										P,R,T, F,I,N,A,L, T,O,T,A,L,S
0,4,0			C,C									@	S,K,I,P, T,O, C,H, 1,2
0,5,0			C,S	0,2,9,9									C,L,E,A,R, P,R,I,N,T
0,6,0			A,	O,N,E				P,G,C,T,R					I,N,C,R,E,A,S,E, P,G, C,N,T
0,7,0			M,C,W	P,A,G,E				0,2,1,1					M,O,V,E, P,A,G,E, T,O, P,R,T
0,8,0			M,C,S	P,G,C,T,R				0,2,1,5					P,A,G,E, N,O, T,O, P,R,T
0,9,0			W										P,R,T, P,A,G,E, N,O
1,0,0		H,A,L,T	H,	H,A,L,T									
1,1,0			H,										
1,2,0	0,1	L,A,S,T,S,W	D,C,W	0,0,8,1		0							L,A,S,T, C,A,R,D, S,W,I,T,C,H
1,3,0	0,2	Z,E,R,O	D,C,W	*		0,0							C,O,N,S,T,A,N,T
1,4,0	0,1	O,N,E	D,C,W	*		1							C,O,N,S,T,A,N,T
1,5,0	0,3	S,9,4	D,C,W	*	S,9,4								S,L,S,M, ,D,E,P,T, ,C,O,D,E
1,6,0	0,4	L,S,T,E,M,P	D,C,W	*	b,b,b,b								S,T,O,R,E,D, E,M,P,L, N,O
1,7,0	0,4	S,A,V,E,H,W	D,C,W	*	b,b,b,b								S,T,O,R,E,D, M,S,T,R, W,A,G,E
1,8,0	0,2	X,1,0	D,C,W	*	1,0								M,U,L,T, B,Y, 1,.,0
1,9,0	0,2	X,1,5	D,C,W	*	1,5								M,U,L,T, B,Y, 1,.,5
2,0,0	0,3	C,T,R,1	D,C,W	*	0,0,0								R,E,G, H,O,U,R,S, C,T,R
2,1,0	0,3	C,T,R,2	D,C,W	*	0,0,0								O,V,E,R,T,I,M,E, H,R,S, C,T,R
2,2,0	0,3	T,O,T,H,R,S	D,C,W	*	0,0,0								T,O,T, R,E,G, &, O,T, H,R,S
2,3,0	0,4	C,T,R,3	D,C,W	*	0,0,0,0								R,E,G, H,R, F,I,N,A,L, T,O,T
2,4,0	0,4	C,T,R,4	D,C,W	*	0,0,0,0								O,T, H,R,S, F,I,N,A,L, T,O,T
2,5,0	0,8	R,E,G,P,A,Y	D,C,W	*	0,0,0,0	0,0,0,0							R,E,G, P,A,Y, C,T,R
2,6,0	1,1	O,T,P,A,Y	D,C,W	*	0,0,0,0	0,0,0,0,0,0,0							O,V,E,R,T,I,M,E, P,A,Y, C,T,R

AREA–DEFINITION CHARACTER COUNT ⟶ 1   5   10   15   20   25   30 32

6402250MSP

Fig. 18-2   Program to produce employee earnings register in Fig. 18-1 (continued).

This is an instruction that turns switch 1 OFF, regardless of its setting. Although we have not covered the use of this switch yet, it is through this switch that overtime is processed or not processed by the time-and-one-half calculation routine. The purpose of switch 1 is to identify department S94 employees, who are all salesmen. In another place in the program overtime is computed without special computation if switch 1 is ON. Otherwise, the switch is OFF and overtime is computed under the time-and-one-half routine.

The *no-operation* instruction causes no action to take place anywhere in the computer. Since this instruction can be made active or inactive, it serves as a switch by its two-state characteristic. That is, it can in effect be turned OFF or ON, thus having the capability of representing a yes or no decision. Let us look at the *no-operation* instruction.

No-Operation Instruction

Instruction format

Mnemonic	OP code	A-address	B-address	d-modifier
NOP	N	XXX	XXX	X

IBM

INTERNATIONAL BUSINESS MACHINES CORPORATION
IBM 1401 SYMBOLIC PROGRAMMING SYSTEM
CODING SHEET
FORM X24-1152-3
PRINTED IN U.S.A.

Program   Earnings Register

Programmed by   I. Q. STUDENT

Date   JAN 1

Page No. |0,6| of   6

Identification E,A,R,N
                76   80

LINE	COUNT	LABEL	OPERATION	(A) OPERAND ADDRESS	±	CHAR. ADJ.	IND.	(B) OPERAND ADDRESS	±	CHAR. ADJ.	IND.	d	COMMENTS
010	0 8	MULTOT	DCW	*		0,0,0 0 0,0,0,0							STRAIGHT OT CTR
020	0 8	CTR5	DCW	*		0,0,0 0 0,0,0,0							REGPAY FINAL CTR
030	0 8	CTR6	DCW	*		0,0,0 0 0,0,0,0							OT PAY FINAL CTR
040	1 1	MASK	DCW	*		$ b b b ,,b b 0 . b b							MONEY EDIT WORD
050	0 1	NOPSW	DCW	*		N							OP CODE FOR SW
060	0 2	LOOP	DCW	*		0,0							LOOP COUNTER
070	1 1	EDITSS	DCW	*		b b b & b b & b b b b							SOC SEC EDIT WD
080	0 5	EDITHW	DCW	*		b b . b b							HR WAGE EDIT WD
090	0 2	C14	DCW	*		1 4							MAX CDS CONSTANT
100	1 1	PAGE	DCW	*		PAGE NUMBER							CONSTANT
110	0 2	PGCTR	DCW	*		0 0							PAGE COUNTER
120	3 2		DCW	*		EMP #		NAME				E	SOC S
130	3 2		DC	*		EC NO		WAGE HRS		REGULAR PAY			
140	3 2		DC	*		HRS		OVERTIME PAY HRS		TOTAL			
150	0 9	COLHDG	DC	*		PAY		DEPT					
160		EMPNO	DS	0,0,0,4									EMPL NUMBER 1-4
170		NAME	DS	0,0,2,3									EMPL NAME 5-23
180		SSNO	DS	0,0,3,2									SOC SEC NO 24-32
190		HRWAGE	DS	0,0,3,6									HR WAGE 33-36
200		REGHR	DS	0,0,6,4									REG HRS 63-64
210		OTHR	DS	0,0,6,6									OVERTIM HR 65-66
220		DEPT	DS	0,0,3,9									DEPARTMENT 37-39
230			END	BEGIN									

AREA—DEFINITION CHARACTER COUNT → 1   5   10   15   20   25   30 32

6402250MSP

Fig. 18-2 Program to produce employee earnings register in Fig. 18-1 (continued).

Function   This code performs no operation. It can be substituted for the operation code of any instruction to make that instruction ineffective. It is commonly used in program modification to cause the machine to skip over specific instructions. The instruction can be from one to eight characters in length. For example, the OP Code may be made a 1 (read a card, which does not require other parts of the instruction) under certain conditions.

Word marks   The program operation resumes at the next operation code identified by a word mark.

Timing $T = N(L_I + 1)$ ms

Address registers after operation

I-add Reg	A-add Reg	B-add Reg
NSI	A_p	B_p

The *no-operation* instruction can be used in numerous ways. If we desire to bypass a particular instruction, such as an *add* instruction, when a certain condition arises, we can simply change the *add* instruction to a *no-operation* instruction. This is done by moving the NOP code of N to the location of the OP code for the *add* instruction. Subsequently, it is actually necessary to set the OP code back to its original state. Therefore, the *add* instruction is executed when the program is repeated, unless a decision again calls for the instruction to be bypassed. Since only the OP code determines what action the computer takes, any other parts of the instruction are ineffective when the OP code is changed to N.

If there are several instructions to be bypassed, as is the case of our sample program, it is best to branch around them. Returning to the next instruction (line 150 page 3) in the program, the switch is turned OFF by moving the NOP code of N to the location of the switch. This is necessary because the switch may have been turned ON from the previous compare. Consequently, if the switch were left ON and the master being compared is a nonsalesman, incorrect processing of the overtime computation would occur. Next, department is compared with a constant S94 (salesman department) and if the indicator tested by the *branch-if-indicator* ON instruction is unequal, the program branches around the instruction that sets the switch. Otherwise, the program falls through to the next instruction, which turns the switch ON. This is done by replacing the OP code at the switch with a B (branch) OP code.

The next seven instructions move employee number, name, social security number, hourly wage, and department to the print area. Three new instructions, *move characters and suppress zeros, load characters to a word mark,* and *move characters and edit,* are introduced to accomplish the desired printing.

The first field, *employee number,* is to have leading or insignificant zeros omitted in the printing. For example, employee number 0050 should print as 50. This movement of data and suppression of insignificant zeros is accomplished by the following instruction.

Move Characters and Suppress Zeros Instruction

Instruction format

Mnemonic	OP code	A-address	B-address	d-modifier
MCS	<u>Z</u>	XXX	XXX	

Function The data in the A-field are moved to the B-field. After the move, high-order zeros and commas are replaced by blanks in the B-field. The sign is removed from the units position of the data field.

Word marks The A-field word mark stops transmission of data. B-field word marks, encountered during the move operation, are erased.

Timing $T = N(L_I + 1 + 3L_A)$ ms

Address registers after operation

I-add Reg	A-add Reg	B-add Reg
NSI	A-L_A	B + 1

Employee name is moved with a familiar *move character to a or b word mark* instruction. However, the movement of social security number requires a new instruction. Although the number is punched in the card as, for instance, 239448143, it is printed on the report as 239 44 8143, as a matter of ease of reading. This form of printing is called *editing,* which has two different meanings. Previously, we defined one meaning as checking source data for validity and accuracy before they are used for further processing. In the other meaning, editing refers to the rearrangement of input information or results of processing by inserting punctuation. This means providing spaces between numbers for ease of reading, or inserting decimal points, commas, and dollar signs to make the number more meaningful.

In editing, two fields are needed, the *data word* and *edit word.* The first step is to load an edit word, also called a *mask,* into the print storage area. The mask in this case is bbb&bb&bbbb and is set up under the label EDITSS by a *DCW* statement. In general, the edit word, or mask, specifies how the data word is edited. It provides the location of punctuation, indicates where zero suppression occurs, if any, and where the characters of actual data go. Loading the mask into the print area is accomplished by the *load characters to a word mark* instruction. This instruction is somewhat similar to other *move* instructions, but with a significant difference in handling of the word mark. The A-field need only have a word mark, B-field word marks are erased and the A-field word mark is transferred to the corresponding position in the B-field. Thus, the need to set a word mark in the print area is eliminated.

Load Characters to a Word Mark Instruction

Instruction format

Mnemonic	OP code	A-address	B-address	d-modifier
LCA	L	XXX	XXX	

Function   This instruction is commonly used to load data into designated printer or punch output areas of storage, and also to transfer data or instructions from a designated read-in area to another storage area. The data and word mark from the A-field are transferred to the B-field, and all other word marks in the B-field are cleared.

Word marks   The A-field must have a defining word mark, because the A-field word mark stops the operation. If the B-field is larger than the A-field, the B-field word mark is not clear.

Timing $T = N(L_I + 1 + 2L_A)$ ms

Address registers after operation

I-add Reg	A-add Reg	B-add Reg
NSI	A-L_A	B-L_A

After the edit word is loaded into the specified printer output area, which is where the edited information eventually goes, the second step in editing is performed. When the *move characters and edit* instructions are executed, the data from the A-field are inserted into blank positions of the mask. The examples in Table 18-2 illustrate what this instruction can do.

Move Characters and Edit Instruction

Instruction format

Mnemonic	OP code	A-address	B-address	d-modifier
MCE	E	XXX	XXX	

Table 18-2   Editing Operations

A-field	B-field before	B-field after
239448143	bbb&bb&bbbb	239 44 8143
00230	$bbb.bb	$002.30
00230	$bb0.bb	$bb2.30
00000	$bb0.bb	$bbb.00
0006012	$bb,bb0.bb	$bbbb60.12
0507398	$bb,bb0.bb	$b5,073.98
00247̄	$bb0.bb&CR	$bb2.47bCR
10247⁺	$&bb0.bb&CR	$b102.47bbb
00247̄	$bb0.bb&—	$bb2.47b—

Function   The *data* field (A-field) is modified by the contents of the *edit-control* field (B-field) and the result stored in the B-field. The *data* field and the *edit-control* field are read from storage character-by-character, under control of the word marks and the editing rules. Any sign in the units position of the *data* field is removed during the operation.

Editing Rules

Rule 1   All numeric, alphabetic, and special characters can be used in the control word. However, some of these characters have special meanings:

Control character		Function
b	**Blank**	This is replaced with the character from the corresponding position of the A-field.
0	**Zero**	This is used for zero suppression and is replaced with a corresponding character from the A-field. The rightmost zero in the control word indicates the rightmost limit of zero suppression.
.	**Decimal**	This remains in the edited field in the position where written. It is removed during a zero-suppress operation if it is to the left of the high-order–significant digit.
,	**Comma**	This remains in the edited field in the position where written. It is removed during a

Control character	Function
	zero-suppress operation if it is to the left of the high-order–significant digit.
CR	**Credit** This is undisturbed if the data is negative (B-bit in units position). It is blanked out if the data sign is positive (other than B-bit in units position). It can be used in body of control word without being subject to sign control.
—	**Minus** This is the same as CR.
&	**Ampersand** This causes a space in the edited field. It can be used in multiples.
*	**Asterisk** This can be used in singular or in multiples, usually to indicate class of total.
$	**Dollar sign** This is undisturbed in the position where it is written.

Rule 2   A word mark in the high-order position of the B-field controls the operation.

Rule 3   When the A-field word mark is sensed, the remaining commas in the control field are set to blanks.

Rule 4   The body of the control word is that portion beginning with the rightmost blank or zero and continuing to the left to the control character that governs the transfer of the last position of the *data* field. The remaining portion of the *control* field is the status portion.

Rule 5   If the data field is positive, and if the CR or — symbols are located in the status portion of the control word, they are blanked out.

Rule 6   The data field can contain fewer, but must not contain more, positions than the number of blanks and zeros in the body of the control word.

Rule 7   Zero suppression is used if unwanted zeros to the left of significant digits in a data field are to be deleted.

Zero-suppression operation   Zero suppression is the deletion of unwanted zeros at the left of significant digits in an output field. A zero is placed (in the body of the control edit word) in the rightmost limit of zero suppression.

All identifying information (employee number, name, social security number, and department) has been moved to the print area and edited as necessary. The next two instructions (line 260, page 3) store employee number and hourly wage from the master into separate working storage areas labeled LSTEMP and SAVEHW. Earlier in the program, we saw that employee number in the master is compared with succeeding details to ensure processing against the corresponding master. The employee-number comparison tells the machine when to take a control break, that is, finish processing the current employee group before continuing processing of the new group. The saved hourly wage is stored until all hours worked have been accumulated from the details and is then used as a calculation factor. Pertinent information from the master has been moved to the print area and working storage. The program branches to REPEAT (line 130, page 1) and begins processing the corresponding details.

The counters that contain the accumulated hours for the previous employee are cleared. The counter used to count the details for the corresponding new master is reset to 14. Of course, it is needless to execute these instructions for the first master card since the counters are already initialized. However, this is necessary due to the nature of the program and henceforth the counters will have been used, thus creating a need for resetting them.

The first detail card is read and the last-card indicator is assumed OFF, so that the program falls through to a *branch-unconditional* instruction. This instruction causes the program to branch to symbolic location SETSW + 007, thus bypassing the setting of the *last-card* switch. Employee number of this detail is compared with employee number stored previously from the master and is found equal. This nullifies the next *branch* instruction, and the program falls through to another *compare* instruction.

Here we perform one of the controls previously described. Recall that we set the loop counter to 14 before reading a new-employee card. The compare is made and we next test the indicator set as a result of the compare. If equal, this means the counter is zero; thus the loop has been executed 14 times and the computer branches to a *halt* instruction. The machine operator corrects the cards, places all details for that group back into the read hopper, and presses the start button, which causes the program to branch to the beginning process. Since this is the first detail, the counter is not zero, and the program branches around the *halt* instruction.

The next instruction subtracts one from the loop counter each time the routine is executed. If the routine that handles the detail cards is performed 14 times, the loop counter contains zero and the computer stops as described above when the counter is tested for zero for the fifteenth card. Regular and overtime hours are accumulated into separate counters and the program branches to read another card if the *last-card* switch is OFF. This program loop continues until a new employee card is recognized or until the last card is processed.

The last-card decision is performed by a *branch if character equal* instruction. Earlier in the program, a 1 is moved to the location called LASTSW when the last-card indicator is recognized. Otherwise, the switch retains the original zero set up with a *DCW* statement when the program is loaded. If the *last-card* switch is found to be ON, the program must branch to a routine that will compute and print the totals for the last employee and accomplish final processing for the overall totals. If the switch is OFF, a branch is taken to read another card and the routine is repeated.

Referring to the flowchart in Fig. 18-1, we see that the program branches to connector P when the *last-card* switch is ON. This happens to be the same point of processing whenever a new employee is recognized. Since we have followed the program through for a master and detail record, let us discuss the processing that takes place in order to compute the hours and money fields and print the results.

Continuing with the program at line 40, page 2, the computer branches to a routine called PRTRTN (line 80, page 2) when the *last-card* switch is ON. Counter 1 (accumulated regular hours) and counter 2 (accumulated overtime hours) are moved to the print-storage area. The total hours for both counters are moved to the final counters 3 and 4. Regular and overtime hours are added into another counter, labeled TOTHRS, and are moved to the print-storage area.

At this point, we are ready to compute the regular pay

and overtime pay. This is accomplished by multiplying hours worked by the hourly wage saved from the master card. Two instructions are necessary for a multiplication operation. The first step is to place the multiplier in the high-order positions of the field where the product is developed. Then the multiplicand is repetitively added to itself in the *product* field the number of times specified by the multiplier.

Since counter 1 contains the accumulated regular hours worked (multiplier), we place the multiplier in the high-order position of a counter labeled REGPAY. Referring to the defining statements at the end of the program, we see that REGPAY counter is eight positions and that CTR1 counter is three positions. Thus, we place the multiplier in the high-order positions of the *product* field by a *zero-and-add* instruction with character adjustment of minus 005. In other words, if the product counter is located at positions 800 to 807, the multiplier will be placed in positions 800 to 802. The multiplier in these positions is destroyed as the product is developed. Next, we multiply the hourly wage, which was stored from the master in an area labeled SAVEHW, by the regular hours.

Multiply Instruction

Instruction format

Mnemonic	OP code	A-address	B-address	d-modifier
M	@	XXX	XXX	

Function   The multiplicand (data located in the A-field) is repetitively added to itself in the B-field. The B-field contains the multiplier in the high-order positions, and enough additional positions (low order) to allow for the development of the product. At the end of the multiply operation, the units position of the product is located at the B-address. The multiplier is destroyed in the B-field as the product is developed. Therefore, if the multiplier is needed for subsequent operations, it must be retained in another storage area.

Rule 1   The product is developed in the B-field. The length of the B-field is determined by adding 1 to the sum of the number of digits in the multiplicand and multiplier fields. For example:

```
XXXX        4-digit multiplicand
 XXX        3-digit multiplier
  +1
            8 positions must be allowed
            in the B-field.
```

Rule 2   A- and B-bits need not be present in the units positions of the *multiplier* and *multiplicand* fields. The absence of zone bits in these positions indicates a positive sign. At the completion of the multiply operation the B-field will have zone bits in the units position of the product only. The multiply operation uses algebraic sign control (Fig. 18-3).

Rule 3   Zone bits that appear in the *multiplicand* field are undisturbed by the multiply operation. Zone bits in the units position of the multiplicand are interpreted for sign control.

Rule 4   The first addition within the multiply operation inserts *zeros* in the *product* field from the storage location specified by the B-address up to the units position of the multiplier. The A-address register and the B-address register indicate positions within the A- and B-fields on which operations are currently being performed.

Timing

$T = 0.0115 (L_I + 3 + 2L_C + 5I_C L_M + 7L_M)$ ms
where L_C = length of multiplicand field
      L_M = length of multiplier field

Word marks   A word mark must be associated with the high-order positions of the multiplier and multiplicand fields.

Multiplier sign	+	+	−	−
Multiplicand sign	+	−	+	−
Sign of product	+	−	−	+

Fig. 18-3 Algebraic sign control for multiplication.

Address registers after operation

I-add Reg	A-add Reg	B-add Reg
NSI	A minus the length of the multiplicand	B minus the length of the *product* field

Overtime pay is similarly computed by multiplying overtime hours times hourly wage. Recall that earlier we computed overtime pay for nonsalesmen by a time-and-a-half multiplication routine. At the time each master is processed, a decision is made to determine if the employee is a salesman. If so, the switch at line 190, page 2 is changed to a *branch-unconditional* instruction which causes the program to branch around the time-and-a-half computation routine. Otherwise, the switch is in effect OFF as a result of the *NOP* instruction. In this case, the instruction is ignored and the next sequential instruction is executed.

To increase the overtime pay by 50 percent, we multiply the field by 1.5 percent. This is accomplished by moving a multiplier factor of 15 into the product counter labeled OTPAY. Again the multiplier is stored in the high-order positions of the counter with character adjustment. Decimal points are kept track of by the programmer, and thus are considered by his logic in the program. The multiplication process is illustrated in Fig. 18-4.

After the computed straight overtime is multiplied by 1.5 percent, the product is rounded to the nearest penny. This is done by setting a word mark at the units position of the 1.5-adjustment factor, adding the units position of 5 to the overtime pay, and clearing the word mark for the next program execution.

Referring to Fig. 18-4, we see that the mills position must be dropped. This is done with character adjustment at the time the overtime pay is added into the final-pay counters and moved to the print area. Consequently, the straight overtime pay for salesmen must be shifted one position to the left to be compatible with the adjusted overtime pay for nonsalesmen. Therefore, the last instruction in the overtime routine for nonsalesmen branches around this shifting operation.

Now let us see what happens when switch 1 is turned ON to bypass the processing of overtime pay as previously described. If the indicator (set as a comparing result of

Regular pay		Overtime pay		Total pay	
$2.28	Hourly wage	$2.28	Hourly wage	$182.40	Regular pay
×80	Regular hours	×9	Overtime hours	30.78	Overtime pay
$182.40	Regular pay	$20.52	Straight overtime pay	$213.18	Total pay
		×1.5	Adjustment factor		
		1 0 2 6 0			
		2 0 5 2			
		3 0 . 7 8 0			
		5	Round		
		3 0 . 7 8 5	Time-and-a-half overtime pay		
			dropped		

Fig. 18-4   Computation of regular pay, overtime pay, and total pay.

department) is found equal by the *branch if indicator* ON instruction at line 170, page 3, the branch is not taken. Instead, the program falls through and sets the switch by moving an OP code of B (branch) to the location of the switch. Thus, the program branches around the time-and-a-half computation routine and begins the shifting operation. This operation is performed by multiplying the overtime hours by 1.0 percent in the same manner as we multiplied previously.

The next several instructions move and edit the regular and overtime pay to the print area. The *amount* fields are moved through the mask causing commas, decimals, and dollar signs to be inserted as necessary. For example, if the regular pay is computed as 18240, this amount moves through the mask of $bbb,bb0.bb and is set up in the print area as $bbbb182.40. Unwanted zeros and commas to the left of significant digits are set as blanks.

We need now to add the regular and overtime pay to final counters 5 and 6, and compute the total pay by adding counter labeled OTPAY into counter labeled REGPAY. When this operation is completed, total pay is standing in the regular pay counter and is then moved and edited into the print-storage area. Next, we print the entire line, including identifying information from the master and all computed *hours* and *pay* fields. The paper is advanced two spaces and a test is made to determine if the last printing line of the page has been reached.

Control of the vertical spacing of lines on a printed report is controlled by a combination of programmed signals

to the printer carriage and a control tape in the printer. Holes are punched in the tape in proper positions to indicate where carriage spacing is to start or stop. A control tape has 12 columns or channels in which these holes are punched. We shall be concerned with two, channel 1 and channel 12. Detection of the hole in channel 12 occurs when the last line is printed at the bottom of the page and turns ON an indicator which can be tested by the *branch-if-indicator* ON instruction. Channel 1 is used to stop the paper movement at the top of a new page when skipping occurs using the *control-carriage* instruction. At line 130, page 3, the program branches to a routine called OVERF if channel 12 was sensed during the previous *write-a-line* Instruction.

The first instruction in the overflow routine (line 30, page 4) is to clear the print-storage area. A 1 is added to the page counter and the words "page number" are moved to the print area. Contents of the page counter are then moved adjacent to the words "page number" and insignificant zeros are suppressed. The page constant and number are written and the paper overflows to channel 1, which is the first printing line of the new page.

A common practice is to print column headings over each field of information at the top of each page. Since there are 11 fields, it would require 11 instructions to move the column-heading constants separately to the print area. However, we shall use another method that requires only one *move* instruction.

We have set up a constant area in storage with column

identification corresponding to the print positions of Table 18-1. For example, EMP# is set up to print in positions 1 to 4, NAME in positions 13 to 16, SOC SEC NO in positions 28 to 37, and so on. The units position of the column heading constant is labeled COLHDG and the high-order position contains a word mark. Notice that the *define-constant* statements (lines 120 to 150, page 6) are carefully set up with *DC* and *DCW* statements that require only one *move* instruction.

The column-identification line is moved to the print area (line 100, page 4) and printed. Three spaces are taken, storage positions used are cleared, and the computer branches to the point in the program where the interruption occurred, which is symbolic location LCTEST.

At line 140, page 3, a test is made to see if the *last-card* switch is ON. We have already followed the path of the program if the *last-card* switch is OFF, so let us assume that the switch is ON and branch to a routine labeled FINAL. Reviewing connector F of the flowchart (Fig. 18-1), we see that this is the final processing and involves computation and printing of the final totals.

The print area is cleared (line 160, page 4) and final counter 3 (regular hours), counter 5 (regular pay), counter 4 (overtime hours), and counter 6 (overtime pay) are moved to the print-storage area. *Hours* fields are zero-suppressed and money amount totals are edited. Next, counter 3 is added to counter 4 giving the final total hours, which is moved to the print area. Likewise, counter 5 is added to counter 6 to obtain the total earnings. After the total earnings are edited to the print area, all totals are printed. The paper is skipped to the bottom of the page where the last page number is printed on the left margin. Since no further processing is necessary, the computer is instructed to halt.

We have followed the program through in its entirety. You are encouraged to trace the program through again and again, following any path you desire. In fact, it is recommended to vary the route each time. It is not necessary to refer to the narrative of the program we have just discussed. Using only the flowchart (Fig. 18-1) and the coded program (Fig. 18-2) and aided by referencing the instructions, one can gain an excellent knowledge of basic programming.

QUESTIONS

1. In Fig. 18-2 if the *last-card* switch were set ON (change constant at LASTSW to 1) initially, what would the computer do?

2. Can the hourly wage be edited without the mask specifically set up at line 80, page 6 in Fig. 18-2? If so, how?

3. Can we tell from Fig. 18-1 if employee number is compared against only the last master or every preceding detail card? How?

4. At what core location will the processor begin loading the program?

5. If the column heading lines at page 6, lines 120 to 150 in Fig. 18-2 are all coded *DCW*, how many *move* instructions are necessary to transfer the entire constant to the print area? If this is the case, what else is required?

6. Will the column heading print at the top of the first page on the employee earnings register? If your answer is yes, explain how. If your answer is no, how can we accomplish this?

7. Write the instruction(s) that will sequence-check the cards by employee number (minor) and department code (major) in Fig. 18-2. The computer is to be stopped on an out-of-sequence condition.

8. Concerning the last question, where are these instructions inserted?

9. What is the technique called that gives us the ability to make a decision at one point in the program and control functions at a later point through storage of the decision?

10. How will the printed result appear if a data field of TOTAL is moved through the mask b&b&b&b&b?

11. What is the technique for repeated execution of program segments called?

12. When is the indicator, set by a *compare* instruction, reset?

13. It is essential to this program that a master be the first card of each employee group. What would happen if the first card were a detail?

14. Concerning the preceding question, what would happen if two masters in a row were processed?

15. How will the instruction MCS AMOUNT 0218 print the data if the contents of AMOUNT contain 040E?

16. What are the characters called in the control-edit word that are replaced by data from the A-field? What is the remaining portion of the edit word called?

17. What is the purpose of the loop counter in the program (Fig. 18-2)?

18. How does the computer keep account of decimal points?

19. In Fig. 18-1 if the end-of-page decision and connector-T symbols are moved to the end of the routine (after save-employee-number-and-hourly-wage symbol), what erroneous effects, if any, will result?

20. Before a *multiply* instruction is executed, where must the multiplier be located?

21. Is it necessary for the programmer to clear the *product* field (B-address) in a multiply operation?

22. At line 170, page 3, can the setting of the switch be accomplished by testing for an equal indicator? If so, write the new instruction(s).

23. Assuming a *data* field of 007931R and a mask of TOTAL&$bb,bbb.bb&CR&**, what will the *printed-output* field look like?

PROBLEM

Draw a program flowchart and write a symbolic program from the diagram to accomplish the following:

a. Write a line for each employee.

Columns	Print positions	Data
1–15	1–15	Employee name
44–52	20–30	Social security number
24–29	35–42	Date of employment
51–57	47–56	Year-to-date earnings
	61–70	Stock bonus
80		Employment status

b. If date of employment is after December 31, 1960 (punched in card as 601231), compute stock bonus as 5 percent of year-to-date earnings; if before January 1, 1961, compute as 15 percent. Drop figures other than dollars and cents.

c. Separate the cards by employment status (P for permanent, T for temporary). If code is in error, select card to middle stacker.

d. Edit all fields as appropriate.

e. Provide for normal overflow.

f. At the end of the report, print the number of employees receiving the 5 percent stock bonus in positions 95 to 97 and the total amount in positions 100 to 106. On the next line in the same positions show the same information for employees receiving the 15 percent stock bonus.

g. Round final totals to the nearest hundred dollars and drop all positions less than $100.00. Mask as X,XXX.X and show the 5 percent total with one asterisk and the 15 percent total with two asterisks.

19

Program timing and magnetic tape operations

It is sometimes necessary to estimate the time that a program will require. The reason may be that the programmer has a choice between two or more ways of coding a program segment or routine. In this case he is interested in using instructions that will result in a minimum amount of processing time. Or the reason may be to properly schedule the work of the computer.

In the first situation an estimate can be reasonably accurate because of the limited number of instructions relative to the estimate. The second situation is more difficult since all of the instructions in the program must be considered. Adding to the complexity is the fact that the program has alternate paths, determined by a decision made by the computer or a decision based on the data. Also, processing may be fully overlapped with input-output operations while others are only partially overlapped. Program timing is essentially an estimate.

Numerous factors are involved in estimating time requirements. Some are volume of records to process, speed of the input-output components, time required to execute each instruction, and minor factors such as whether spacing is single or double. As an example, the printing rate is 600 lines per minute when single spacing, but drops to 572 lines per minute when double spacing. So we shall keep our discussion simple instead of entering into a complete and detailed explanation of all these considerations.

TIMING FORMULA

The internal processing speed of the 1401 EDPS is 11.5 μs or 0.0115 ms. *Processing speed* is described in

terms of the time required for one complete core-storage cycle. The processing time required for any internal processing instruction is always a multiple of 0.0115 ms. You will recall that every instruction we have covered had a formula to be used in calculating the timing for that instruction. The timing formulas are given in terms of certain characteristics of the instruction under consideration and of the data fields being operated on. The key to abbreviations used in those formulas is shown in Table 19-1.

Let us consider how these formulas are applied with a few examples. The equation for the *set-word-mark* instruction is $T = N(L_I + 3)$ ms. Looking at Table 19-1, we see that N stands for 0.0115 ms and that L_I stands for length of instruction. Referring to the instruction in Chap. 16, we see that the length of the instruction can be 4 or 7 positions, depending on whether one or two

Table 19-1 Timing-formula Codes

Abbreviation	Meaning
L_A	Length of the A-field
L_B	Length of the B-field
L_C	Length of multiplicand field
L	Length of argument field
L_I	Length of instruction
L_M	Length of multiplier field
L_Q	Length of quotient field
L_R	Length of divisor field
L_S	Length of sector
L_S	Number of significant digits in divisor (exclude high-order zeros and blanks)
L_W	Length of A- or B-field, whichever is shorter
L_X	Number of characters to be cleared
L_Y	Number of characters back to rightmost zero in *control* field
L_Z	Number of zeros inserted in a field
I/O	Timing for input or output cycle
F_m	Forms movement times. Allow 20 ms for first space, plus 5 ms for each additional space
N	System-processing cycle time (0.0115 ms)
N_S	Number of sectors
S_S	Size of sectors
T_M	Tape-movement times
Σ	Number of fields included in an operation

word marks are set. Thus, the instruction ‚ XXX would have a formula of $T = 0.0115 (4 + 3)$ ms or a timing of 0.0805 ms. The instruction ⨀ XXX XXX has a formula of $T = 0.0115 (7 + 3)$ ms or a timing of 0.115 ms.

Looking at the *move characters to A or B word mark* instruction, also in Chap. 16, we see that the equation is $T = N (L_I + 1 + 2L_W)$ ms. Thus, the instruction M XXX XXX (where A-field is four positions and B-field is six positions) has a formula of $T = 0.0115 (7 + 1 + 2 \cdot 4)$ ms. Therefore, the timing of this *move* instruction is 0.184 ms.

We said earlier that the formulas are given in terms of certain characteristics of the instruction under consideration and of the *data* fields being operated on. Let us explain this fact using the previous move-instruction formula for illustration. As we said in the discussion of registers in Chap. 16, it takes one storage cycle or 0.0115 ms to get each instruction character from storage to the control registers, plus one extra to get the OP code of the next instruction. Remember that the word mark of the OP code in the next instruction signals the end of the I-phase (instruction phase) and beginning of the E-phase (execution phase). This is the basis of the $L_I + 1$ in the formula.

The movement of each character of the data field takes two storage cycles, one to get it from the A-field and one to place it in the B-field. So the number of cycles spent in data movement is two times the number of characters moved, which in turn is the number of characters in the shorter field of the MCW instruction.

ESTIMATING CHAINED INSTRUCTIONS

In this example of the chaining technique, we shall prove that both processing time and storage space are saved. Assume that three 5-position fields in the card are to be added to three adjacent locations in storage. The operation can be done using three 7-character instructions:

```
A   080   500
A   075   495
A   070   490
```

Using the formula for the *add* instruction, $T = 0.0115 (L_I + 3 + L_A + L_B)$, 60 storage cycles are required to execute these instructions, using up 0.690 ms. Twenty-one storage positions are required to store these instructions.

At the completion of the first instruction, the A-address register contains 075 and the B-address register contains 495. Since these are the same numbers that are in the A- and B-addresses of the second instruction, we can take advantage of this fact and write the instructions as follows:

```
A   080   500
A
A
```

This type of operation requires only 48 storage cycles and takes only 0.552 ms. In addition, the three instructions require only 9 storage positions. Therefore, the net saving has been 0.138 ms and 12 storage positions. To conclude chaining instructions, we can say that optimum programming is realized because both processing time and core storage are saved.

INPUT AND OUTPUT TIMING

The 1402 card reader performs card reading at a maximum speed of 800 cards per minute or 75 ms per card. The 75 ms are divided into three parts. The *read-start time* of 21 ms is the interval between the starting of the cycle and the time when information actually begins to move into the card read-in area of storage. It is spent in moving the card from the hopper to the point where the 9 row is under the reading brushes.

The *card-reading time* of 44 ms is taken up with the reading of the 12 rows on the card and the transfer of information into storage. The remaining 10 ms are used for *processing time*. Thus if processing is completed within 10 ms, the maximum speed of 800 cards per minute is attained. Otherwise, the card reading speed drops to 400 cards per minute.

Card punching is accomplished at a maximum speed of 250 cards per minute or 240 ms per card. This cycle is also divided into three parts. The *punch-start time* of 37 ms is the interval of time between the start of the card motion and the beginning of actual punching. Since the cards are fed into the punch hopper 12-edge first, the *punching-time* of 181 ms begins with the 12 row of the card. The 22 ms remaining are available for *processing*. If the instruction to punch another card is not given before the end of processing time, the speed of punching is slowed to 125 cards per minute.

Printing is performed at 600 lines per minute or 100 ms per line. The cycle is divided into two parts, printing and processing, with form or paper movement overlapping one of these. The *printing time* is 84 ms and the remaining 16 ms are available for *processing*. The *form movement* is 20 ms. The printer is able to accept an impulse to print a line at any time. If the instruction to print the next line can be given before the end of processing, printing of 600 lines per minute is attained. Otherwise, the only time penalty is the excess of processing time.

As we have seen, input-output operations slow the computer considerably and corroborate the need for buffered storage. However, in the absence of buffered input-output operations, the total time of this bottleneck can be reduced by the use of combination instructions listed below.

Write-and-Read Instruction

Instruction format

Mnemonic	OP code	A-address	B-address	d-modifier
WR	3			

Function This instruction combines the functions of *read-a-card* (OP code 1) and *write-a-line* (OP code 2). The printer takes priority, and the print cycle is completed before the actual card-reading operation takes place. However, the signal to start the reader can be accepted before the end of the print cycle. Read-start time thus overlaps the print cycle.

Word marks Word marks are not affected.

Timing $T = N(L_I + 1) \text{ ms} + I/O$

Address registers after operation

I-add Reg	A-add Reg	B-add Reg
NSI	A_p	081

Write-and-Punch Instruction

Instruction format

Mnemonic	OP code	A-address	B-address	d-modifier
WP	6			

Function This code combines the *write-a-line* (OP code 2) and *punch-a-card* (OP code 4) instructions. The printer always operates first, but the signal to start the punch is automatically given before the end of the print operation, so that actual card punching starts soon after the print cycle is complete.

Word marks Word marks are not affected.

Timing $T = N(L_I + 1) \text{ ms} + I/O$

Address registers after operation

I-add Reg	A-add Reg	B-add Reg
NSI	A_p	181

Write, Read and Punch Instruction

Instruction format

Mnemonic	OP code	A-address	B-address	d-modifier
WRP	7			

Function Printing, reading, and punching operations are performed when this command is given. The printer takes priority, and the reading and punching cycles start before the end of the actual print operation.

Timing $T = N(L_I + 1) \text{ ms} + I/O$

Address registers after operation

I-add Reg	A-add Reg	B-add Reg
NSI	A_p	181 or 081

Each combination instruction has a corresponding instruction that permits automatic branching to a predetermined instruction address after the functions are completed. The I-address is coded to make this *branch* instruction effective.

MAGNETIC TAPE OPERATIONS

There are several means of coping with expanding business problems. Timely processing and accuracy are gained when a change is made from a manual system to a punched-card data processing system. As volumes of business data grow, additional machines are acquired and finally the data processing department is converted to or augmented with electronic data processing machines. This latter group of machines is capable of handling data by media other than punched cards. Their processing speed is increased tremendously by magnetic tape, which provides compact storage for large amounts of data and allows faster reading and writing than punched cards.

Before proceeding with a tape-program problem, we should review a few basic characteristics about magnetic tape, covered in Chap. 15. Each character on tape is recorded in a six-bit binary-coded decimal form with a seventh bit for even parity check (Fig. 15-11). Characters are recorded in groups called records (Fig. 15-12). One record is distinguished from another on tape by a ¾-inch space of unrecorded tape, called an interrecord gap.

A series of records can be grouped together without interrecord gaps (Fig. 15-12), thus conserving tape space. The number of records in each group, called a block, is determined by the programmer. Each block is separated by interrecord gaps. Another advantage of blocking is that an entire block consisting of several records can be brought into core at the same time and handled at electronic speeds. When the tape is unblocked, records are brought into core storage one at a time; consequently, processing is slowed somewhat by the mechanical speed of the tape unit. Since tape records can be blocked or unblocked, single records on unblocked tape are often called a block.

Magnetic tape is read or written in a tape unit (Fig. 15-10) by a read-write head assembly at a typical speed of 41,667 characters per second. The beginning and end of the tape are each detected by a reflective spot, which consists of an aluminum strip. The location of the reflective spot at the beginning of the tape is called the load point while the location of the reflective spot at the end of the tape is called end-of-reel. Detection of the end-of-reel reflective spot turns ON an indicator in the computer during writing only. This indicator can be tested by the program, and when recognized, a tape mark (8421 bits) is written. The tape mark can be detected by the program during later reading operations to signal the end-of-reel.

Since a collection of data frequently does not fill an entire reel, a tape mark is also written after the final record or block to indicate the end-of-job. The same end-of-reel indicator turned on by the reflective spot when writing is also turned on by the word mark. Thus the end-of-reel or end-of-job can be tested by the program with a *branch-if-indicator* ON instruction. The end-of-job is also called end-of-file because a collection of records is a file.

Like other storage devices, writing onto tape is destructive while reading from tape is nondestructive. When data is read from tape, an exact copy of the contents is transferred to internal core storage and the data on tape remain unaffected. When writing onto tape, the new information is recorded over the old information, thus destroying it. To protect files of permanent information that could be inadvertently destroyed, a removable plastic ring, called a file protection ring, must be placed on the back side of the tape reel in order to write.

Reading and writing on tape are opposite to processing or storing of data within core memory. Information is stored, processed, and read out of storage in reverse order. That is, the units or low-order position of the field of information is specified in the instruction and data are acted upon character-by-character from right to left until a word mark is sensed. Data are written onto tape from the high-order or leftmost position of the record in storage. If we could see the information recorded on tape, it would appear backward. When data are read from tape, they are transferred back to the higher-order position of the tape read-in area of storage, thus restoring the original sequence.

UPDATING A TAPE FILE

We shall now discuss a problem involving both reading of and writing onto magnetic tape. The customer account master tape must be updated periodically. This involves adding new accounts and deleting old accounts.

If the file is composed of punched cards, the operation is performed by a collator by placing the transaction cards (new-account and deleted-account cards) into one feed and the master file in the other feed. Then the new cards are inserted in the master file while equal cards (deletions) are selected to separate pockets.

Merging records onto tape is not quite this simple. They cannot be physically inserted or removed as can punched cards. Tape files are updated by writing an entirely new tape, even though only a few records must be added, deleted, or changed. The updating job requires transactions cards (one card for each new or deleted account), a tape unit for the original customer-account tape file, and a second tape unit with which to write the new tape file. To keep the logic uncomplicated, we assume that the last card is a deletion transaction.

Three conditions, shown in Table 19-2, determine the processing to be done. If account number in the card is *equal* to account number on the tape record, the program branches directly to read another card and another tape record, thus deleting the canceled account by not writing that record on tape. A *low* condition (card account number is less than tape account number) resulting from a card-to-tape comparison indicates a new account and the information from the card is written on tape. If a *high* condition (card account number is higher than tape account number) occurs, the information from the old tape record is merely copied onto the new tape.

The flowchart in Fig. 19-1 presents the solution of updating the customer-account master tape. All records on the old tape are unblocked and are written also as single-record blocks. Because of the different courses of action, such as writing onto the new tape from either card storage area or tape storage area and reading the next card or next tape record or both, address modification and

program switches are used. Otherwise the program would require different write-tape subroutines to handle the alternate actions.

A single write-tape routine is permitted if two conditions are satisfied. The program switches satisfy one condition by controlling the reading of the next card or next tape record or both. Of course, the *write-tape* instruction must specify the address in storage of the data to be written. This can be two different areas, depending upon whether the record being written is a new record (stored in card area) or an old record (stored in tape area). A technique called address modification satisfies the latter condition.

The program provides for two tape error routines, one for reading tape and the other for writing tape. Another routine provides a temporary interruption while the operator mounts a new output reel on the second tape unit in case one tape reel does not hold the newly written master file. We should point out that a write-tape error routine and a routine to check for end-of-reel would be necessary for *each* of the write-tape routines that would be required in case program switches were not used.

Table 19-2   Conditions and Action To Be Taken to Update Customer Account Tape File

Customer account no.			
Card	Tape	Condition	Action
0312	0314	Card < Tape	Write new record and read next card
0313	0314	Card < Tape	Write new record and read next card
0315	0314	Card > Tape	Write old record and read next tape record
0315	0315	Card = Tape	Delete record and read next card and next tape record
0316	0316	Card = Tape	Delete record and read next card and next tape record
0318	0319	Card < Tape	Write new record and read next card
0320	0319	Card > Tape	Write old record and read next tape record

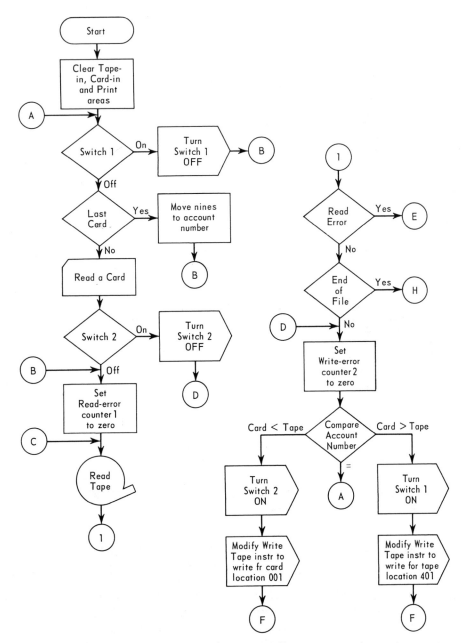

Fig. 19-1 Flowchart to update customer account tape file.

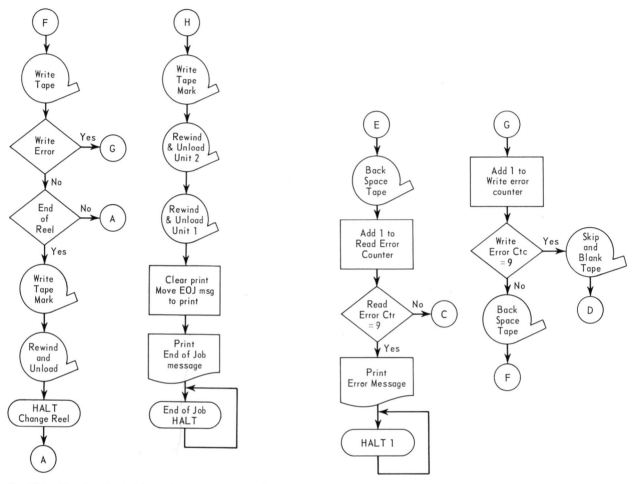

Fig. 19-1 Flowchart to update customer account tape file (continued).

TAPE PROGRAM TO UPDATE CUSTOMER ACCOUNT FILE

Switch 1, switch 2, and last-card indicator are OFF as the program begins. Therefore the program falls through without taking any of the branches specified in the I-address. A card is read into the read area 0001 to 0080. The *clear counter-1* instruction is associated with the read-error subroutine and will be discussed later.

The first tape record is read into a tape storage area, 0401 to 0480, by the *read-tape* instruction whose OP

code is MU (move unit). This operation code assembles to the same OP code as the *move* instruction, but is essentially unrelated. The d-character, R, specifies that the tape unit is to read. We must provide three items of information to the computer:

1. Which of the tape units contain the tape reel, hence the information being read. This is specified in the A-address in the form of %Ux. The %U specifies magnetic tape operation and x is the tape unit on which the tape being read is mounted. The tape unit number can be set by a dial (Fig. 15-10) for any number from 0 to 9. In the case

of the sample program, the dial of the tape unit containing the source tape reel is set to 1.

2. Where in storage is the first character of the block to be stored. This is specified by the address of the high-order core position of the tape read-in area. The first tape record, consisting of 80 characters, is read into a tape storage area specified by the program. In this case the area is 0401 to 0480, since TAPEIN has been defined as location 0480. The area could have been any other area specified by the programmer as long as the area chosen is not required by the stored program.

3. What the length is of the block to be read. Once a tape reel starts moving forward it is stopped by an *inter-record gap* or by sensing a group mark with word mark (BA8421W bits, Fig. 15-7) in core storage. In the sample program, tape reading is stopped by the interrecord gap because each block consists of a single record.

Read-Tape Instruction

Instruction format

Mnemonic	OP code	A-address	B-address	d-modifier
MU	M	%Ux	XXX	R

Function The tape unit specified in the A-address is started. The d-character specifies a tape-read operation. The B-address specifies the high-order position of the tape read-in area of storage. The machine begins to read magnetic tape, and continues to read until either an interrecord gap in the tape record or a group mark with a word mark in core storage is sensed. The interrecord gap indicates the end of the tape record, and a group mark (CBA 8421 bits) is inserted in core storage at this point. If the group mark with a word mark occurs before the interrecord gap is sensed, the transfer of data from tape stops, but tape movement continues until the interrecord gap is sensed.

Word marks Word marks are not affected.

Timing $T = N(L_I + 1)$ ms $+ T_M$. Time varies for type of tape unit and tape density used.

Address registers after operation

I-add Reg	A-add Reg	B-add Reg
NSI	%4x	group mark + 1

Next a test (line 170, page 1) is made to see whether the information was readable. If the tape was not readable, the program branches to a read-error routine (line 140, page 2) that provides for backspacing the tape and reading the same record several times. This often eliminates the trouble, especially when the tape error is the result of dust particles. If a good read is made within the number of times specified by counter 1, processing continues without interruption. Otherwise the operator is notified by a message written on the printer and the computer stops for more extensive action on the operator's part. Counter 1 is cleared before the next record is read, but not while the read-error loop is being repeated.

Backspace-Tape Instruction

Instruction format

Mnemonic	OP code	A-address	B-address	d-modifier
CU	U	%Ux		B

Function The tape unit specified in the A-address backspaces over one tape block. The first interrecord gap encountered stops the backspace operation specified by the d-character of B.

Word marks Word marks are not affected.

Timing $T = N(L_I + 1)$ ms $+ T_M$

Address registers after operation

I-add Reg	A-add Reg	B-add Reg
NSI	%4x	dbb

The end-of-file is tested at line 180, page 1, and if the indicator has been set by sensing the tape mark, the program branches to the end-of-job routine. If found OFF, the write-error counter is cleared. This instruction is associated with the write-tape error routine and is explained later.

Now that a card record and a tape record are in core

IBM

INTERNATIONAL BUSINESS MACHINES CORPORATION
FORM X24-1152-3
PRINTED IN U.S.A.

IBM 1401 SYMBOLIC PROGRAMMING SYSTEM

CODING SHEET

Program __Update Magnetic Tape__

Programmed by __I. Q. STUDENT__   Date __OCT 13__

Page No. |0, 1| of __4__

Identification __T A P E__
                76   80

LINE	COUNT	LABEL	OPERATION	(A) OPERAND ADDRESS	±	CHAR. ADJ.	IND.	(B) OPERAND ADDRESS	±	CHAR. ADJ.	IND.	d	COMMENTS
0 1 0			C T L	3 3									
0 2 0		*											
0 3 0		* U P D A T E		C U S T O M E R A C C O U N T T A P E				F I L E . P R O G R A M					
0 4 0		* D E L E T E S		C A N C E L L E D A C C O U N T S A N D				A D D S N E W A C C T S					
0 5 0		* B A S E D		U P O N C A R D T R A N S A C T I O N S .				A C C O U N T S W I T H					
0 6 0		* N O C O R		R E S P O N D I N G C A R D A R E W R I T				T E N O N N E W T A P E					
0 7 0		*											
0 8 0			O R G	0 4 8 2									
0 9 0		S T A R T	C S	0 0 8 0								C L E A R C A R D A R E A	
1 0 0			C S	0 4 8 0								C L E A R T A P E A R E A	
1 1 0		S W 1	N O P	S E T 1								B R I F S W 1 I S O N	
1 2 0			B	M O V E 9							A	B R I F L A S T C A R D	
1 3 0			R									R E A D A C A R D	
1 4 0		S W 2	N O P	S E T 2								B R I F S W 2 I S O N	
1 5 0		C L E A R	S	C T R 1								C L E A R R D E R R C T R	
1 6 0		T A P E	M U	% U 1				T A P E I N	-	0 7 9		R	S T O R E T A P E R C D
1 7 0			B	E R R 1								L	C K T A P E R D E R R
1 8 0			B	E O J								K	C K E N D O F F I L E
1 9 0		R E S E T	S	C T R 2								C L R R I T E E R R C T R	
2 0 0			C	T A P E N O				C A R D N O					T E S T A C C T N O
2 1 0			B	S W 1								S	E Q D E L E T E R C D
2 2 0			B	C R D R T N								T	G O T U R N S W 2 O N
2 3 0			M C W	B R A N C H				S W 1					T U R N S W I T C H 1 O N
2 4 0			M C W	A D D 4 0 1				W R I T E	+	0 0 6			M O D I F Y T A P E I N S T
2 5 0		W R I T E	M U	% U 2				0 0 0 0				W	B - A D D M O D I F I E D
2 6 0			B	E R R 2								L	T A P E W R I T E E R R

AREA—DEFINITION CHARACTER COUNT ⟶ I   5   10   15   20   25   30 32

6402250MSP

Fig. 19-2   Program to update customer account tape file.

storage, they are compared by customer-account code to determine whether the card record is lower than, higher than, or equal to, the tape record. This is the only field within the 80-character record we are concerned with, so we shall consider the account number to be in columns 1 to 4 of the card and positions 1 to 4 of the tape record. By reviewing Table 19-2, we see that an equal compare calls for the program to read another card and tape record. This action bypasses the *write-tape* instruction and in effect deletes the record.

If the compare is low, a branch is taken to the symbolic

I-address labeled CRDRTN. This routine sets the B-address (which specifies where the data are to be written from) of the *write-tape* instruction at line 250, page 1. A low condition indicates that the card is lower than the tape record, hence a new-customer account. The information from the card is written onto tape. Now a new card must be read but not another tape record. To cause the program to carry out this action, switch *2* is turned ON. This results in branching around the *read-tape* instruction when the program is repeated.

To comprehend the program logic discussed in the

IBM

INTERNATIONAL BUSINESS MACHINES CORPORATION
IBM 1401 SYMBOLIC PROGRAMMING SYSTEM
CODING SHEET

FORM X24-1152-3
PRINTED IN U.S.A.

Program __Update Magnetic Tape__

Programmed by _____I. Q. STUDENT_____

Date __OCT 13__

Page No. |0,2| of __4__

Identification T,A,P,E (76–80)

LINE	COUNT	LABEL	OPERATION	(A) OPERAND ADDRESS	±	CHAR. ADJ.	IND.	(B) OPERAND ADDRESS	±	CHAR. ADJ.	IND.	d	COMMENTS
0 1 0			B	CHGTP								K	END OF REEL
0 2 0			B	SW1									GO TO REPEAT PGM
0 3 0		* B R A	N	C H	S	U	B	R O U T I			N	E S
0 4 0		SET1	MCW	NOPSW				SW1					TURN SW 1 OFF
0 5 0			B	CLEAR									TO READ TAPE
0 6 0		SET2	MCW	NOPSW				SW2					TURN SW 2 OFF
0 7 0			B	RESET									BYPASS TAPE READ
0 8 0		CRDRTN	MCW	BRANCH				SW2					TURN SW 2 ON
0 9 0			MCW	ADD001				WRITE	+	0 0 6			MODIFY TAPE INST
1 0 0			B	WRITE									TO WRITE NEW RCD
1 1 0		MOVE9	MCW	NINES				CARDNO					HIGHEST ACCT NO
1 2 0			B	CLEAR									TO READ TAPE
1 3 0		* R E A	D	T A P	E			E R R O R			R	O U T I N E
1 4 0		ERR1	CU	%U1								B	BACKSPACE TAPE
1 5 0			A	ONE				CTR1					READ ERROR CTR
1 6 0			B	PRTMSG				CTR1				9	TRY 9 TIMES
1 7 0			B	TAPE									READ TAPE AGAIN
1 8 0		PRTMSG	W										PRT ERROR MSG
1 9 0		HALT1	H	HALT1									CLOSED LOOP
2 0 0		* W R I		T E	T A	P	E	E R R	O	R		R	O U T I N E
2 1 0		ERR2	A	ONE				CTR2					WRITE ERROR CTR
2 2 0			B	SKIP				CTR2				9	TRY 9 TIMES
2 3 0			CU	%U2								B	BACKSPACE TAPE
2 4 0			B	WRITE									WRITE TAPE AGAIN
2 5 0		SKIP	CU	%U2								E	SKIP & BLANK TP
2 6 0			B	RESET									CLR CTR & WRITE TP

AREA–DEFINITION CHARACTER COUNT ——→ 1   5   10   15   20   25   30 32

6402250MSP

Fig. 19-2   Program to update customer account tape file (continued).

previous paragraph, follow the program through the flow-chart solution (Fig. 19-1), taking only the switch-*2* branch. In order to understand how the B-address of the *write-tape* instruction is modified to handle a card from core locations 0001 to 0080 or a tape record from core locations 0401 to 0480 (tape read-in area), we must first understand the *write-tape* instruction.

The actions of writing tape are very similar to reading tape, except that the operation is ended in a slightly different way. The main difference between the two instructions is the d-character of W, which stands for write. The

A-address specifies the tape unit in which the new tape is to be written, in this case tape unit 2. The B-address contains the location of the high-order character of the record in storage. This will be 0001 (card-storage area) or 0401 (tape-storage area) depending upon which record is being written.

When transmitting characters from core storage to tape, a group mark with a word mark stops the operation. Since we are writing records sometimes from 0001 to 0080 and other times from 0401 to 0480, we need a group mark with a word mark (BA8421W bits) one posi-

194 Data processing concepts

IBM

INTERNATIONAL BUSINESS MACHINES CORPORATION
IBM 1401 SYMBOLIC PROGRAMMING SYSTEM
CODING SHEET

FORM X24-1152-3
PRINTED IN U.S.A.

Program: Update Magnetic Tape   Page No. |0 3| of 4

Programmed by: I. Q. STUDENT   Date OCT 13   Identification T A P E (76–80)

LINE	COUNT	LABEL	OPERATION	(A) ADDRESS	CHAR. ADJ.	(B) ADDRESS	CHAR. ADJ.	d	COMMENTS
0 1 0		* E N	D	O F R E E		L R O U T		I	N E
0 2 0		C H G T P	C U	% U 2				M	W R I T E T A P E M A R K
0 3 0			C U	% U 2				U	R E W I N D & U N L O A D
0 4 0			H	S W 1					C H G R E E L A N D G O
0 5 0		* E N	D	O F J O B		R O U T		I	N E
0 6 0		E O J	C U	% U 2				M	W R I T E W O R D M A R K
0 7 0			C U	% U 2				U	R E W I N D N E W T A P E
0 8 0			C U	% U 1				U	R E W I N D O L D T A P E
0 9 0			C S	0 2 9 9					C L E A R P R I N T
1 0 0			M C W	E O J M S G		0 2 9 9			M O V E T O P R I N T
1 1 0			W						P R T E O J M E S S A G E
1 2 0		H A L T	H	H A L T					E N D O F J O B
1 3 0		* C O N	S	T A N T S					
1 4 0	0 3	A D D 0 0 1	D C W	*	0 0 1				C A R D – I N A D D R E S S
1 5 0	0 3	A D D 4 0 1	D C W	*	4 0 1				T A P E – I N A D D R E S S
1 6 0	0 1	N O P S W	D C W	*	N				N O O P E R A T I O N
1 7 0	0 1	B R A N C H	D C W	*	B				B R A N C H O P E R A T I O N
1 8 0	3 2		D C	0 2 5 0	B A D	T A P E ,	R E R E A	D	9 T I M E S . S E E R E
1 9 0	3 2		D C	0 2 8 2	C O V E R Y	I N S T R U C T I		O	N S I N O P R G U I D E
2 0 0	0 1	C T R 1	D C W	*	0				R E A D E R R O R C T R
2 1 0	0 1	C T R 2	D C W	*	0				W R I T E E R R O R C T R
2 2 0	2 9	E O J M S G	D C W	*	C U S T O M E R A C C O U N T				J O B F I N I S H E D
2 3 0	0 1	O N E	D C W	*	1				
2 4 0		T A P E N O	D S	0 4 0 4					T A P E A C C T N O
2 5 0		C A R D N O	D S	0 0 0 4					C A R D A C C T N O
2 6 0	0 4	N I N E S	D C W	*	9 9 9 9				

AREA–DEFINITION CHARACTER COUNT ⟶ I

6402250MSP

Fig. 19-2 Program to update customer account tape file (continued).

tion to the right of the last character to be transmitted to tape. This is accomplished by two *DCW* statements at lines 040 and 050, page 4.

Write-Tape Instruction

Instruction format

Mnemonic	OP code	A-address	B-address	d-modifier
MU	M	%Ux	XXX	W

Function The tape unit designated in the A-address is started. The d-character specifies a write-tape operation. The data from core storage is written onto the tape record. The B-address specifies the high-order position of the record in storage. A group mark with a word mark in core storage stops the operation. The group mark with a word mark causes an interrecord gap to be created on tape.

Word marks Word marks are not affected.

Timing $T = N(L_I + 1)$ ms $+ T_M$

IBM

INTERNATIONAL BUSINESS MACHINES CORPORATION
IBM 1401 SYMBOLIC PROGRAMMING SYSTEM
CODING SHEET
FORM X24-1152-3
PRINTED IN U.S.A.

Program UPDATE MAGNETIC TAPE

Programmed by I. Q. STUDENT

Date OCT 13

Page No. |0, 4| of ___4___

Identification T, A, P, E

LINE	COUNT	LABEL	OPERATION	(A) OPERAND ADDRESS	±	CHAR. ADJ.	IND.	(B) OPERAND ADDRESS	±	CHAR. ADJ.	IND.	d	COMMENTS
0,1,0	3,2		DCW	0,4,3,2									T,A,P,E
0,2,0	3,2		DC	0,4,6,4									R,E,A,D,I,N,-
0,3,0	1,6	T,A,P,E,I,N	DC	0,4,8,0									L,O,C,A,T,I,O,N
0,4,0	0,1		DCW	0,0,8,1	≠								G,P M,A,R,K W,D M,A,R,K
0,5,0	0,1		DCW	0,4,8,1	≠								G,P M,A,R,K W,D M,A,R,K
0,6,0			END	S,T,A,R,T									B,R T,O B,E,G,I,N P,G,M
0,7,0													
0,8,0													
0,9,0													
1,0,0													
1,1,0													
1,2,0													
1,3,0													
1,4,0													
1,5,0													
1,6,0													
1,7,0													
1,8,0													
1,9,0													
2,0,0													

AREA-DEFINITION CHARACTER COUNT ⟶ 1   5   10   15   20   25   30 32

6402250MSP

Fig. 19-2 Program to update customer account tape file (continued).

Address registers after operation

I-add Reg	A-add Reg	B-add Reg
NSI	%4x	group mark + 1

ADDRESS MODIFICATION

We are now ready to see how only one *write-tape* instruction is used to write information from two different areas. We have seen in Chap. 16 that instructions are stored in much the same way that data is stored. Since an instruction is composed of the same characters that are available for storing data, the only thing that actually distinguishes one from another is the time at which each is brought into the control unit, that is, I-phase and E-phase.

This being the case, we can operate on instructions in storage as though they were data. We have previously seen how the program can be modified by changing the OP code of one instruction by another instruction. In fact, we exercise this technique in the form of switches in this program. To cause the program to modify itself, to write tape from the card area, we move (line 90, page 2) a constant of 001 to the B-address of the *write-tape* instruction in the subroutine labeled CRDRTN.

We shall next discuss the subroutine resulting from a high compare (line 200, page 1). If the equal branch or low branch is not taken, the program falls through to the card-greater-than-tape routine. Here, switch *1* is turned ON to permit bypassing the reading of another card. Again, refer to Fig. 19-1 for a pictorial view of the action resulting from setting switch *1* ON. Next the B-address of the *write-tape* instruction is modified to location 401, which is the high-order position of area we have set aside for tape storage.

Whether the condition be a card or tape record, the *write-tape* instruction is modified to accept the one at hand when a record is transferred to tape. After writing tape, a check is made for tape transmission error. If a write error is detected, the I-address labeled ERR2 is the next executable instruction.

ERR2 is a write-error tape subroutine (line 210, page 2) that backspaces the tape one record and attempts to write the record correctly several times. If a record is written correctly before the tenth attempt, the program continues without interruption. However, if the loop is repeated the maximum times specified by counter 2, the tape is advanced 3½ inches and erased. The bad area of tape is meaningless to the computer since it recognizes the erased area as just a longer interrecord gap. Note that loop counter 2 is not reset until either a *skip and blank tape* instruction is executed or until the program is repeated for the next record.

Skip and Blank Tape Instruction

Instruction format

Mnemonic	OP code	A-address	B-address	d-modifier
CU	U	%Ux		E

Function   The tape unit, designated by the A-address, spaces forward and erases approximately 3½ inches of tape. The actual skip occurs when the next *write-tape* instruction is given. This instruction makes it possible to bypass defective tape areas.

Word marks   Word marks are not affected.

Timing $T = N(L_I + 1)$ ms

Address registers after operation

I-add Reg	A-add Reg	B-add Reg
NSI	%4x	dbb

After checking to see if the tape was written accurately, the program tests (line 10, page 2) for an end-of-reel indicator which is automatically set internally when the reflective spot is sensed. If the branch is taken to the subroutine labeled CHGTP (line 20, page 3), we must write a tape mark for the final block. Earlier in the chapter, we said that a tape mark is the only means of recognizing the end-of-reel, or if the tape is only partially written, the end-of-job, when reading tape.

A tape mark is created by the *write tape mark* instruction. This instruction writes the tape mark (8421 bits) in a separate block, preceded by an interrecord gap. Thus, the tape mark is not detected when the last record or block is read, but on the next tape reading.

Write Tape Mark Instruction

Instruction format

Mnemonic	OP code	A-address	B-address	d-modifier
CU	U	%Ux		M

Function   This instruction causes a tape-mark character (8421 bits) to be recorded immediately following the last record on tape. When the tape mark is read back from a tape, the end-of-reel indicator is turned on. This signals the program that the end of a major group of records has been reached (end-of-file) or the end of utilized tape has been reached.

Word marks   Word marks are not affected.

Timing $T = N(L_I + 1)$ ms $+ T_M$

Address registers after operation

I-add Reg	A-add Reg	B-add Reg
NSI	%4x	dbb

When the tape mark is written, the tape must be re-wound and another tape manually mounted if the operation is not yet completed. Rewinding is accomplished automatically by the *rewind tape and unload* instruction. After the new tape reel is mounted, the operator presses the *start* key to resume the operation. This instruction makes it impossible for the computer to use the tape unit until a button on the tape unit is manually depressed. This prevents the program from destroying the newly written information by mistake.

Rewind Tape and Unload **Instruction**

Instruction format

Mnemonic	OP code	A-address	B-address	d-modifier
CU	U	%Ux		U

Function This instruction causes the tape unit specified in the A-address to rewind its tape to the load point. At the end of the rewind, the tape is out of the vacuum columns, and the reading mechanism is disengaged. The unit is effectively disconnected from the system, and is not available again until the operator restores it to a ready status.

Word marks Word marks are not affected.

Timing $T = N(L_I + 1)$ ms. Rewind time is 1.2 minutes for the IBM 729 II unit.

Note The d-character, R, causes the selected tape unit to rewind without unloading. Processing may continue during the rewind.

Address registers after operation

I-add Reg	A-add Reg	B-add Reg
NSI	%4x	dbb

To end the job a branch is taken from the end-of-file instruction (line 180, page 1) to an end-of-job routine that closes the files. This entails writing a word mark on the output tape, rewinding both tape reels, notifying the operator by a printed message, and halting.

QUESTIONS

1. What is the processing time for the instruction A 069 875? A word mark is set in locations 066 and 871.

2. Write a short program that will take advantage of the *write, read, punch,* and *branch* instruction.

3. Without changing the d-modifier, 9, at line 160, page 2 in Fig. 19-2, how would you change the program to reread the tape 10 times?

4. At line 160, page 1, in Fig. 19-2, what is the symbolic B-address of TAPEIN−079 assembled as?

5. What causes the creation of the interrecord gap between tape records or blocks?

6. The source tape for the complete customer-account file is slightly less than one reel. If the end-of-reel branch is ever taken (Fig. 19-1), how must the program be altered for future updating cycles of the customer-account file?

7. In Fig. 19-1, how many attempts will the computer make to write a correct record before halting?

8. In Fig. 19-2, why must the *ORG* statement cause the program to be stored beginning at core location 0482?

9. How is the end-of-reel detected during reading? During writing?

10. In relation to the sample program what stops the reading of tape? The writing of tape?

11. How does the addressing of information during tape operations differ from those of nontape operations?

12. What must the tape number dial of the output tape unit for the sample program be set to?

13. If a tape has a blocking factor of five records, how

far does the tape backspace during a *backspace-tape* instruction?

14. If switch 1 in Fig. 19-1 is turned ON, what is the B-address of the *write-tape* instruction?

15. When switches *1* and *2* are OFF during a complete program execution in Fig. 19-2, what were the settings of the comparing indicators for the record(s) just processed and the previous record(s)?

16. In Fig. 19-1, how many times is the subroutine at connector H executed?

17. How many times is the routine at connector G executed?

18. In the read-tape error routine of Fig. 19-2, the information to be printed is not moved to the print area. How do you account for this?

19. What is the purpose of the two *DCW* statements at lines 40 and 50, page 4 of Fig. 19-2?

20. Does the group mark on magnetic tape have a parity bit? Why?

20
Data processing management

We have defined data processing as electronic machines and people organized and working together to process the data requirements of a business firm. Our discussion thus far has dealt primarily with the machines. In this chapter we shall speak of a data processing department in terms of people and organization. This, with your accumulated knowledge of the machines, will give an indication of the true meaning of data processing.

An effective manager is one who has proven himself by fulfilling the firm's objectives. Although he may never wire a control panel or write a program, a manager must be knowledgeable in the art of data processing. Without this understanding, he cannot meet the objectives set by higher management. In order to do so he must know what the company's punched-card machines and computers can and cannot do. He must also be able to methodically determine the cost of each requirement, one time or recurring, before committing his department to it. His findings must then be analyzed as to the value of the requirement and a decision made as to the method (manual or mechanized) that will produce acceptable results. In short, the most successful businesses are those with managers who are knowledgeable in, and are aware of the capabilities of, the data processing department, nerve center of a company's operation.

Considerable attention must be given to the many details involved in a data processing application. The data must be created, if unavailable; most likely they are on file and can be made usable with little alteration. The volume of the data and the deadline of the finished product are most important. The input data must be available at the proper time, procedures and programs must be tested and ready. The biggest problem will likely be scheduling the work on the machines. Hence, the manager must know when machine time is available in relation to other work, how important the job is so as to assign operators and programmers with commensurate experience, and what to do in case problems arise that threaten to result in a late report.

People with varying experience are needed to assist the manager in making all of these pieces fall together properly and on schedule. In a large installation assistance comes from many people, each with specialized skills. In a small data processing department this same planning is necessary, but with assistance to the manager coming from only a few people, each having several skills.

Since management is so dependent upon the data processing department, it must be composed of at least some truly professional technicians with several years of experience. Other subordinate personnel vary in experience, some being skilled workers, some helpers. Because the business role has grown from manual systems to standard punched-card data processing systems to electronic data processing systems in such a short span, some companies are fortunate in having managers with experience in all three types of systems.

Let us delve into the maze of responsibilities that must be borne in operation of a data processing installation. We shall first see how the data processing department is organized in relation to the overall structure and next isolate and identify the positions within the facility.

POSITION OF DATA PROCESSING IN THE ORGANIZATION

In the beginning of mechanization, data processing machines were used primarily for record keeping. Consequently, the data processing activity was merely an extension of the accounting department. As the capabilities of these machines became more evident, their usages were expanded into other applications. Data processing thus became a servicing agency.

In most organizations it is unfeasible for each department to have its own data processing facility, mainly because of the excessive cost of multiple facilities. If decentralization *is* attempted, some departments will be swamped with peak work loads while others are in slow periods. And small departments that cannot justify their own machine facility may have difficulty in obtaining data processing support. Even if this difficulty is resolved, their work is likely to come second to the prime user of the machines.

For these reasons, a centralized data processing installation is better for the majority of organizations. When set up as a separate department, it is of prime importance that it be on an equal level with other departments, with the data processing manager responsible to at least one higher level of authority than the departments he services. This ensures unbiased service to all departments. From a management standpoint, an independent data processing department is perhaps more important because pressure that could be brought to process data incorrectly in order to cover up dishonesty is reduced.

INTEREST OF TOP MANAGEMENT

Although data processing installations do fail from lack of support from middle and top management, they can fail just as quickly from overcontrol by management. Too often, the data processing manager has the responsibility for a project, but not the authority. After a complete systems study, the data processing manager knows as much about the project as, or even more than, the department heads who have initiated the project. Yet someone else may decide to alter the solution, even though he does not have enough information to make a logical decision, perhaps producing something less useful than expected.

On the other hand, the data processing manager may have a parochial view of the overall organization, with little comprehension of the objectives of the project. This is possible for various reasons. The manager may have

been hired for his technical ability and not given the opportunity to gain depth and understanding about company operations and management goals. Regardless, the computer manager, or even a technician, can gain limited control of facts that vital decisions are based upon simply by the manner in which the mechanized system is programmed. Top management must actively participate in data processing and must encourage the data processing manager to become knowledgeable in all aspects of the company, to close any gap between technical and professional managers.

Data processing's great potential for dollar savings and other contributions toward profits make it important that all levels of management, including top management, take a vital interest in its operation. Too, the data processing budget is not small. It is estimated that in 1970 computer shipments will exceed 10 billion dollars and programming costs are often as much or more than the hardware cost.

Employees of a data processing department are generally well paid. The extra salary paid for their efficiency can save thousands in company operations. Let us consider a one-time programming requirement. At an hourly rate of $35.00, a medium-sized computer can print a stack of paper three feet high in two hours. The cost of the job, excluding manhours, is $128.00. Since a computer must be given every minute detail, the programmer must consider and plan for all possibilities. If the programmer fails to consider even one condition, it could produce a completely valueless report, resulting in a loss of $128.00 plus operator and programmer salary.

There are no set rules as to assignment of responsibilities, for no two projects are the same. Nor are the people involved the same. But guidelines do have to be set. As a general rule, we can say that top management must be responsible for planning and controlling. Their decisions are based upon the cost of the project, the purpose to be served, and the advice of each department head involved. The department heads in turn rely upon the guidance of their specialists, the impact upon their work load and people, their accumulated knowledge and past experience, and the value of the project to the organization as a whole.

RESPONSIBILITIES OF THE DATA PROCESSING FUNCTION

Let us now turn our attention more specifically to the responsibilities of the data processing function. Data processing can contribute to management planning and controlling by participating in the daily operations of the company. It can maintain customer accounts by processing orders, preparing invoices, and crediting accounts when payments arrive. It can support departments within the company by controlling inventory and production, preparing the payroll, and providing analyses and statistical studies of sales. Support of this nature is essential to any business. As an example, sales forecasts affect production scheduling, which in turn affects financial requirements.

The data processing function provides the personnel department with placement information when selecting new employees, personnel statistics on turnover of employees, and routine record keeping. It maintains accounts receivable and accounts payable for the accounting department and forecasts budget estimates for the budget department. It is truly a service function. We can say, in fact, that the data processing department is the nerve center of the organization.

Systems design is a major function of data processing. It involves analysis of proposed applications and subsequent design of programs and operating procedures. We can define *systems analysis* as the art of determining precisely what must be done and how to do it effectively at the lowest possible cost, keeping in mind the overall picture. The last part is of particular importance. For it is here that duplication is detected and action taken to eliminate or combine overlapping reports.

Another objective of the systems study is to look for overall organization implications. As an example, that which is acceptable to the accounting department may not be acceptable to the auditor because a suitable audit trail has not been provided. As potential problem areas or unanswerable questions arise, a combined team of those involved studies the situation and corrects the problem. This precludes having to frantically correct the problem in the early stages of implementation, or worse still, after results are being produced.

The first step of the systems study is problem definition. All information regarding application objectives, controls to be included in the design, estimated cost, volumes of data, additional machine hours needed, and similar factors are compiled. The existing system is reviewed to gain an understanding of what is being done and what is needed to give the desired results. During these stages any misunderstanding of terms or objectives comes to light. After everyone is in agreement as to when, how, and where the project is going, design of the system is begun. This involves coming up with the best solution, flowcharting the solution, writing and testing the program, documenting the job, preparing operating procedures, and finally implementing the system.

Programming takes into account the data entering the system, processing of this data to give the desired output, and careful documentation of the system to allow for easy program modification. The original program design rarely remains unchanged. Periodic changes will be needed because of a desire for additional information as the business grows and conditions change. However, it is the responsibility of the initiating department or management to make known expected major changes during the systems study. This permits the system to be designed in such a manner that its scope can be increased without needless reprogramming effort. The program could otherwise become obsolete as a result of normal business changes, such as new discount practices.

Standardization in programming allows changes to be made to the program with a minimum of effort. Since the job of revising a program may fall on someone unfamiliar with the system, it is desirable to have uniform subroutines that all programmers are familiar with. For example, the read-tape and write-tape error routines need not be customized for each individual program, but instead, can be identically prepunched in several copies and merely inserted in each new program at the proper locations. Other types of standard subroutines are clear storage, page overflow and numbering, end-of-job, end-of-tape reel, and restart procedures for programmed halts and input-output areas. Such subroutines are called *utility routines;* many are available from equipment manufacturers.

Program revision can be devastating, even for seemingly minor changes. To avoid it, the user should be alerted, whenever a change is made, to check for possible errors. In addition, every program revision, regardless of its simplicity, should be desk checked and tested as if it were a new program.

Desk checking is a term that describes examining the program for obvious errors and manually following the paths that the computer can take for every possible condition. For example, if the programmer uses the symbolic constant of REGHR, but has defined the constant as REGHRS, the assembler will tag each place used as being in error. Here the program flowchart also proves its worth. It provides a means of visualizing and following the path of any condition exactly as the program will execute it. Program switches are exceedingly difficult to keep track of using only the program assembly listing, so it is best to analyze them using the flowchart.

The main area of activity in data processing is the day-to-day operation of machines for established systems. This includes card and tape handling during input-output, set up and control of the equipment, and operation of a variety of auxiliary machines. Very few jobs would be processed accurately if all the details were left up to the memory of the machine operators. There are simply too many jobs that are run in any given period.

To avoid this problem each job is fully documented. This documentation is usually filed in looseleaf notebooks by job number or in separate binders, one for each job. Called *procedures* or *operation manuals,* they serve several purposes. They enable machine operators to process a job from beginning to finish with little or no supervision. They also simplify the turnover of the job to another operator, even in the middle of processing. Just as important, these procedures provide a permanent record of the application, which facilitates correction, modification, and program improvement.

It is essential that a duplicate copy be maintained to reconstruct lost or worn pages in the working procedure. The best time to construct a procedure is concurrently with the systems design and program-planning stages.

Otherwise, there is an obvious danger of forgetting pertinent facts.

Most procedures are used for long periods of time and survive many improvements and revisions. During these changes, updating is sometimes neglected, especially of routine procedures familiar to everyone, leaving the documentation nearly worthless. This leads to the wasted effort of making major revisions and is especially serious if the original planners are tied up with other projects or have left the company.

Adequate documentation consists of at least these elements:

1.   Identifying procedure number, name of the application and specific program, magnetic tape reel, or control panel number to be used.

2.   Written description and explanation of the purpose of the run.

3.   Memos on decisions reached during the systems study and agreements for solutions of problems encountered.

4.   Factors relative to input-output, such as estimated volume, input-output formats, description of codes used, keypunch instructions, due-in and due-out dates, and labeling and disposition of output.

5.   Accounting controls to protect company assets and controls that edit the data to ensure correct processing.

6.   Systems flowchart showing data movement between machines from beginning to final processing.

7.   Program flowchart showing detailed computer operations performed by the program.

8.   Sample runs of each program. These are suitable for checking against each actual run for obvious errors in format, machine, or data.

9.   Assembled program in source and machine language to include programmer name and date of last change.

10.   Wiring diagrams, planning charts, or instructions suitable for wiring and testing control panels.

11.   Computer operating instructions to include console switch settings, program halts with corrective action and recovery instructions, identity of cards in selective operations, number of copies of report, control carriage tape

instructions, and console display forms to record unexpected halts.

12. Precise punched-card equipment instructions to include identification of columns to be sorted, special handling of selected cards, collator instructions, such as control columns and an indication of which file goes in the primary or secondary feed.

DATA PROCESSING POSITIONS

It is impossible to describe a data processing installation that is tailored for every concern. Companies vary in size, environment, and organizational philosophy. It is possible, however, to define positions according to function. Figure 20-1 is a typical organizational chart for a combined computer and punched-card machine installation, but it could be a punched-card operation with minor changes, namely the elimination of computer and programming functions.

The data processing manager is responsible for carrying out the objectives established by company management. He must have the authority to plan, organize, control, and direct overall activities. Under the hypothetical organization in Fig. 20-1, he directly supervises the managers of systems and programming, production control, and machine operations. In actual practice, he allows these highly trained and technically competent section heads to function without hindrance as long as they maintain high standards of performance. In so doing, he relies heavily upon their judgment and management experience. Their efficiency enables him to advise other

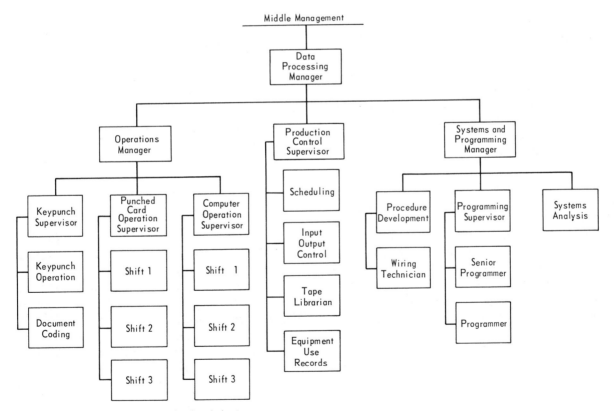

Fig. 20-1 Data processing organizational chart.

departments and management on technical decisions, to concentrate on long-range planning, and to utilize equipment with as few people as possible. To effectively service all departments and accomplish the objectives of management he must have the complete cooperation of all department heads.

The data processing manager keeps management informed of current operations, problems, and progress made on projects. He has responsibility for selection and training of personnel, effective utilization of equipment through machine scheduling, systems studies of proposed projects, operation of the installation, documentation, and program maintenance of all applications, and continuing analysis of existing systems for improvements. He advises other departments on the feasibility of new applications and on costs.

The programming and systems manager supervises and schedules the development or improvement of programs; the study, analysis and systems design of new or revised applications; the preparation of procedures, and the wiring of control panels. He assigns program requirements to the programmers, instructs them in complex problems, and enforces programming and flowcharting standards to ensure effective documentation. In the systems analysis unit he consults with and advises other departments on findings of a systems studies, cost savings with recommended changes, and practicability of the proposed systems.

When a system is completed, he reviews the programs, flowcharts, off-line processing and operation procedures. When he is satisfied that everything is thoroughly tested and complete, he turns over to the operations manager one copy of the fully documented procedure and related programs. A duplicate copy is generally maintained in the systems and programming section.

The operations manager is responsible for operating the computer, punched-card, and keypunching-verifying equipment. In this capacity he works closely with the systems and programming section, and with the departments supported. He assists in establishing a machine schedule and in using this schedule to assign personnel to obtain maximum efficiency. We can say that he produces specified results through coordination of both machines and people. To have an efficient balance of experienced operators, he may interchange personnel between the computer and punched-card machine rooms. His ability to coordinate machine usage results in timely and accurate reports.

In the final analysis the management positions in a data processing structure are overlapped in both function and responsibilities. It is only through harmonious team effort that successful data processing operation emerges to fully support management's objectives.

Machine operators and programmers vary in qualifications. Each section and shift usually has a senior technician who doubles as assistant supervisor. In this capacity he furnishes technical guidance to section managers and assigns, instructs, and checks the work of others. Some machine operators and programmers are sufficiently competent to work with only general guidance. Others need close supervision, and a few are in training positions. With this in mind, let us outline the broad responsibilities of a machine operator and programmer.

Under general guidance the programmer defines the problem in terms of what is to be done, analyzes the facts for an optimum solution, and flowcharts the solution. After checking and rechecking the flowchart for correct logic, he codes the program. Next he develops test data to include every possible condition in the program and tests and debugs the program. To preclude inadequate testing, final testing should be done with actual data which are representative of true conditions. Last, he prepares or assists the procedure writer in preparation of the console operating instructions.

Most machine operators are versatile. They may be called upon to sort and sequence-check cards, merge them with a master deck, intersperse gangpunch information from the masters into the details, calculate them, or list them. This usually requires wiring one or more simple control panels since only complex panels are permanently wired. As each machine is used, pertinent details such as the start time, stop time, and job number are recorded on the time-utilization logs.

The machine operator's duties include more than just loading cards and pushing buttons. He must follow a procedure that includes balancing and correction steps, processing of unique cards in a special manner, and, at specific points, adding or removing cards. Throughout processing he must look for the unexpected, which may result in erroneous processing. While the finished product is being processed, he checks the printed or punched output for format errors. Consequently, the operator's job is far from simple.

Final processing is accomplished on an accounting machine or computer. The operator sets up the machine by loading the cards, tape reels, or both, inserts the proper type of paper or forms, and makes the correct switch settings on the console. If the machine stops, he must be able to take corrective action and continue according to the procedure. The machine may occasionally halt for no apparent reason. In these cases he must have a knowledge of wiring or programming, in order to analyze the situation.

Systems analysis is a part of everyone's job, especially of those in supervisory positions. If the installation is large enough to warrant a separate position for this function, it will likely be filled by someone with a well-rounded technical knowledge of all data processing operations, as well as knowledge of the company's general operation. The systems analyst, in cooperation with the user of the application being studied, analyzes new and current projects and improves the value of the results being produced while lowering the cost of processing.

The systems analyst may be assigned a few projects with top priority, or he may be directed to examine the organization as a whole. In either case the analyst studies the present processing methods and determines if each report is really needed and, if so, checks to see if it shows enough information. Or he may change the structure of the report. For example, management may have asked for an analysis of sales, but really received a pile of unmanageable information. What management really needed was a compact tabulated report showing percentages of current sales in relation to last month's sales.

If information reaches management late, decisions must be made without factual data, meaning that decisions are made without the full picture. The reports are left to history, unsound decision having already been made, and man-hours and machine hours have been wasted. The analyst, therefore, strives to give the users the information they can effectively use, and on a timely basis. In doing this he recommends that certain reports no longer needed be eliminated, while others be combined or expanded.

In order to evaluate and manage a data processing department, certain control information must be available. The manager needs to know how many late reports were encountered and if they were caused by late input from the using department or by backlogged work. This function is best located separately from the operations section. Called production control, it is a multiple function section as we see from the organization chart in Fig. 20-1.

Production control is responsible for ensuring that the input data are available at the proper time. At this stage the authenticity and accuracy of the input documents are of minor importance since this is the responsibility of the originating department. Upon receipt, these documents are sent to the keypunch section for punching and verifying. Making sure that each processing function is completed in time for the next processing step is called *scheduling*. The schedule is prepared by production control with the assistance of the operations personnel and the departments receiving the reports. The using department usually establishes the due-in and due-out date in relation to the processing needed, as determined by the operations section. Upon receipt of the completed output product, the report is reviewed by production control for neatness and format consistency, and dispatched to the user. This is normally the extent of the auditing by production control because of the invisible nature of the recording medium and its processing.

SCHEDULING

One of the major responsibilities of a data processing manager is getting every job out on time. He does this with the assistance of one of two types of schedules. One form of schedule consists of a breakdown by machine type and the scheduled time each job is to be processed. This type of schedule is the most difficult to plan because of unexpected developments. Some of these uncertainties are late input data, machine downtime for unscheduled maintenance, unexpected one-time priority jobs, and an increase in volume of data to be processed.

Another form of schedule leaves the manipulation of machines and times up to the skill of the operations manager. He is furnished a daily list of jobs that are to be processed with such indications as volume, average processing time, priority of importance, and due-out date. Thus the sequence and timeliness of processing are left up to him.

An ideal schedule would be a constant work load without day-to-day fluctuations. Unfortunately, this is seldom possible. Much can be done, though, to smooth out processing time by redistributing part of the work load in peak periods to days with idle machine time, thus reducing or eliminating the need for overtime.

There are several ways this can be done. The easiest method, naturally, is to change the due-out date. Of course, this must be with the approval of the using agency and cannot be changed in many cases. Another method makes use of *preprocessing*. By this technique, the procedure is changed so that idle time before the peak work load is used to prepare the cards for final processing. For example, a large volume of transaction cards can be summarized during slow periods, reducing the number of cards that must be worked with and permitting faster processing when machine time is at a premium.

A schedule must make provision for program testing, but the manner and time at which it is done can assist in balancing the schedule. Enforced desk checking results in the location of many errors before work reaches the machine-testing stage. Debugging at the console, also, can be reduced to a minimum during rush periods. Advance planning by the program manager in many cases can result in scheduling program testing during idle time. For example, instead of developing one program at a time from start to finish, several programs can be flowcharted, coded, and set aside for later testing when machine time is available.

In conclusion, optimized scheduling calls for fitting regular processing runs, program or control panel testing, rerun time due to error, unscheduled maintenance, buffer time for one-time requests, and machine setup time within the processing time available. The objective of scheduling is to eliminate personnel and machine overtime while meeting all processing commitments.

REPORTS FOR MANAGEMENT

The basic ingredient of a successful business is vital information, upon which decisions are made.

Management information comes in many forms and must reach all concerned, but go no farther. Some may be in the form of forecast or summary facts which are the criteria for top management's decisions. Some may be comparative data covering a short period, which is the barometer of middle management. The bulk of information is for accounting purposes, and is of interest to management only from the historical or fiscal standpoint.

It is not enough for the data processing manager to know that all machines are scheduled so as to eliminate peak work loads, for much of that time may have been rerun time due to errors. So the manager turns to comparative and control data to operate efficiently. He needs to know the productive use time, rerun time and its causes, program testing time, machine downtime, and so on. From this data, he determines the cause of reruns and initiates corrective action.

Since his department is run on a budget, he also needs to know cost per transaction processed, per machine hour, per report processed, for overtime due to special requests, for overtime for machine rental and manhours, etc. With these tools, he judges the efficiency of his department, and, where possible, implements measures to contribute to a profitable business. Without these tools, operating cost grows to unrealistic proportion.

To evaluate machine usage, the manager resorts to recording the time required for every job by machine type. This is accomplished with a simple log located on every machine (Fig. 20-2). The operator records his identity, job number, shift, and time started. Each machine normally has a meter similar to an automobile speedometer, which operates only when the machine is running. This time is recorded under the column labeled meter start time. When he finishes the job, the clock stop time and meter

MACHINE UTILIZATION LOG   Machine ______   Date ________

Job Number	Oper No.	Shift	Use Code	Clock Time		Meter Time		Remarks
				Start	Stop	Start	Stop	

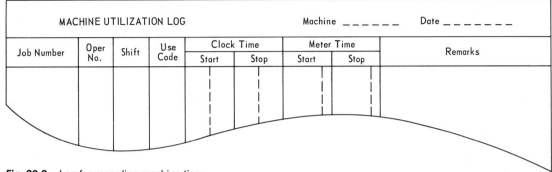

Fig. 20-2 Log for recording machine time.

time are recorded. Then he proceeds to another machine or another job and repeats this recording process. The time utilization cards are keypunched and edited by machine, elapsed and setup time are computed, and management reports are run. Setup time (includes loading card reader, punch, printer, and tape units) is derived by subtracting the total elapsed meter time from total elapsed clock time. As examples of editing principles, elapsed clock time must exceed elapsed meter time and start time must be earlier than stop time.

Distinction between categories of time is recorded in order to evaluate the machine utilization. Some of the typical codes normally used are listed in Table 20-1. From these time cards, management data can be run showing machine time and use code by operator. This report is used to distribute and equalize the work load among operators and to identify competent as well as incompetent operators.

Another management tool reflects the time spent on each job by use code by machine type. Figure 20-3 illustrates the report. The manager expects answers to questions such as: Why did job number 159 take twice as long to run this month? What was the program error that caused a rerun on job number 490? What can we do about the overtime continually caused by job number 263?

Prepared July 1   MACHINE TIME ANALYSIS BY JOB   As of June 30

Job No	Use Code	26 Punch	84 Sorter	557 Interp	88 Collator	514 Reproducer	407 Acctg Mach	1401 CPU	1402 Read-Pch	1403 Printer	729 Tape	Total	Overtime

Fig. 20-3 Management report showing time spent on each job.

Table 20-1   Use Codes for Recording Machine Time

Production		Rerun	
01	Complete run	20	Operator error
02	Incomplete run (operator error)	21	Program error
		22	Procedure error
03	Incomplete run (program error)	23	Input error (incorrect data)
04	Incomplete run (procedure error)	24	Keypunch error
05	Incomplete run (input error, data)	25	Material error (e.g., bad cards)
06	Incomplete run (keypunch error)	26	Machine error
		27	Other
07	Incomplete run (material error, e.g., bad tape)	**Idle**	
		30	Not scheduled
		31	Nonworkdays
08	Incomplete run (machine error)	**Maintenance**	
09	Incomplete run (other)	40	Scheduled
		41	Unscheduled

Preparation	
10	Machine setup
11	Program assembly
12	Program testing
13	Checkout
14	Demonstration
15	Other

Data processing answers endless questions for top management through numerous other reports. For example:

In the accounts payable area   What cash discounts have we lost? Which vendor had the largest dollar value of returns?

In the cost area   How much does each of our departments cost? Which departments run over their budgets? Which departments reduced their budgets?

In the sales area   In what geographic area are sales growing? Which salesman had the greatest dollar sales? Which salesman had the largest percentage increase in sales?

In the payroll department   How much overtime is paid by department? What were our payroll dollars spent for?

In the personnel area   What is the accident rate per department? How many people did we retrain due to turnover?

In the inventory area   Have we lost sales on out-of-stock orders? What is on order and how much? What is the dollar value of our inventory?

In the production area   How much does it cost to produce product A? What was the cost last year?

ADVANCED PROGRAMMING SYSTEMS

Each data processing installation is unique to some extent. A manager may have more than one computer system to operate, which means he may have to write programs in two quite different languages, or his departmental service may involve scientific or mathematical problems which, by the very nature of the application, suggest that many of the programs will be run only once. Indeed, these unrelated situations could produce an unmanageable installation, not to mention the increased cost under conventional programming methods. Let us see how recent technology has solved these unique data processing problems.

To allow programmers to express their problems in a language more easily comprehensible than machine language, the symbolic programming system (SPS) was developed. This language employs easy-to-remember, mnemonic operation codes and English words instead of machine addresses. Even so, this is still a machine-oriented programming system because the programmer must think in terms of the machine instructions of the computer. Other programming languages have been developed that are problem oriented. That is, the program language and the method of using it are similar to the problem being solved. The programmer need know very little about the technical characteristics of the computer, and can concentrate more on the problem and less on the computer.

As before, programs written in problem-oriented languages are called source programs. Consequently, they must be translated into machine language before the machine can utilize the program. The absolute program resulting from the translation is called an object program. The program which does the translating is called a *compiler,* not an assembler. Recall that an assembly program used in the SPS language is a one-for-one translator. That is, the assembler produces one machine-language instruction for each source-language instruction written by the programmer.

A compiler is a one-to-many translator. This means that several machine-language instructions are produced for each single source-language instruction written by the programmer. This is made possible by macroinstructions. A macroinstruction is an instruction in the compiler program which is capable of producing a series of machine instructions from a single instruction written by the programmer.

Perhaps the most widely used program language employing macroinstructions and compilers is Cobol (*Com*mon *Business Oriented Language*). Cobol (pronounced as co-ball) was developed to overcome a problem associated with multiple-computer installations. Suppose a firm has two types of computers. Since computers differ, a program written for one will not necessarily run on the other. Two programs must be written if a problem is to be processed on two or more incompatible models. Writing programs in Cobol eliminates the time and cost of rewriting when a job must be run on a computer that will not accept the original program. The translation is done by the compiler. Individual compilers have been developed for different types of computers. A source program written in Cobol can be translated into the machine language of another computer by using that computer's compiler.

Cobol bears little resemblance to the two languages, machine and symbolic, that we have learned. For instance, if we wish to multiply two fields called *savings* and *interest,* the machine-language instruction would be @ H76 /99 and the symbolic instruction would be M SAVING INTRST. In Cobol, the business English used permits us to specify this problem by writing the statement MULTIPLY SAVINGS BY INTEREST. Remember that this is a source program written by the programmer, so it is necessary to compile or produce a machine-language program before this problem can be executed and solved by the computer.

The Fortran (*for*mula *tran*slation) language is similar in concept to Cobol. Whereas business English is used in Cobol, mathematical language is used in Fortran. For example, a formula may be expressed as $B = (C + D) *$ $(A - E)$. This causes the computer to multiply (asterisk means multiply) the result of C plus D times the result of A minus E and store the result at the location of B.

When these systems are used, the program is written in terms more readily understood by the programmer. As a result, experts in other fields can be taught the art of programming with little concern about the characteristics of the computer. For example, an engineer may need to solve an equation while designing a bridge. A computer, with its speed and power, is available, but he finds communication with it a barrier. For the computer to solve his equation, someone must define each single step and then write the program accordingly. But if the engineer and others in this situation are trained in one of the problem-oriented languages, they have the computer at their disposal.

Cobol was designed for commercial data processing and Fortran for mathematical data processing. In effect, the business and mathematical statements merely say logically what is to be done by the program, not how the function is to be performed. This aspect is left to the compiler of the particular machine that will solve the problem.

CONCLUSION

Some data processing installations are poorly designed and some are mismanaged. Nevertheless, they continue operating, perhaps even at a loss. Others operate efficiently. In all cases, successes or failures are directly attributable to people first, machines second. Today's machines are more complex than those of yesteryear and future machines may be even more complex. Therefore, the quality of personnel selected is the key to success, not quantity. The most important attributes include the prospect's interest in the field, past performance, education, and desire for self-improvement.

Bibliography

IBM Technical Publications

A24-0520-2	IBM 24, 26 Card Punch
A24-1034-1	IBM 82, 83, 84 Sorter
A22-0510-0	IBM 108 Card Proving Machine
A24-0516-1	IBM 557 Interpreter
A24-1013-2	IBM 88 Collator
A24-1072-2	IBM 188 Collator
A24-1002-2	IBM 514 Reproducer
A24-1017-1	IBM 519 Document Reproducing Machine
A26-1507-1	IBM 604 Electronic Calculating Punch
D26-1512-0	IBM 609 Electronic Calculator
A24-1011-1	IBM 407 Accounting Machine
A24-1007-0	IBM Functional Wiring Principles
A24-1010-0	IBM Operators Guide
F22-6517-2	IBM Introduction to Electronic Data Processing Systems
A24-3144-2	IBM 1401 EDPS Operators Guide
C24-1480-0	IBM 1401 Symbolic Programming System 1 and 2
A24-3067-2	IBM 1401 (Programming Instructions) Reference Manual
A24-3069-2	IBM 1401 Tape Input/Output Instructions
C24-3319-0	IBM 1401 AUTOCODER (On Tape) Language
F28-8053-2	IBM Common Business Oriented Language (COBOL)
F28-8074-x	IBM FORTRAN
A24-1495-3	IBM Index of 1401 Publications
A22-6810-1	IBM System 360 Summary
A22-6821-1	IBM System 360 Principles of Operation (Programming Instructions)

Reading References

Andree, Richard V.: "Computer Programming and Related Mathematics," John Wiley & Sons, Inc., New York, 1967.

Arnold, Bradford H.: "Logic and Boolean Algebra," Prentice-Hall, Inc., Englewood Cliffs, N.J., 1963.

Auerback Corp.: "Required Cobol—1961 (Programmed Instruction)," U.S. Government Printing Office, Washington, D.C., 1963.

Brandon, Dick H.: "Management Standards for Data Processing," D. Van Nostrand Company, Inc., Princeton, N.J., 1963.

Cashman, Thomas J., and William J. Keys: "Data Processing: A Text and Project Manual," McGraw-Hill Book Company, New York, 1967.

Chapin, Ned: "An Introduction to Automatic Computers," D. Van Nostrand Company, Inc., Princeton, N.J., 1963.

————: "Programming Computers for Business Applications," McGraw-Hill Book Company, New York, 1961.

Crowder, Norman A.: "The Arithmetic of Computers," Doubleday & Company, Inc., Garden City, N.Y., 1960.

Davis, Gordon B.: "An Introduction to Electronic Computers," McGraw-Hill Book Company, New York, 1966.

Dearden, John: "Computers in Business Management," Richard D. Irwin, Inc., Homewood, Ill., 1966.

Dimitry, Donald L., and Thomas H. Mott, Jr.: "Introduction to Fortran IV Programming," Holt, Rinehart and Winston, Inc., New York, 1966.

Flores, Ivan: "Computer Software: Programming Systems for Digital Computers," Prentice-Hall, Inc., Englewood Cliffs, N.J., 1965.

Gregory, Robert H., and Richard L. Van Horn: "Automatic Data-Processing Systems," Wadsworth Publishing Company, Inc., Belmont, Calif., 1965.

Gruenberger, Fred, and George Jaffray: "Problems for Computer Solution," John Wiley & Sons, Inc., New York, 1965.

Leeson, Daniel N., and Donald L. Dimitry: "Basic Programming Concepts and the IBM 1620 Computer," Holt, Rinehart and Winston, Inc., New York, 1962.

Lytel, Allan: "ABC's of Computers," Howard W Sams & Co., Inc., Indianapolis, Ind., 1966.

Martin, E. Wainright, Jr.: "Electronic Data Processing—an Introduction," Richard D. Irwin, Inc., Homewood, Ill., 1965.

McCracken, Daniel D.: "Guide to Fortran Programming," John Wiley & Sons, Inc., New York, 1961.

———: "Guide to IBM 1401 Programming," John Wiley & Sons, Inc., New York, 1962.

Nelson, Oscar S., and Richard S. Woods: "Accounting Systems and Data Processing," South-Western Publishing Company, Cincinnati, Ohio, 1961.

O'Neal, Leeland R.: "Autocoder Programming for the IBM 1400 Series Computers," Dickenson Publishing Company, Inc., Belmont, Calif., 1966.

Prager, William: "Introduction to Basic Fortran Programming and Numerical Methods," Blaisdell Publishing Company, Waltham, Mass., 1965.

Raun, Donald L.: "An Introduction to Cobol Computer Programming for Accounting and Business Analysis," Dickenson Publishing Company, Belmont, Calif., 1966.

Saxon, James A., and William S. Plette: "Programming the IBM 1401," Prentice-Hall, Inc., Englewood Cliffs, N.J., 1962.

Schmidt, Richard N., and William E. Meyers: "Electronic Business Data Processing," Holt, Rinehart and Winston, Inc., New York, 1963.

Sprague, Richard E.: "Electronic Business Systems: Management Use of On-Line Real Time Computers," The Ronald Press Company, New York, 1962.

Van Ness, Robert G.: "Principles of Punched Card Data Processing," Taplinger Publishing Company, Inc., New York, 1966.

Periodicals

Business Automation: OA Business Publications, 288 Park Avenue West, Elmhurst, Ill., 60126.

Datamation: F. D. Thompson Publications, Inc., 35 Mason Street, Greenwich, Conn.

Data Processing Digest: Data Processing Digest, Inc., 1140 South Robertson, Los Angeles, Calif., 90035.

Data Processing for Management: American Data Processing, Inc., Book Tower, Detroit, Mich.

Data Processing Magazine: 134 North 13th Street, Philadelphia, Pa., 19107.

Data Processor: IBM Data Processing Division, 112 East Post Road, White Plains, N.Y. 10601.

Glossary

absolute Refers to actual machine language. For example, an absolute address indicates the actual location in memory where the word is stored.

accounting machine The most important machine in a punched-card system. Capable of detail or group printing, accumulating totals, and summary punching when connected to a reproducing punch. Also called a *tabulator*.

address A designation, in either symbolic or machine language, a location in storage, or a device where information is stored. Also called the *operand* of an instruction.

address, absolute A machine-language designation which indicates the true location of data or an instruction in storage.

address, symbolic A name or label assigned by the programmer which represents a storage location. The symbolic address is translated into an absolute address by an assembly program.

alphabetic characters A set of symbols arranged to express the letters A to Z, which are designed for communicating between people and machines and are intelligible to both.

alphameric Data which may consist of alphabetic characters A to Z, numeric characters 0 to 9, or special characters for punctuation such as $, . and % symbols.

arithmetic unit A section in the central processor where addition, subtraction, multiplication, and division are performed. Also where logical operations, such as comparing, are performed.

assembly program A program provided by the computer manufacturer which converts a non-machine-language program, such as a symbolic program, written by the programmer, into machine language. An assembler assigns absolute addresses to symbolic labels and converts mneumonic operation codes to a language the computer can act upon.

binary A numbering system using a base of 2, as opposed to the base of 10 in the decimal system. Used by computers because of its two-state, zero or one, characteristic.

binary-coded decimal (BCD) A system of binary notation in which each decimal digit or alphabetic character is represented by the binary digits 0 and 1. BCD is the language of most computers.

bit The smallest element in a binary character. Each bit has two states, either OFF or ON, thus the representation of 0 or 1.

branch One of two or more paths the computer can take when a decision is made under control of the program.

brush A group of thin wires used for reading the punches in a card.

card column One of 80 vertical divisions of a card normally accommodating one numeral or letter. Each column, consisting of 12 rows, is divided into two parts. The bottom 10 rows contain punching positions for decimal digits 0 to 9; three top rows, 0, 11, and 12, are combined with a digit punch to represent an alphabetic character.

card feed That portion of a machine which moves cards into the machine for reading. Cards are immediately stacked into pockets after being read.

central processing unit The computer without the input-output components. The CPU houses the control, internal storage, and arithmetic-logic sections. Also called the central processor.

character A set of symbols specially arranged to express the decimal digits 0 to 9, the letters A to Z, and several special symbols used for punctuation.

coding Changing data to an abbreviated form before punching in cards by assigning letters and numbers to classify the data for machine processing. Also refers to writing a series of computer instructions, usually on a special coding form, which makes up a program.

collator A machine which has two card feeds and four

stackers, and is capable of comparing two fields in a card to perform sequence checking, matching, merging, or card selection.

comparing Examining two or more fields to establish if one field is equal to, lower than, or higher than the other field.

compiler A special program which converts a non-machine-language program written by a programmer into an object program that the computer can use to process information.

computer A group of machines interconnected to function under the control of a program. Once the program is stored in the computer's memory, processing of data, such as reading, comparing, computing, and punching or printing of the results, is controlled and accomplished without human intervention. The computer is electronic except for input and output units.

console A separate component or a display panel located on the computer which consists of lights, buttons, and switches for manual control and observation of the system.

control panel A removable device in the machine into which wires are plugged to complete electrical circuits, thus controlling machine operations.

control unit A component of the computer which controls the entire system by decoding each instruction in the program and carrying out the action called for by the instruction.

cycle An interval of time that a machine requires to complete a series of operations. There are many types of cycles, such as card cycle, read cycle, print cycle, or program cycle; some are repeated and some are not.

data A collection of numeric, alphabetic, or special characters denoting facts and information, in particular that which is to be processed or produced by machine.

data processing A group of people and machines organized and acting together to process data by recording, sorting, calculating, tabulating, and summarizing, thus producing the desired output. Such a system strives to minimize the need for manual handling of data with primary emphasis on elimination of retranscription of data and duplication of effort.

debugging Data processing terminology that refers to locating and correcting errors in control panel wiring or programs.

detail printing Printing all or a portion of the information from each record.

digital computer A computer which operates on digits represented in a binary form of ones and zeros, as opposed to an analog computer which performs calculations on physical measurements.

document A typed or handwritten representation of source information, such as an invoice form which must be converted to an input medium acceptable to the machine.

editing Checking of data for impossible elements to ensure accuracy. Also, the rearrangement, deletion, or addition of data to improve the appearance and meaning, such as punctuation of money amount fields.

electronic data processing system See **computer.**

execute To carry out a machine operation based upon given instructions.

field A predetermined number of columns set aside in a record for similar information. For example, a card field containing customer name.

file A collection of facts or information about related items recorded in machine media, such as card file or tape file. A master file contains semipermanent data whereas a detail file contains transient data for recent transactions.

fixed word length Refers to a computer, thus a program, where the number of characters in a word is constant, determined by the design of the machine.

flowchart A graphic representation using symbols to show step-by-step machine operations. A system flowchart shows the flow of information between machines whereas a program flowchart shows the flow of information within the machine.

gangpunching Punching repetitive information in all cards of a file.

garbage Data processing jargon for unwanted and meaningless data recorded in input media or produced by a machine. May consist of double-punched cards, reports with overprinting, or an inaccurate product produced by the machine.

group printing Printing a single line with accumulated

totals for a group of identical items. Also called tabulating.

hardware The mechanical devices and components of which a machine is constructed.

high-order Leftmost position of a field, storage location, or machine word. Also referred to as left-justified.

housekeeping Pertaining to instructions, usually at the beginning of a program, which are necessary but do not directly contribute to the solution of a problem and which are normally executed only once.

hubs Holes in a control panel into which wires may be plugged to connect an electrical circuit.

indicator A hardware feature that records certain machine conditions. For instance, the last-card indicator is turned ON when the last card is fed into the machine.

information See **data.**

in line Descriptive of processing whereby an entire file, usually stored permanently on magnetic disk or drum, is updated as soon as the transactions occur; opposed to sequential processing. See also **random access.**

input Any form of input media containing data which are used to provide the machine with information for processing.

input device A unit that reads cards, tape, and other input media and moves the data to the component where processing is being accomplished.

instruction Precise direction, in the form of either a wired or stored program, which is an element of a program and which causes the machine to perform a specific operation. In a wired program one wired impulse, hence an instruction, causes a counter to add two amount fields. In a stored program a set of absolute or symbolic characters consisting of operation code and one or more operands cause the computer to perform the indicated operation upon the data located at the address.

intermediate Of three fields or totals, the one of middle importance.

internal memory Storage directly addressable and located normally within the central processor.

interpreter A machine used for printing information onto cards.

interpreting Converting the holes punched in cards into alphanumeric characters and printing them onto the same or succeeding cards.

intersperse gangpunching Punching the same data in individual groups of cards.

keypunch Machine with a keyboard similar to a typewriter, which is used for punching data from source documents in cards. Sometimes called a card punch.

label A name, representative of the data, given by the programmer to the address where data are located in memory. As an example, storage location 500 to 504 containing account number may be given the label of ACCTNO.

location See **address.**

loop A set of instructions in a routine or program in which the last instruction can cause the previous instructions just executed to be repeated if certain conditions exist.

low-order The units or rightmost position of a storage location or field. Also called right-justified.

machine language The vocabulary which engineers have given the machine. To simplify communication between man and machine, non-machine programming languages were developed, which are convertible by assembly or compiler programs to a language the machine understands.

machine word See **word.**

magnetic core A form of high-speed storage capable of storing one binary bit. The core is magnetized in one direction or the other, thus the binary 1 or 0 representation.

magnetic core plane Screen strung with several thousand magnetic cores. A stack of planes comprises a storage unit in which each column of cores represents a storage location, thus a BCD character.

magnetic disk An auxiliary memory device for mass storage consisting of a stack of up to 50 disks. On each disk surface information is recorded in binary on tracks similar to a phonograph record, which permits random access processing.

magnetic tape A reel of tape, usually ½ inch wide and 2400 feet in length, on which several hundred characters are recorded per inch in the form of seven binary bits.

major The most important field or total.

mark sense Refers to information handwritten on a

card by a special pencil which can be automatically converted to punches.

matching   Operation of examining two or more fields to see if there are corresponding records or a group of records.

memory   See **storage.**

merging   Filing or combining two files into a single file. Selection can be accomplished during the same operation.

microsecond   One millionth of a second; 0.000001 second, abbreviated as μs.

millisecond   One thousandth of a second; 0.001 seconds, abbreviated as ms.

minor   The least important field or total.

mnemonic operation code   That part of an instruction designating the operation to be performed, which is written in an easy-to-remember symbolic notation. For example, the operation code MCS means *move character and suppress zeros,* but MCS must be converted to the absolute operation code Z by an assembly program before execution.

numeric characters   A set of symbols arranged to express the decimal digits 0 to 9, which are designed for communication between people and machines and which are intelligible to both.

object program   A machine-language program ready for execution by the computer.

octal   A numbering system with a base of 8.

off-line   Processing operations performed by auxiliary equipment not under control of the primary computer. For example, transferring data from cards onto tape by conversion machines or reproducing and printing on more economical machines. Smaller computers are often used to support larger computers, and thus are directly off-line from the main computer.

on-line   Processing operations performed by various machines under direct control of the main computer. Commonly used to describe random access processing or operations that are normally done off-line, such as card-to-tape conversion.

operand   See **address.**

operation code   That portion of an instruction designating the operation to be performed.

parity check   A system where the total number of binary-1 bits in a character determines its accuracy. Accuracy can be checked by either odd-parity or even-parity depending upon the hardware design of the computer.

printing   See **detail printing** and **group printing.**

procedure   Written narrative instruction, usually accompanied by flowcharts, giving step-by-step directions how a job is processed.

processing   The handling of data from the point where source documents are converted to punched cards until the final product is completed. This includes such operations as sorting, sequence checking, gangpunching, calculating, summarizing, and printing reports or document forms.

program   A series of steps in the form of instructions which are arranged and automatically executed in a prescribed sequence to accomplish reading and storing of data, calculating, and decision-making operations necessary to give the desired results and providing the solution in the desired format.

programmer   A person who defines and solves a problem, draws a flowchart of the solution, and writes a program from the flowchart. Usually one who writes programs for computers as opposed to a project planner who is a wiring technician and procedure writer.

punched card   A card, usually consisting of 80 vertical columns, used to record data by punching characters in each column. The punched holes are read electronically by wire brushes or a photosensing mechanism located inside the machine.

punched-card data processing system   A set of conventional machines consisting of sorters, interpreters, collators, reproducers, calculators, and accounting machines.

random access   Refers to data stored usually on magnetic disks which is processed randomly as opposed to data stored in punched cards or on magnetic tape, which is processed sequentially. In this type of processing one record is available as quickly as another, thus, is suitable for applications where files must be updated as transactions occur. See also **in-line.**

record   A group of characters and fields relative to a specific item which is processed as a unit.

record density The number of characters that is written per inch on magnetic tape.

register A hardware component of the central processor used to temporarily store and act upon data or instruction words.

reproducer A machine capable of punching information from an original deck of cards in a new deck of cards.

routine A set of instructions which solves a problem when executed in sequence by the computer. A program is often called a routine. See also **subroutine.**

selector Electromechanical relay with the capability of assuming either of two states. A selector has three hubs called *common, normal,* and *transfer.* The *common* hub is connected to either the *normal* or *transfer* hub, but not both.

sequential processing Accumulating transactions or documents until the number warrants machine processing, then processing them in a predetermined sequence. Opposite of random access.

software Programs associated with a computer such as assemblers, compilers, and certain subroutines, including square root routines available from a centralized program library.

solid state Refers to a machine whose circuitry consists of transistors and similar devices with the advantage of higher reliability and lower power consumption than vacuum tubes.

sorting The function of arranging records into numeric, alphabetic, or alphanumeric sequence, either ascending or descending.

source program A program written in a non-machine language which must be converted to machine language by a compiler or assembler before execution by the computer.

statistical machine A sophisticated sorter which compiles facts and prints or punches the statistics. Also called card proving machine because of its editing function.

storage A device, such as magnetic core or magnetic disk, in which information can be kept for later use. Internal storage is the same as memory. External storage can be in the form of punched cards or magnetic tape.

stored program A program which is executed from instructions stored inside the computer.

subroutine Part of a program consisting of a set of instructions that deviates from the main program to accomplish alternate processing. Usually a subroutine is used repetitively to solve part of a problem and is programmed so that it can be repeated as often as necessary with program control being returned to the main routine after the last instruction in the subroutine is executed.

summarize Punching accumulated totals along with identifying information from a group of cards in a single card.

symbolic program A source program written in the symbolic programming system language.

system A group of machines united to process the requirements of a business. Also an assembly of people, machines, procedures, and methods by which a business is run.

systems analyst A person skilled in initiating or improving machine solutions to business problems.

unit record See **punched card.**

variable word length Refers to a computer in which the number of characters or storage positions comprising a machine word is set by the programmer in the program.

verifier A machine similar to a keypunch which verifies the data previously punched into cards.

wired program A set of step-by-step instructions provided to the machine by a wired control panel.

word A predetermined set of characters which occupies one area of storage and is treated by the machine as a unit. Word lengths can be fixed or variable.

zero-print control Eliminating unwanted zeros in a numerical field.

zone punch One of three top punching rows in a card, 0, 11, and 12 punches.

Index

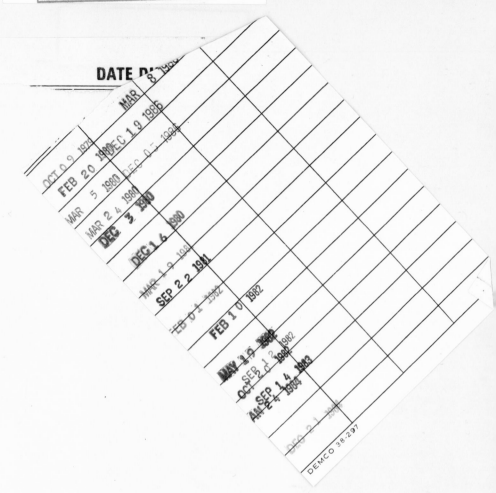